THE PROLIFERATION OF NUCLEAR WEAPONS

Extending the U.S. Umbrella and Increasing Chances of War

Edited by

DEMETRIOS JAMES CARALEY

ROBERT JERVIS

THE ACADEMY OF POLITICAL SCIENCE
NEW YORK

Published by
The Academy of Political Science
475 Riverside Drive, Suite 1274
New York, NY 10115

Cover design: Loren Morales Kando

Cover credits: U.S. Air Force, U.S. Navy, and Missile Defense Agency photos.

Library of Congress Cataloging-in-Publication Data

Names: Caraley, Demetrios James. | Jervis, Robert.
Title: The proliferation of nuclear weapons : extending the U.S. umbrella and
   increasing chances of war / edited by Demetrios James Caraley, Robert
   Jervis, The Academy of Political Science.
Description: New York, NY : The Academy of Political Science, [2018]
Identifiers: LCCN 2018039452 | ISBN 9781884853135 (pbk.)
Subjects: LCSH: United States--Military policy. | Nuclear weapons--United
   States. | Nuclear arms control--United States. | Nuclear
   nonproliferation--Government policy--United States. | United
   States--Foreign relations--Middle East. | United States--Foreign
   relations--Pacific Area. | Deterrence (Strategy)
Classification: LCC UA23 .P77 2018 | DDC 355/.033573--dc23 LC record available at
   https://lccn.loc.gov/2018039452

Printed in the United States of America
P 5 4 3 2 1

CONTENTS

Publisher's Preface

DEMETRIOS JAMES CARALEY

THIS BOOK IS ONE OF A SERIES of publications released by the Academy of Political Science on timely subjects of special importance in the fields of public and international affairs. *The Proliferation of Nuclear Weapons: Extending the U.S. Umbrella and Increasing Chances of War* brings together essays from *Political Science Quarterly* that explore topics of central and ongoing importance in American nuclear policy toward the Middle East and Asia Pacific regions. In addition to examining the proliferation of nuclear capacity and the increased risk of nuclear war, the book explores the links between nonproliferation, arms control, and extended deterrence.

The Academy of Political Science is a nonpartisan, nonprofit organization founded in 1880 with a threefold mission: to contribute to the scholarly examination of political institutions, processes, and public policies; to enrich political discourse and channel the best social science research in an understandable way to political leaders for use in public policy making and the process of governing; and to educate members of the general public so that they become informed participants in the democratic process. The major vehicles for accomplishing these goals are its journal, *Political Science Quarterly*, Academy conferences, and special books.

Published continuously since 1886, *PSQ* is the most widely read and accessible scholarly journal on government, politics, and policy, both international and domestic. Dedicated to objective analysis based on evidence, *PSQ* has no ideological or methodological slant and is edited for both specialists and general readers who have a serious interest in public and foreign affairs.

DEMETRIOS JAMES CARALEY is Editor of the *Political Science Quarterly* and President Emeritus of the Academy of Political Science. He is also Janet H. Robb Professor of the Social Sciences Emeritus at Barnard College and Professor of International and Public Affairs Emeritus at Columbia University.

I thank the authors of the essays in this collection. As is normal, the views expressed are those of the authors and not of the institutions with which they are affiliated. I am especially grateful to Robert Jervis, a long-term member of *PSQ*'s editorial board, for writing the introductory chapter. I am equally grateful to Marylena Mantas, *PSQ*'s Managing Editor, for contributing to the editing and production of this volume. Others on the small staff at the Academy who warrant my warm thanks are special assistant Caroline Monahan and Loren Morales Kando, who as Vice President for Operations and Executive Director oversaw final details of the book's publication and distribution. Ms. Kando also designed the cover.

Introduction

ROBERT JERVIS

NUCLEAR WEAPONS ARE BACK. They never completely disappeared, but with the end of the Cold War they lost their central place in American concerns as the danger of a civilization-ending war disappeared. Other nuclear-related dangers remained, of course. Indeed, with the dissolution of the Soviet Union new ones appeared. Not only were Belarus, Ukraine, and Kazakhstan now nuclear powers, but the sprawling Russian nuclear installations and, even more, Soviet nuclear scientists who were now unemployed, raised the danger of "loose nukes" and nuclear proliferation. Fortunately, the former Soviet republics saw nuclear weapons as difficult to maintain, unnecessary, and a ticket to Western assistance, and the United States also moved creatively to do what it could to develop cooperative arrangements with Russia that would secure nuclear sites and keep nuclear scientists usefully employed. Although far from complete and perhaps having unintended consequences (could Moscow have seized Crimea and Eastern Ukraine in 2014 if Ukraine had maintained a nuclear arsenal?), these efforts were largely successful, which may account for the fact that we now take this denuclearization for granted rather than studying it and praising its architects.

Even during the Cold War, there were fears that terrorists would get nuclear weapons and, lacking a "return address" that could be attacked in retaliation, could not be deterred from using them. The terrorist attacks of September 11, 2001 greatly magnified these fears. Looked at in the light of cool hindsight, September 11 appears less like an epical event than a demonstration that unless they have nuclear (or biological) weapons, terrorists can only inflict limited damage. But at the time it appeared quite differently, especially because these attacks were followed by rumors that al-Qaeda had

ROBERT JERVIS is Adlai E. Stevenson Professor of International Politics at Columbia University. His latest book is *How Statesmen Think* (Princeton University Press, 2017).

planted atomic bombs in Washington or New York, anthrax attacks in October 2001, and the near-miss of the "shoe bomber" attempt to bring down a transatlantic flight two months later. The discovery that al-Qaeda leaders had met with Pakistani nuclear scientists drove home the fear that this or other organizations could get the bomb. Debates about whether this would be merely very difficult or next to impossible have not been resolved, but the passage of time has served to diminish the fears.

By bringing other fears to the fore, the rise of great power conflict after the turn of the twenty-first century has similarly pushed concerns about nuclear-armed terrorists further down our worry list. The hope for a peaceful, rules-based liberal order, so strong after the end of the Cold War and reinforced by the united anti-terrorist stance that followed from September 11, now seems a mirage. Whether one sees this order as largely a cover for American dominance, a marvelous idea for the entire world that was doomed due to the eternal features of domestic and international politics, or an opportunity that was missed due to faulty leadership, the old pattern of rivalry among major powers has returned. Ratification was provided by President Donald J. Trump's 2017 National Security Strategy that proclaimed Russia and China as displacing terrorism as the major threats to American security.

The fact that these states are armed with nuclear weapons both increases the threat that they pose and makes American nuclear policy more salient. Under the presidency of Barack Obama, the United States moved to try to push nuclear weapons to the background of world politics. Obama re-stated with greater fervor the American desire to eventually rid the world of these weapons. Of course, he also said that this was not a goal that could be reached in the foreseeable future and he undoubtedly realized that in a nuclear-free world American conventional superiority would loom even larger. But even if political pressures and perhaps a change in outlook led him to propose a large nuclear modernization program in his last years in office, he nevertheless avoided flaunting American nuclear weapons or expanding their possible missions.

This changed with Trump's presidency. He not only called for increases in the American stockpile, according to some reports enraging Secretary of State Rex Tillerson by asking why it should not be ten times larger, but also issued a Nuclear Posture Review calling for a new generation of lower-yield warheads to thwart a possible Russian attack on the Baltic republics and suggesting that a massive cyberattack against the United States might be met by a nuclear response. Trump also reminded North Korea's Kim Jong Un that his nuclear button was much larger. Ironically, the increased salience of nuclear weapons seeds attention to nuclear arms control. This is not to say that what arrangements are possible and in the American interest are uncontroversial. Far from it. As was true during the Cold War, many people who are skeptical of Russian intentions doubt that meaningful arms control agreements with Moscow can be reached. In parallel, a coming issue is likely to be whether the goal of forcing or enticing Kim to give up his nuclear stockpile is really possible and whether the United States instead should aim for an arms control agreement with North Korea. While such negotiations have important technical aspects that only specialists can love, they are always rooted in broad political calculations that should be the focus of our attention.

A good start on these broader questions, and an indication of how things looked before the sharp deterioration of relations between the United States and Russia and China, is provided by Regina Karp's "Nuclear Disarmament: Should America Lead?" Important for this volume are the arguments that arms control can alter as well as reflect relations between the parties and that nonproliferation and arms control have always been tightly linked, albeit in hotly debated ways. Three considerations are involved. First, the non-proliferation treaty (NPT) couples the non-nuclear states' renunciation of these weapons to the promise that the nuclear weapons states will both facilitate access to peaceful uses of nuclear energy and make progress toward their own disarmament. Second, the initial American efforts at post-war arms control (the Baruch Plan of 1946) can readily be seen as a nonproliferation measure. Third and related, nonproliferation was always a central consideration for American policy during the Cold War and has emerged as even more important since the end of that conflict.

American policy toward proliferation, although generally hostile, has not been uncontroversial or entirely consistent. During the Cold War, there were reasons to favor nuclear weapons in the hands of countries allied to the United States or at least hostile to the USSR. The argument that anything that complicated the defense problems of the latter would make it less of a threat to the United States, although too simple, had obvious appeal. Nevertheless, the United States greatly feared China getting the bomb even at a time when the Sino-Soviet split was growing. These fears were great enough to motivate the United States to ask the USSR for permission for the United States to launch a preventive strike. The Soviets responded negatively, only to make a similar overture several years later to which the United States demurred.

The use of force has not been an effective tool to prevent proliferation. Israel's attack on the reactor in Syria in 2007 may be the outstanding case to the contrary, but even here we cannot be sure that Syria would have gone on to develop nuclear weapons had the reactor not been destroyed. The attack on Saddam Hussein's Osirak reactor in 1981 appears to have speeded up rather than retarded his program, and while one can argue that the 1991 and 2003 American-led invasions prevented Saddam from developing nuclear weapons, here too it is unclear whether he would have been able to fulfill his nuclear ambitions had the United States not prevented him. Of course if the threat of force is sufficiently credible, it does not have to be used to be effective. It may be that one reason why Kim Jong Un agreed to freeze his missile and nuclear tests was that he feared an American military strike, and the possibility of a military confrontation may have similarly contributed to Iran's agreement to a nuclear deal with the United States and its allies in 2015.

These are matters for speculation. Two other aspects of the struggle over proliferation are clearer. First, in order to have a serious chance at developing nuclear weapons, states that are hostile to the United States and its allies must either operate in deep secrecy or have some other shield behind which they can launch their program. In the years between the Israeli raid on Osirak and the Gulf War, Saddam followed the former path, with some success. North Korea followed the latter route. It was and continues to be very hard for the United States to credibly threaten a military strike against North Korean facilities when that country holds Seoul hostage with its conventional (and chemical) artillery.

Economic sanctions, then, often appear a more viable instrument than force in curbing a country's nuclear ambitions. Most observers feel that economic sanctions were important in bringing Iran and North Korea to the negotiating table. But Scott Helfstein's "Friends Don't Let Friends Proliferate" shows that sanctions are less efficacious in cases like these than they are when threatened or levied against friends (e.g., the American efforts to pressure South Korea and Taiwan into abandoning their nuclear weapons programs). Economic ties are usually much more important to countries with which the United States had good relations than they are with adversaries. Indeed, as Helfstein shows, while a necessary (but not sufficient) condition for sanctions to have significant effect on adversaries is that they be agreed to by a very broad coalition, the United States by itself can exert major pressure on allies.

Of course, pressures are of multiple types and can flow in both directions. Although initially opposing India's drive for nuclear weapons, the United States came to accept it both because it seemed irreversible after the nuclear tests in 1998 and because a nuclear-armed India had significant value as a counterweight to China. But recognizing India's nuclear status was controversial because doing so would contravene the principled American opposition to proliferation and could encourage other states to follow a similar path. So when President George W. Bush signed a nuclear cooperation agreement with India, Congressional assent was not guaranteed. Dinshaw Mistry's "The India Lobby and the Nuclear Agreement with India" examines the role of Indian Americans in this effort, showing that their impact was less direct than it was in helping form a broader India lobby that included business interests, strategic affairs experts, and lobbying firms employed by the Indian government. The case is a good reminder that foreign policy in the United States is never entirely foreign and that domestic interests, processes, and politics always play a large role.

Nonproliferation is closely tied to the strategic problem of extended deterrence. The United States seeks to deter not only attacks on its own territory, but on those of its allies as well, and extending deterrence to them is more difficult because the threat of retaliation, especially against a nuclear-armed adversary, is less credible than that of retaliating to a direct attack. This problem loomed large in the Cold War, especially in Europe where the Soviets had an advantage in conventional military forces. "Would we trade New York for Berlin," as the question was often phrased. With the end of the Cold War, concern about the credibility of extended deterrence has largely moved to northeast Asia because of China's and North Korea's nuclear weapons and to the Persian Gulf because of the danger that Iran will stage a nuclear breakout.

Nonproliferation and extended deterrence are tightly linked in that the latter is a fundamental instrument to pursue the former. That is, the American security guarantees, during the Cold War to West Europe and today to Japan, South Korea, and Middle East states, are designed to in part convince American allies that they do not need nuclear weapons of their own because the United States will protect them. Although the desire to prevent proliferation is not the only impulse behind American presence throughout the world, it is one of the significant motivations. A proliferated world is believed to pose dangers, both direct and indirect, to the United States as well as to humanity at large. Extending the American nuclear umbrella over others, although not without costs and risks, seems preferable to the alternative.

But doing so does not seem preferable to all observers and leaders, even American ones. The most important modern theorist of international politics, Kenneth Waltz, (in)famously argued that proliferation would make the world safer, reproducing the Soviet-American stalemate of the Cold War around the globe.[1] One obvious benefit would be to permit the United States to end or to at least limit extended deterrence. These security guarantees not only risked dragging the United States into quarrels of no direct importance to it, they also allowed allies to engage in provocative behavior. Furthermore, the guarantees required the United States to spend money for the

---

[1] Scott Sagan and Kenneth Waltz, *The Spread of Nuclear Weapons: An Enduring Debate*, 3rd ed. (New York: W.W. Norton, 2012).

needed military forces, and the difficulty in making the threats credible pushed it into behaving dangerously in order to demonstrate that it would in fact protect others even at great risk to itself.

Although no decision-maker has taken Waltz's ideas on this point seriously, in order to reduce the burdens on the United States they have flirted with encouraging others to get their own weapons. Both Richard Nixon and Donald Trump encouraged Japan to consider acquiring nuclear weapons, although the former backed away and the latter appears to have done so as well. The possibility that Japan will decide that nuclear weapons are a better source of security than the American guarantee, while worrying to many, may play an important role in moderating the behavior of China and North Korea. So from the standpoint of most American policymakers, a Japan that refrains from building bombs but is not completely averse to doing so may represent the best posture. In "Japan's Nuclear Hedge: Beyond 'Allergy' and Breakout," Richard J. Samuels and James L. Schoff explore the changes and intricacies in Japan's stance. In private discussions with American leaders, Japanese prime ministers and other officials often explained that their strictly anti-nuclear posture was less than entirely sincere and immovable. Even before the advent of the Trump administration, serious questions about the American commitment had been raised and while the barriers to producing nuclear weapons remain high, they are vulnerable to domestic changes and international challenges.

As important as Japan is, the country that is most on the front lines in Asia is South Korea, which in the past reacted to doubts about the American commitment by seeking its own nuclear weapons. In "The U.S. Nuclear Umbrella over South Korea: Nuclear Weapons and Extended Deterrence," Terence Roehrig outlines the history of the deployments and maneuvers by which the United States tried to maintain the credibility of its promise to protect its ally. Despite the threat posed by North Korean nuclear weapons to South Korea and the U.S. and President Trump's ambivalence toward the alliance, the strong American conventional military posture in the area combined with the continuing ties between the United States and South Korea mean that extended deterrence retains sufficient credibility to be effective.

The other area where extended deterrence and nonproliferation intersect is the Persian Gulf. Ever since the United States discovered that Iran was developing the ability to enrich uranium in August 2002 it has focused on preventing that country from getting nuclear weapons, which the United States believes would provide it with a shield behind which it could gain sway over the region and support terrorism. But nuclear weapons and the problems of extended deterrence may not be enough to explain the adamant American stance. Relations between the two countries have been very bad ever since the Iranian Revolution of 1979, and this plays into the propensity for the United States to demonize its adversaries. In "The Role of Villain: Iran and U.S. Foreign Policy," Paul R. Pillar examines the unhelpful pattern of Iranian and American attitudes and initiatives toward each other. Written before the 2015 nuclear agreement that seemed to break this malign cycle, Pillar's analysis foreshadowed Trump's withdrawal from the bargain. Of course the United States and Iran are not the only players involved. The Persian Gulf states are more than the objects of American protection, they are active players with their own interests and plans. As Zachary K. Goldman and Mira Rapp-Hooper show in "Conceptualizing Containment: The Iranian Threat and the Future of Gulf Security," the obvious American strategy of uniting the Gulf states in a joint effort to contain Iran is unlikely to succeed in the face of regional rivalries and obstacles to the United States taking a highly visible leadership position. More likely are bilateral arrangements between the United States and individual Gulf states.

The future of proliferation probably depends on what happens with North Korea and Iran. Both are unfolding as I write in mid-July 2018, and indeed the situation with the latter changes almost day-to-day. More stable is the point that proliferation might well end if Iran's neighbors are confident that it will not get nuclear weapons and if the North Korean program can be contained, if not rolled back. Although Pillar is correct that the American concerns about Iran are extreme, its neighbors, especially Turkey and Saudi Arabia (not to mention Israel), are worried as well. The latter already has nuclear weapons, but the former two might well seek them if Iran seems on the verge of becoming a nuclear power. Were they to start down this path, other countries in the Middle East, especially Egypt, might join them, driven by concerns over status and security. What lessons this would teach the rest of the world is impossible to tell at this stage, but it is possible that with this many countries joining the nuclear club, this behavior would seem like the new normal, and even states in other regions might seek entry.

Two of North Korea's neighbors are major nuclear states, but two others are more menaced by that country. Japan has an enormous stockpile of fissile material, great scientific and technical skill, and a highly trained Air Force. While there are major ideological and bureaucratic inhibitions against developing nuclear weapons, as Samuels and Schoff explain, they might not be the last word. If the negotiations between North Korea and the United States break down and the former continues its program and resumes threats against Japan, the inhibitions might be overcome. Of course a breakdown of negotiations might also lead the United States to seek to destroy the North Korean nuclear program, and Japan's reaction would probably be strongly influenced by the outcome of this war. A successful surgical attack could reassure Japan, but one that failed or led to a larger war could easily undermine Japanese faith in the American nuclear umbrella and lead it to seek its own weapons. The impact of successful negotiations would largely turn on the extent to which they served Japanese interests. If the United States were able to completely end the North Korean program, Japan's desire for these weapons would presumably recede. But if Japan believed that the United States had ignored its interests, most obviously by not limiting North Korea's medium-range missiles that could strike their island or by paying no attention to the issue of Japanese citizens who had been abducted by North Korea, Japanese elite and public opinion might believe that they had been abandoned by the United States and that obtaining nuclear weapons was the only way to ensure their long-term security.

If Japan does get nuclear weapons, South Korea is likely to resume its quest for them, although a great deal would depend on its domestic politics, its relations with Japan, and the American stance. In any case, however, being the only country in the region without nuclear weapons is not likely to be appealing. Under the current leadership of Moon Jae-In, South Korea is as worried that aggressive American policies will entrap it as it is of being abandoned. Both fears highlight the advantages of nuclear weapons.

Aside from the unlikely possibility that North Korea will give up all of its nuclear weapons, the best outcome from the standpoint of nonproliferation would be a formal or tacit agreement that while the North would keep a stockpile of weapons and missiles, it would not export them, maintain its moratorium on testing and cease, or at least limit, bragging about its arsenal. This could be stable in the static sense of giving all the affected countries an acceptable measure of security, but probably would not be stable in the dynamic sense of being able to maintain itself in the face of shocks generated by domestic and international politics. Nevertheless, it may be the best of the feasible outcomes, at least for the short run, and could push nuclear weapons and the possibility of nuclear war comfortably into the background.

Even under the most optimistic assumptions, this is not likely to be the case in American dealings with Russia and China. These countries hold American cities hostage, as the United States holds theirs. This produces a form of stability, but as I noted earlier brings with it the difficulty of making extended deterrence credible. Whether this is a real as opposed to a theoretical problem and how to cope with it remain topics of debate, just as they were in the Cold War. Indeed, much of the current debate parallels that in the Cold War. Both broad political arguments and narrower debates over nuclear strategy are involved. In the former category are disagreements about Russian and Chinese intentions and risk-taking propensities. The Cold War classification of hawks and doves is even cruder now than it was then, but still provides serviceable labels. Hawks believe that Russia—or at least Putin—is committed to recreating the territory of the Soviet Union and extending influence into as much of the rest of Europe as he can, while doves believe that although his regime is authoritarian and repressive, his foreign policy is largely defensive and to a significant extent a reaction to his fears, exaggerated but not totally imaginary, that the West is trying to undermine him. The threat he presents is limited and the United States should take care not to over-react.

In parallel, hawks see a rising China as a fundamental threat to American allies, security, and values and believe that it must be contained by bolstering our arms and alliances. Doves do not dispute the judgment that China wants a much greater say in its region, but believe that peaceful accommodations can satisfy each side's basic interests, that patient diplomacy is the best tool, and that a belligerent stance will set off a spiral of misunderstanding and dangerous tensions.

More relevant to this volume are the differences in proposed nuclear policies. Hawks believe that the problem of extended deterrence is severe and, as the NPR argues, requires the United States to have at its disposal a broad spectrum of possible nuclear responses to Russian or Chinese aggression. The United States must be able to match and preferably over-match the adversary at any rung of violence on the escalation ladder in order to convince the adversary that moves in areas in which it may have local preponderance, such as against the Baltic republics or in the South China Sea, could not succeed. Doves see this as a dangerous solution to an illusory problem, one that not only is a fantasy world, but that brings with it dangers of self-fulfilling prophecies. To the extent that Russia and China need to be deterred by the anticipation of military consequences, it is the understanding that violence cannot be readily controlled and the fear of escalation that operates most strongly.

If this debate sounds familiar to readers of a certain age, it should: the parallels to the arguments in the last twenty years of the Cold War are striking. Whether this represents the lack of imagination of American analysts or the objective dilemmas posed by nuclear weapons is unclear. What is clear, however, is that the linked problems of extended deterrence and the spread of nuclear weapons have resumed a central place in contemporary international politics and are likely to be with us for the indefinite future.

Nuclear Disarmament: Should America Lead?

REGINA KARP

NUCLEAR ARMS CONTROL IS BACK—OR SO IT SEEMS. The conclusion of the 2010 New START treaty follows a hiatus of two decades during which arms control was relegated to the margins of statecraft and all but disappeared from the political agenda. The question is why and to what end has arms control returned. For arms control to make a difference to the quality of international security in the twenty-first century, it must be meaningful and sustainable, contribute to tackling primary security threats, and build consensus on the rules of security governance.

Together with deterrence, arms control was a Cold War staple. When the Cold War ended and preoccupations with deterrence yielded to the demands of a different international environment, arms control was adrift, its specific role lost. Its connection with an era that had come to a close contributed to a sense of death by association. After all, what could be arms control's contribution to a world in which the Soviet Union no longer existed, systemic conflict was a rapidly fading memory, and the United States and Russia no longer threatened one another with nuclear annihilation? Though there was plenty of arms control going on, including negotiations for START II and for a Comprehensive Test Ban Treaty (CTBT), establishment of the Missile Technology Control Regime, and the indefinite extension of the Nuclear Non-Proliferation Treaty (NPT), there was a pervasive sense that arms control's best days lay behind it. When the United States failed to ratify the CTBT in 1999 and left the Anti-Ballistic Missile (ABM)

REGINA KARP is an associate professor of political science and the director of the interdisciplinary Graduate Program in International Studies (GPIS) at Old Dominion University. She has published books and articles on international security including works on German security policy and the transformation of war.

Treaty in 2001, not even the conclusion of the Strategic Offensive Reductions Treaty in 2003 was able to rekindle arms control embers. It no longer appeared to be part of the *fabric* of international relations.

Recent efforts to bring back arms control have tried to do just that. In their already legendary article in *The Wall Street Journal* in January 2007, George P. Shultz, William J. Perry, Henry A. Kissinger, and Sam Nunn lent their combined weight as elder statesmen to the idea of "A World Free of Nuclear Weapons" and called upon the United States to bring its "moral heritage" to bear on bold initiatives toward the elimination of nuclear weapons. The time to act is now, they argued, to prevent proliferation "into potentially dangerous hands." A new nuclear era has dawned, in which countries like North Korea and Iran set dangerous proliferation examples and non-state actors are likely to "get their hands on nuclear weaponry."[1] To stem the spread of nuclear weapons and strengthen the Non-Proliferation Treaty regime, Shultz et al. proposed a number of broad initiatives. Together, they believed, these steps would reduce reliance on nuclear weapons among states that have them and support non-proliferation efforts.

Their call for nuclear abolition found broad support among other elder statesmen, all erstwhile members of the Cold War strategic community, and included such illustrious names as former Soviet leader Mikhail Gorbachev; British politicians Malcolm Rifkind, Douglas Hurd, and David Owen; and George Robertson, former North Atlantic Treaty Organization (NATO) Secretary General; from Germany, Helmut Schmidt, Richard von Weizsäcker, Egon Bahr, and Hans-Dietrich Genscher joined; and from Poland, former president Lech Walesa.[2] In January 2008, Shultz et al. published a follow-up piece in *The Wall Street Journal* in which they showed the wide echo their 2007 article had produced, now including a growing and impressive list of individuals familiar to students of American foreign policy.[3]

In December 2008, a group of international military, political, and business leaders founded Global Zero, a world-wide action group that quickly

---

[1] George P. Shultz, William J. Perry, Henry A. Kissinger, and Sam Nunn, "A World Free of Nuclear Weapons," 4 January 2007, accessed on the website of *The Wall Street Journal Online* at https://www.wsj.com/articles/SB116787515251566636, 5 February 2010.

[2] Douglas Hurd, Malcolm Rifkind, David Owen, and George Robertson, "Start Worrying and Learn to Ditch the Bomb," 30 June 2008, accessed on the website of *The Times Online* at http://www.timesonline.co.uk/tol/comments/columnist/guest_contributors/article4237387, 5 February 2010; "Mikhail Gorbachev Calls for Elimination of Nuclear Weapons as Soon as Possible," 31 January 2007, accessed on the website of the *Wall Street Journal Online* at https://www.wsj.com/articles/SB117021711101593402, 5 February 2010; Helmut Schmidt, Richard von Weizsäcker, Egon Bahr, and Hans-Dietrich Genscher, "Toward a Nuclear-free World: A German View," 9 January 2009, accessed on the website of the *International Herald Tribune Online* at https://www.nytimes.com/2009/01/09/opinion/09iht-edschmidt.1.19226604.html, 5 February 2010.

[3] George P. Shultz, William J. Perry, Henry A. Kissinger, and Sam Nunn, "Toward a Nuclear-Free World," 15 January 2008, accessed on the website of *The Wall Street Journal Online* at http://online.wsj.com/public/article_print/SB120036422673589947.html, 5 February 2010.

gained momentum. In July 2009, the group launched the Global Zero Action Plan, calling for specific steps to eliminate all nuclear weapons by 2030. The Plan envisions four phases of ever more comprehensive disarmament goals, including the participation of all nuclear-weapons-capable countries and extensive verification and enforcement measures.[4]

Arguably, none of the individuals currently lending their support to the elimination of nuclear weapons subscribed to a vision of nuclear abolition during their time in office. Nonetheless, their standing in the policy community makes their support especially noteworthy. The dangers to international security they described are real: nuclear proliferation and the possibility of nuclear weapons in terrorist hands are a concern to the international community as a whole. Everyone's security is affected unless steps are taken to keep nuclear arsenals secure and to counteract proliferation in all its forms.

In April 2009, President Barack Obama added a sense of urgency. Speaking in Prague, he reflected that "in a strange turn of history, the threat of global nuclear war has gone down, but the risk of nuclear attack has gone up. More nations have acquired these weapons. Testing has continued. Black market trade in nuclear secrets and nuclear materials abound. The technology to build a bomb has spread. Terrorists are determined to buy, build or steal one. Our efforts to contain these dangers are centered on a global non-proliferation regime, but as more people and nations break the rules, we could reach a point where the center cannot hold."[5] America was committed, the President stated, "to seek the peace and security of a world without nuclear weapons."[6] He laid out an ambitious policy agenda: the United States would reduce the role of nuclear weapons in its own security strategy, embark on new arms control negotiations with Russia, aggressively pursue ratification of the Comprehensive Test Ban Treaty by the U.S. Senate, take steps toward a Fissile Material Cut-Off Treaty, strengthen the NPT by increasing the cost of defiance and defection, and create an international nuclear fuel bank that gives equal access to the peaceful uses of nuclear energy. Adding momentum to the abolitionist dynamic, the Norwegian Nobel Committee awarded the 2009 Nobel Peace Prize to President Obama.

---

[4] Accessed on the website of *Global Zero* at http://www.globalzero.org/en/getting-zero, 15 February 2010. Developing a strategy and fostering a global public campaign for Global Zero was the subject of a summit meeting 2–4 February 2010 in Paris, http://globalzero.org/en/2010-paris-summit. Similarly, see *Eliminating Nuclear Threats: A Practical Agenda for Global Policymakers*, Report of the International Commission on Nuclear Non-Proliferation and Disarmament (Canberra, November 2009), http://www.icnnd.org/reference/reports/ent/index.html, accessed 25 June 2010.

[5] The White House, "Remarks by President Barack Obama," Hradcany Square, Prague, 5 April 2009, accessed on the website of the *White House* at http://www.whitehouse.gov/the_press_office/Remarks-By-President-Barck-Obama-In-Prague, 10 February 2010.

[6] Ibid.

Can arms control once again become part of the fabric of international relations? This paper argues that to ask this question is to ask about principles of world order, its foundational assumptions, and its durability. Earlier arms control initiatives took their cues from the particular circumstances that governed relations between the United States and the Soviet Union. As a result, arms control was able to serve the security needs of both states. Due to their unique position in the international system, ensuring the security of the United States and the Soviet Union yielded essential benefits for the survival of all. Building on the work of Arnold Wolfers and Hedley Bull, both concerned with the relationship between national security and world order, I argue that the changes in the international system since the end of the Cold War challenge the established balance between nuclear possession goals and non-proliferation milieu goals. Traditional arms control no longer generates system-wide security benefits. Hence, the new security environment compels a reassessment of how national security and international security governance inform one another. I contend that new theorizing on arms control and disarmament is possible and yields fresh insight into the shifting relationship between arms control that regulates security choices and arms control that transforms international security.

The first part of the paper questions the continued utility of nuclear deterrence strategies against the background of the post-Cold War security environment. The second part explores how possession goals are increasingly less able to generate milieu goals; the third part advances the notion that the possession of nuclear weapons must become responsive to the rising need for global security governance. American leadership in recognizing the growing rivalry between nuclear possession and non-proliferation provides new perspectives on the role of nuclear weapons in international security. However, I conclude that the role of disarmament in effecting global security governance is at best ambiguous. For disarmament to become a shared vision of international governance and world order, the United States must invite others to shape the rules that govern them. Sharing rule-making power is critical for advancing a disarmament agenda. It is also consequential for American leadership. Hence, in the final analysis, the challenge of eliminating nuclear weapons is likely to be evaluated on the merits of America's role in a future security order.

ARMS CONTROL AND AMERICAN LEADERSHIP

The resurgence of arms control lends itself to a number of observations. First, arms control initiatives center on America's leadership and its ability to shape international order. Cold War prescriptions of deterrence and containment are to be replaced by "engagement based on common interests, shared values, and mutual respect."[7] As it has done on past occasions, Secretary Hillary Clinton argues, America can lead on an issue vital to the quality of international relations. It will do so in concert with others, fully recognizing that no country can solve global challenges on its own. With American leadership, arms control is to speak to salient concerns in international politics, enhance global stability, and extend the network of rules that shape global governance.[8] Back at the heart of statecraft, arms control serves as a beacon for the mission to create a better world and a signpost against which accomplishments are judged. Re-fashioned to engage a vastly different security environment, arms control gives purpose and direction to the international community. Putting the neo-conservative revolution of unilateralism behind it and against the backdrop of a national image tarnished by wars in Iraq and Afghanistan, the United States seeks to reconnect with its neglected soft-power capacities. A renewed commitment to arms control, engaging other players, showing restraint, and living by the rules one preaches to others, allows the United States to exercise consensual leadership, reclaiming its "moral heritage" on the world stage.

ARMS CONTROL AND DISARMAMENT

A second observation is the explicit link forged between arms control and the elimination of nuclear weapons. There is a critical conceptual difference between arms control that *regulates* state behavior and arms control *that transforms* international relations. In its regulative role, arms control aims to curb potentially destabilizing behavior especially in the areas of military procurement and deployment. It plays a crucial but essentially modest role that is conservative and status quo-oriented.[9] Arms control that aims at disarmament has its intellectual roots in the belief that the anarchic state system can be transformed, that security competition can be replaced by security cooperation, and that such a cooperative system can be maintained. Hence, in a globalized, interdependent world, arms control linked with disarmament would re-cast the relationship between national security and world order, between what states claim for themselves and the environment

---

[7] Hillary Rodham Clinton, "Foreign Policy Address at the Council on Foreign Relations," Washington, DC, 15 July 2009, accessed on the website of the State Department at http://www.state.gov/secretary/rm/2009a/july/126071.htm, 6 February 2010.

[8] Charles D. Ferguson, "The Long Road to Zero. Overcoming the Obstacles to a Nuclear-Free World," *Foreign Affairs* 89 (January–February 2010): 86–94.

[9] The best source on the debate about the goals of arms control remains the Fall 1960 special issue of *Daedalus*, the Journal of the American Academy of Arts and Sciences. A revised and enlarged version in book form appeared in 1961 under the same editor, Donald G. Brennan, *Arms Control, Disarmament, and National Security* (New York: George Braziller, 1961), 23. In his introduction, Brennan points out that "the doctrine of deterrence has assumed paramount and explicit importance in contemporary strategic thinking." Hence, arms control is about managing the armaments policies that serve deterrence and avoiding nuclear war.

within which these claims are made. In short, the new promise of arms control is to do more than *stabilize* relations between states, more than lock in the status quo. It is about *transforming* these relations.[10] To seek the elimination of nuclear weapons as President Obama has proposed is to undertake those steps of arms control and disarmament that eventually lead to a world without nuclear weapons.

Though there are notable examples of both arms control leading to disarmament and cooperative security displacing years of war and mistrust, these are either issue specific or regionally bound. In 1987, for example, the United States and Russia agreed to rid themselves of intermediate-range nuclear forces (INF), a step that facilitated the credibility of Mikhail Gorbachev in the eyes of the West and ushered in the vast transformation that ultimately came to be known as the end of the Cold War. While the INF Treaty was certainly a milestone in the history of arms control and the Cold War, it is less clear whether this particular "confidence-building measure" lends itself to global application.[11] Cooperative security too appears compelling, especially in the context of European integration, where it transformed traditional balance-of-power politics. Yet even this remarkable achievement lacks global traction. Fifty years after Europeans took the first cautious steps toward integration by establishing the European Coal and Steel Community, their security community has remained regional, lacking notable imitators elsewhere.[12]

ARMS CONTROL AND WORLD ORDER

A third observation relates to the rising prominence of world order questions in international relations. Recent history is replete with efforts to understand the role of power and its relationship to the use and legitimacy of force in international politics. The experiences in the Balkans, Iraq, and Afghanistan have starkly exposed the limitations of force and highlight the connection between security and development. Interdependence and globalization are reshuffling established hierarchies. Transnational actors erase the boundaries between the international and the domestic spheres. Failed states threaten to become safe havens for terrorists. The information revo-

---

[10] Philip Noel-Baker, the most prominent of early advocates of nuclear disarmament, rejects as a matter of principle the notion that the management of nuclear balances is superior to striving for the elimination of nuclear weapons. See his response to the chapters in Brennan's book: Brennan, *Arms Control*, 451–456.
[11] Harald Mueller, "The Future of Nuclear Weapons in an Interdependent World," *The Washington Quarterly* 31 (Spring 2008): 63–75, at 66. Mueller argues that the new role of arms control is "to help move the world from an era of self-help into an era of cooperative and collective security," 65.
[12] Emanuel Adler and Michael Barnett, eds., *Security Communities* (Cambridge, UK: Cambridge University Press, 1998). Though Europe may be unique, the contributions to this volume demonstrate that the concept of security communities, broadly defined, offers fresh insight into how cooperative security can shape perceptions of what is possible in international relations.

lution empowers individuals globally, increasing the spread of social networks, the demands of civil societies, and opportunities for crime and terrorism. Climate change signals resource competition and uncontrolled refugee flows. States and their institutions are grappling with unprecedented change. Though produced under the cloak of urgency, some of the strategies proposed are themselves a reflection of the longer-term challenges faced and constitute serious attempts to shape world order. Thus the European Union promotes itself as a civilian power projecting European preferences for governance structures that de-emphasize the use of military force.[13] NATO's debate about a new strategic concept highlights the alliance's struggle to balance collective global responsibilities and collective defense.[14] Both the EU and NATO have each adopted a comprehensive approach that develops more-nuanced understanding of the changing nature of conflict.[15] The U.S. military has embarked on "winning the narrative," an explicit recognition of the limited role force plays in building stable societies.[16] Government agencies and think tanks have engaged in future-oriented studies, invariably predicting greater complexity in international relations and emphasizing the need for cooperation.[17]

Taken together, these observations about the renewed interest in arms control reveal widespread concern about the state of international/global order, concern that is heightened by the sheer complexity of the issues and the absence of easy solutions. There is in addition a pervasive sense that the international system has so profoundly changed that a return to business as usual is not an option. In the critical area of national security, states are no longer the only actors, and individual states are less and less able to provide

---

[13] Helene Sjursen, ed., *Civilian or Military Power? European Foreign Policy in Perspective* (New York: Taylor and Francis, 2007).

[14] Klaus Wittmann, "Towards a New Strategic Concept for NATO," NATO Defense College Forum Paper 10, NATO Defense College, Rome, 2009. For an extensive bibliography, see the collection of publications at http://www.nato.int/strategic-concept/strategic-concept-bibliograpy.html#strategic_concept_recent_articles, accessed 15 May 2010.

[15] Peter V. Jakobsen, "NATO's Comprehensive Approach to Crisis Response Operations," DIIS Report 15, Danish Institute for International Studies, Copenhagen, October 2008; Eva Gross, "EU and the Comprehensive Approach," DIIS Report 13, Danish Institute for International Studies, Copenhagen, 2008.

[16] General James T. Mattis, US Joint Forces Commander and former NATO Commander Allied Command Transformation expressed this sentiment well when he said, "We do not want the US forces to be dominant and irrelevant in the future." "Joint Warfare in the 21st Century," 12 February 2009, accessed on the website of U.S. Joint Forces Command at http://www.jfcom.mil/newslink/storyarchive/2009/sp021209.html, 4 February 2010.

[17] General (ret.) Klaus Gaumann, et al., *Towards a Grand Strategy for an Uncertain World: Renewing Transatlantic Partnership* (The Netherlands: Noaber Foundation, 2007); Bob Graham and Jim Talent, *World At Risk: The Report of the Commission on the Prevention of Weapons of Mass Destruction Proliferation and Terrorism* (New York: Vintage Books, 2008); National Intelligence Council, *Global Trends 2025: A Transformed World* (NIC 2008-003, November 2008); Giovanni Grevi, "The Interpolar World: A New Scenario," Occasional Paper 79, (Paris: European Union Institute for Security Studies, June 2009); "Multiple Futures Project. Navigating towards 2030," Final Report (Norfolk, VA: Headquarters, Supreme Allied Command Transformation, April 2009); *The JOE 2008. Joint Operating Environment. Challenges and Implications for the Future Joint Force* (United States Joint Forces Command, November 2008).

security on their own. Now great powers too have to come to grips with the fact that they need to build coalitions in order to be effective players.[18] Last, there is a blurring of how the international relates to the national. Questions of world order have challenged national definitions of security, ushering in ideas of collective enterprise and responsibility.

It is in this context that we need to explore the calls for linking arms control with disarmament, for presenting it as an intellectually coherent and compelling case. In light of currently projected developments in world order, the questions must be these: What contribution does nuclear disarmament make? What makes nuclear disarmament more compelling now than before? And, even if it could be shown that nuclear disarmament were to make a significant contribution to world order, what is different now that should lead us to think that counter-arguments might be put to rest successfully?

NUCLEARISM AS FICTIONAL UTOPIA

Nuclear disarmament as a process and a goal has a history long in effort and thin in results. Not unlike other notions that envision transformative change such as collective security and security communities, it spans the divide between two different conceptions of security. One advocates state security through the augmentation of capabilities; the other believes state security derives from collective efforts to ameliorate anarchy.[19] Most states find themselves somewhere along this spectrum, building capabilities and hedging against a deterioration in their security environment. Throughout the history of the modern state system, we see a prioritizing of capabilities trumping efforts to shape a more-benign international order, less reliant on power politics.

Two decades ago, engaging the dominance of nuclear weapons and thinking "beyond nuclearism," Ken Booth and Nicholas Wheeler proposed that the real challenge to notions of world order transformation was not to imagine a perfectly peaceful world, in which dissent is absent and where all incentives for defection are perfectly deterred, but to envision a less than perfect world without nuclear weapons.[20] "The very idea," they knew, "confronts almost all mainstream theories and assumptions about state and human behavior." Nonetheless, they set out to challenge what they called an "academic hegemony," namely, the assertion that to think seriously outside the "mainstream

---

[18] In recognition that American forces will most likely be employed as part of a larger coalition, General Mattis requested U.S. Secretary of Defense Robert Gates to re-name U.S. Joint Forces Command the U.S. Joint Forces and Coalition Command, January 2010.

[19] Sverre Lodgaard, "Toward a nuclear-weapon-free world," *Daedalus* (Fall 2009): 140–152.

[20] Ken Booth and Nicholas J. Wheeler, "Beyond Nuclearism" in Regina C. Karp, ed., *Security Without Nuclear Weapons? Different Perspectives on Non-Nuclear Security* (London: Oxford University Press, 1992), 21–54, 28. This chapter was part of a multi-year project on the future of nuclear weapons at the Stockholm International Peace Research Institute, SIPRI.

framework" is unworthy of serious scholarship.[21] They were particularly taken aback by the conclusions reached by the Harvard Nuclear Study Group, which declared that nuclear weapons had to be coped with indefinitely. "Humanity has no alternative but to hold this threat at bay and to learn to live with politics, to live in the world we know: a world of nuclear weapons, international rivalries, recurring conflicts, and at least some risk of nuclear crisis. The challenge we face is not to escape to a fictional utopia where such problems do not exist."[22] Though the Harvard Nuclear Study Group reached these conclusions in 1983 during a resurgence of Cold War politics, they hold up well today when Robert Kagan cautions the Obama administration's foreign policy on "the perils of wishful thinking," ignoring "the clashing interests of great powers with competing ambitions and different world views."[23] Then as now, it seems, there simply is no room for thinking about world order in terms different than competition and rivalry.

In this sense, calls for disarmament have remained the "fictional utopia," rendered irrelevant by the cyclical nature of international politics. International politics is not about change but the management of relations to national advantage. Yet, such thinking rests more on forceful assertion than evidence and does not reflect the fact that significant transformations have taken place in international relations throughout modern history. Examples are well known and cannot easily be dismissed. They include decolonization in the 1950s and 1960s and the end of empires that in their heyday were legitimate and a powerful demonstration of a nation's place in the international hierarchy. They also include the European integration process, wholly unimaginable before World War II, when power politics was ingrained in the very nature of the European state system.

Perhaps even more important for a discussion about transformation in international relations are those changes that are usually not mentioned but that are nonetheless critical indicators that a cyclical view of world politics is less and less warranted. These have to do with the decline of war between major powers, the rise of non-state actors, the changing nature of conflict, the use of information technology in all sectors of public and private life, and a rising awareness that only cooperation among actors can deliver solutions to global problems.[24] None of these transformations are complete, and their

---

[21] Ibid, 21, 23, 24.

[22] Albert Carnesale, et al., *Living with Nuclear Weapons* (Cambridge, MA: Harvard University Press, 1983), 19, quoted in Booth and Wheeler, 23.

[23] Robert Kagan, "The Perils of Wishful Thinking," *The American Interest* (January–February 2010), accessed on the website of the *Carnegie Endowment* at http://carnegieendowment.org/publications/index.cfm?fa=view&id=24303, 1 February 2010.

[24] For excellent recent scholarship on the question of war between major powers see Raimo Vaeyrynen, ed., *The Waning of Major War: Theories and Debates* (London: Routledge, 2006).

endpoints, if they exist, are yet unknown. They all had relatively modest be-
ginnings, and their potential impact upon the choices of actors could not be
easily projected. Few predicted a global financial crisis, but everyone now
understands the dark side of interdependence and globalization. Most people use cell phones to talk to family and friends. Now we are also perfectly
aware that a call from a cell phone can set off a chain of events that culmi-
nates in the kind of destruction witnessed on September 11. Many people
used to believe that providing for their security is the government's job. With
the right weapons and the right alliances, their security could be assured.
Now they understand that the very way they live and the values they hold
make them targets of militant ideologies far away.

The point here is to appreciate that the "nuclearism" exposed by Booth
and Wheeler 20 years ago as an intellectual straitjacket has now become un-
sustainable. Indeed, the world has changed so profoundly that it is no longer
those who call for nuclear disarmament but those who resist it who must be
called to account. In a curious twist of history, it is those who believe in the
undiminished utility of nuclear weapons and the ability to manage international relations to their advantage who pursue a "fictional utopia." It is they
who should be asked what the role of nuclear weapons now is and what warrants their trust in nuclear management.

Holding the advocates of "nuclearism" accountable is not the same as
endorsing nuclear disarmament. Indeed, dissatisfaction with "nuclearism"
alone does not make nuclear disarmament a viable proposition. What it
does, however, is juxtapose a vastly changed world with a belief system developed during an entirely different era. Given the prevailing opposition to
nuclear disarmament, this is no small feat. The almost reflexive rejection of
nuclear disarmament must be countered by the critical review of the arguments that continue to endorse nuclear weapons in a world that no longer
has an obvious niche for nuclear weaponry.

This is not to suggest that there is anything "fictional" or "utopian" about
nuclear weapons and the dangers they pose. Nor is the aim to diminish any
of the steps taken to reduce accidental or inadvertent use of nuclear weapons
or to secure nuclear materials and prevent their trafficking as demonstrated
by the Proliferation Security Initiative. Rather, it is to question the continued appropriateness of the nuclear management approach itself and the ex-
clusion of alternative thinking that it entails.

Second, holding advocates of nuclear weapons to account allows us to
engage the perennial tension between national security policies and world
order goals, between one's own power and the choices one offers others. If
nuclear weapons are to stay, it needs to be shown that they make a positive
contribution to world order. Since the current international environment

differs greatly from the one that gave nuclear weapons prominence, it would be naïve to presume that environments are mutable but policy tools are not.

RECONCILING DISARMAMENT AND SECURITY?

Half a century ago, Arnold Wolfers provided a useful distinction between "possession goals" and "milieu goals." The former are goals that nations claim in competition with others, such as a share of power or security or, in this case nuclear weapons, that privileges one state over another. The latter are about shaping the rules by which nations play.[25] The spread of democracy, for example, is largely seen as a milieu goal, since it is believed to lead states to adopt more peaceful foreign policies. A fostering of interdependence, since it is believed to increase the cost of war and thereby reduce violent conflict, is also a milieu goal.

Wolfers's distinction between possession and milieu goals is useful. Great powers, especially, have the resources and the ambition "to devote their resources to the benefits they may hope to derive from helping to preserve or improve conditions prevailing beyond their borders."[26] Wolfers rightly points out that milieu goals are not altruistic; they serve state goals. The difference is that milieu goals are inclusive. They reflect an approach to the national interest that embraces the environment within which states operate. It is this that leads states to pursue international law, international organizations and institutions. An exclusively defined national interest is all about possession goals, where national capabilities are treasured and no alternative ideas are compelling. Possession goals not tempered by milieu goals generate fears of losing one's advantage, lead to anticipation of challenge, and promote an atmosphere of uncertainty. Milieu goals do not signal weakness nor do they compromise national security.[27] On the contrary, they demonstrate that positive synergies can be created between national and international security. U.S. foreign policy in the aftermath of World War II shows that investment in the economic and political recovery of Western Europe served U.S. interests and shaped the evolution of peaceful relations among European nations. Likewise, Simon Bulmer shows that post-unification Germany's pursuit of milieu goals in Europe generated trust in German foreign policy among its neighbors and allowed Germany to develop

---

[25] Arnold Wolfers, *Discord and Collaboration. Essays on International Politics* (Baltimore, MD: The John Hopkins University Press, 1962), 67–80.

[26] Wolfers, *Discord and Collaboration*, 75.

[27] Robert Kagan makes the opposite argument. Milieu goals are the preferences of states that do not have the material capabilities to acquire possession goals. In Kagan's universe, capabilities shape possibilities. Milieu goals are not absent, but their pursuit is entirely instrumental. Robert Kagan, "Power and Weakness. Why the United States and Europe see the World Differently," *Policy Review* (June–July 2002), accessed on the website of the Hoover Institution, Stanford University at http://www.hoover.org/publications/policyreview/3460246.html, 12 February 2010.

national interests that do not threaten others. Had Germany opted for possession goals alone, European integration would not long have survived and the historic problem of the German question would have returned.[28]

Milieu goals require a degree of voluntary self-restraint, an understanding that strategies of dominance alone do not yield desired results. Milieu goals also require cooperation. You cannot be multilateralist on your own; but it makes more sense to expect cooperation from others when they too share the benefits of cooperation. Possession goals in the guise of milieu goals are likely to be exposed for what they are, mainly efforts to reap relative gains, to market policies to others that may use the language of milieu goals but disproportionately allocate the gains of cooperation. Realists and nationalists are not troubled by this. In blunt fashion, Charles Krauthammer's 2004 speech at American Enterprise Institute expresses the belief that multilateralism is "to reduce American freedom of action by making it subservient to, dependent on, constricted by the will—and interests—of other nations. To tie down Gulliver with a thousand strings."[29] Following this logic, milieu goals only make sense if they support preferred strategies of dominance. This same logic also forestalls serious consideration of nuclear disarmament, because it would constitute a dangerous weakening of American capabilities. There would simply be no reason for the United States to lead in this area, as called for by Shultz et al. and supporters. Holding on to nuclear weapons is justified on the grounds that great powers must not be constrained in their range of action.[30]

If, as has been argued here, the changes in international relations make nuclearism no longer sustainable as an approach to global problem solving, and if there is evidence to suggest that these same changes allow us to revisit the balance between possession and milieu goals, the possibility of nuclear disarmament is no longer unthinkable. From this follows that we need to

---

[28] Simon Bulmer, et al., *Germany's European Diplomacy: Shaping the Regional Milieu* (Manchester: Manchester University Press, 2000).

[29] Charles Krauthammer, *Democratic Realism: An American Foreign Policy for a Unipolar World* (Washington, DC: American Enterprise Institute Press, 2004), 6.

[30] Lieber and Press, for example, make the argument that for the United States to uphold its alliance commitments and defend its interests, it needs to maintain a robust deterrence force in the form of credible counterforce options. Were the United States involved in a conventional war with a nuclear-armed adversary, it would need to offer its leaders military options that would deter nuclear escalation. This is a powerful argument against the notion that the rationale for having nuclear weapons is deterrence only. Lieber and Press contend that deterrence must be militarily credible to be effective in time of crisis. Keir A. Lieber and Daryl G. Press, "The Nukes we Need," *Foreign Affairs* 88 (November–December 2009): 39–51. The problem with this line of argument is that although it does permit nuclear force reductions, it rules out reducing reliance on nuclear weapons. Its logic is that U.S. national security strategy must be developed not to deter likely but all possible contingencies. Reminiscent of counter-force arguments during the Cold War, Lieber and Press reify a nuclearist determinism that leaves little to no space for alternative thinking. For a different argument see Hans M. Kristensen, et al., "From Counterforce to Minimal Deterrence: A New Nuclear Policy on the Path Towards the Elimination of Nuclear Weapons," Occasional Paper No. 7, (Washington, DC: Federation of American Scientists & The Natural Resources Defense Council, April 2009).

ask whether nuclear disarmament is a viable milieu goal in the Wolfers sense. That is, it has to be shown that nuclear disarmament serves the *common* interest and the *national* interest. This is not to suggest that, of course, everyone will be better off in the absence of nuclear weapons. Such reasoning only works in an abstract setting, not in the real world, where the task is to start with an existing security slate. Instead, we have to proceed with the knowledge that the altruistic state does not exist and that any scheme of world order will at best remain imperfect. *The issue is whether the imperfections of a world without nuclear weapons are preferable to those we confront in the presence of nuclear weapons.* Clearly nuclear disarmament is a milieu goal. But its desirability must not be judged on the presumption that milieu goals are superior to possession goals. Such thinking only nurtures realist and nationalist fears. Instead, we need to explore whether and how a *new* balance between possession and milieu goals can be struck and whether nuclear disarmament is a useful tool for striking this new balance.

This is the issue Hedley Bull wrestled with in his seminal 1976 essay, "Arms Control and World Order."[31] Bull was keenly aware that a discussion of nuclear disarmament had to proceed not just from where we are but with a thorough appreciation of how we got here. His analysis of the role of arms control in international relations revealed that the state of international order did not readily lend itself to a distinction between possession goals and milieu goals. The Soviet Union and the United States were cooperating in arms control for the purpose of avoiding nuclear war, but that cooperation was decidedly skewed to serve their own interests. As Bull argued, "These special or bilateral purposes reflect the preference of the two great powers for a world order in which they continue to enjoy a privileged position."[32] Hence, the milieu goal of war avoidance through arms control maintained the existing distribution of power in the international system, the possession goal of the superpowers. Though everyone benefits from the success of arms control, it is the possession goal of securing their privileged positions that "leave the existing political structure of the world intact."[33] Both sides have a vested interest in enlisting the support of others for arms control, but this support also means an affirmation of superpower status. It was the milieu goal of avoiding nuclear annihilation through arms control cooperation that legitimated the possession goal of having nuclear weapons.

Bull was concerned that the practice of arms control, though it contributed to the stabilization of superpower relations, locked in place a security system resistant to change "whose effect is to formalize the claims of these

---

[31] Hedley Bull, "Arms Control and World Order," *International Security* 1 (Summer 1976): 3–16.
[32] Ibid., 4.
[33] Ibid., 5.

two states to a special position in the hierarchy of military power."[34] International security is entrusted to those who hold nuclear weapons and "we are choosing arms control arrangements which leave those countries which now possess preponderant military power secure in the enjoyment of their position."[35] In other words, arms control has an inherent anti-proliferation bias that is supported and legitimated by the milieu goal of keeping down the number of states with nuclear weapons *and* the possession goal of maintaining a privileged security status for nuclear weapons states.

Obviously, this is not quite what Wolfers had in mind when he spoke of a link between possession goals and milieu goals. The latter are about international structures of governance, not the perpetual maintenance of a differentiated security system. Yet Bull cautions against rejecting the existing international order out of hand. Arms control cooperation, he argues, has reduced the nuclear danger, "however inadequately and imperfectly."[36] These imperfections should not lead to the presumption that an international order could be constructed in which imperfections would no longer exist. In fact, Bull has little time for ideas that ignore the role of power and capabilities in international politics. The challenge, he says, is "how to make the state system work."[37] At the same time, he does not believe that a grossly hierarchical international order is stable. A world order viewed as fundamentally unjust by the majority of states would inevitably attract challengers. It would foster dissent and calls for fundamental change. Foreshadowing the *Anarchical Society*, Bull advocates that "making the state system work is a matter of preserving and nurturing what remains of a rudimentary consensus about 'minimum order,' not of advancing towards some 'optimum order' about which, at the global level, no consensus exists or is in prospect."[38]

Nurturing consensus is not synonymous with settling for second best because the big prize remains unattainable. Rather, it gets back to Bull's point that any system of order has to use the building blocks it finds itself with, not invent grand schemes bereft of mechanisms to bring them about and likely to be creating new lines of division. What Bull is ultimately arguing for is the evolution of an international order that rebalances the interests of great powers with the aspirations of the international community. A system of international order that primarily caters to the advantage of some is unable to accommodate dissent. It can manage that dissent but at considerable risk of either further alienation or outright failure. In other words, world

---

[34] Ibid.
[35] Ibid., 6.
[36] Ibid., 7.
[37] Ibid., 9.
[38] Ibid., 10.

order is about nurturing a consensus on the balance between possession goals and milieu goals.

The Nuclear Non-Proliferation Treaty, for example validates Bull's call for attending to a sustainable balance between rights and responsibilities. The NPT locks in place an agreement between nuclear weapons states and non-nuclear weapons states based on restraint and privileges. Non-nuclear weapons states agree not to proliferate, and gain unrestricted access to civilian nuclear energy. Nuclear weapons states are obligated to engage in serious nuclear disarmament efforts. The agreement projects a world order in which, at some point, all states are non-nuclear and all have unimpeded access to civil nuclear energy. Forty years of NPT history show that nuclear weapons states have a long way to go toward realizing their disarmament obligation. Their number has grown to now include India, Pakistan, North Korea, Israel (though unconfirmed), and possibly Iran in the near future. Few states trust the ability of the international community to manage proliferation temptations successfully. Holding on to nuclear weapons, or efforts to acquire them, continue to demonstrate their high value; nuclear possession continues to be rewarded with enhanced status.[39]

Recognizing that balance between possession and milieu goals is critical to international order makes Bull's work of enduring value. Balance respects the irreducible need of states to attend to national security even under conditions of globalization; balance also asserts the need for structures of governance that legitimate possession goals. Bull's recommendations of how to strike a stable balance are necessarily modest and reflect his belief that international politics is inherently imperfect. He emphasizes not large-scale transformation but small, sustainable steps that nurture consensus. Hence to Bull, the milieu goal of nuclear disarmament can only be compelling if the structures of governance necessary to sustain it establish a balance between possession goals and milieu goals reflective of the need for both.

THE RETURN OF ARMS CONTROL: TWENTY-FIRST CENTURY SECURITY AND WORLD ORDER

Arms control earned its credentials at a time when regulating the competition between the United States and the Soviet Union was to everyone's benefit. The imperative to avoid nuclear war created a perfect match between the possession goals of the two powers and the milieu goals of the international community. Though of overriding importance and perfect in that sense, profound changes in the international system warrant examination

---

[39] Kurt M. Campbell, et al., eds., *The Nuclear Tipping Point: Why States Reconsider their Nuclear Choices* (Washington, DC: Brookings Institution Press, 2004), esp. pts 1 and 3.

of *how* nuclear weapon use is to be avoided in the future. We have also recognized that a new international or global order must resonate with the distribution of power, the "imperfections" of any world order currently conceivable and into which globalization in all its different forms introduces new variables. Third, we have learned that relations between possession goals and milieu goals are complex; establishing rules of *global* governance and maintaining *national* security is not an easy bargain, especially since the self-serving needs of national security demand cooperation with others and turn arms control into a multilateral effort. Fourth, there is little doubt that a return to Cold War arms control would not address current problems of security. Simply too much has changed. For one, attention has shifted away from a concern with nuclear great-power relations toward relations between new nuclear states, proliferation issues generally, and the possibility of nuclear weapons in the hands of non-state actors. Hence, arms control must address a much larger and more-diverse spectrum of problems, must be able to tackle nuclear issues across a broad front. For another, during the Cold War, the United States had little choice but to accept a relationship of mutual deterrence with the Soviet Union. In the new security environment, this mutuality does not apply to would-be proliferators. Hence, the United States is not interested in finding new ways to regulate new deterrent relationships that would replicate U.S.–Soviet relations. Such regulatory arms control would fail to address the desire on the part of state and non-state actors to seek nuclear capabilities in the first place. No conceivable milieu goal is served by proliferation in the guise of new deterrent relationships.

There is, of course, a whole host of unfinished arms control business, including a follow-on agreement to the New START Treaty between the United States and Russia concluded in April 2010; U.S. ratification of the CTBT; strengthening the International Atomic Energy Agency's ability to detect and act on NPT safeguard agreements; comprehensively following through with United Nations Security Council Resolution 1540 of 2004 that calls for nations to improve the security of weapons of mass destruction–related materials, equipment, and technology; and institutionalizing the 2006 Russian–American Global Initiative to Combat Nuclear Terrorism.[40]

Interestingly, with the exception of the CTBT, none of these measures constitutes new arms control. They are about establishing leverage over new actors and foreclosing their nuclear options. They are in the *tradition* of Cold War arms control even if they encompass a broader agenda. They *regulate* behavior; they do not *transform* the existing order. The thrust of current arms control measures is about fostering milieu goals: keeping down

---

[40] Kenneth N. Luongo, "Making the Nuclear Security Summit Matter: An Agenda for Action," *Arms Control Today* 40 (January–February 2010): 15–21.

the number of proliferators, and reducing the potential for terrorists to gain access to nuclear technology. They do little in the area of possession goals, nor do they come close to rebalancing milieu goals and possession goals.

For that to happen, entry into force of the CTBT would be an important first step. Ending nuclear testing for all is a de facto disarmament measure for nuclear weapons states. The CTBT's future, however, is not promising, nor does arms control appear to be headed toward embracing a transformative agenda. Conservative, regulatory measures remain firmly entrenched. This is nowhere more clearly demonstrated than by the 2009 *Final Report of the Congressional Commission on the Strategic Posture of the United States.*[41] Reminiscent of the Clinton presidency's nuclear posture review to "lead but hedge," the Commission recommends that the United States "move in two parallel paths—one path which reduces nuclear dangers by maintaining our deterrence, and the other which reduces nuclear dangers through arms control and international programs to prevent proliferation."[42] The Commission recognizes that progress in stemming nuclear proliferation is significantly shaped by perceptions of two different kinds of security systems, one for nuclear weapons states and one for the rest. To secure the cooperation of others in the area of non-proliferation, the Commission argues that the United States and Russia must be seen as moving seriously to "reduce the salience of nuclear weapons in their own force posture and are continuing to make significant reductions in their nuclear arsenal."[43]

To a large extent, the formulation of two parallel paths toward security in the twenty-first century reflects divisions within the Commission on how to reap the benefits of deterrence *and* roll back proliferation. To achieve the latter, the Report places much emphasis on American engagement of the international community that is extending the nuclear dialogue far beyond U.S.–Russian negotiations. Deterrence will be maintained as the bedrock of American security and as the premise upon which U.S. leadership is based. Though the Commission firmly rejects American unilateral disarmament measures, it acts on the conviction that the nuclear weapons states must do more to reduce their reliance on nuclear weapons. But caution rules. Arms control must rest on "rigorous analysis of the requirements of security and

---

[41] Positions in favor and opposed to a CTBT have remained as far apart as they were in 1999. Then as now the principal contention between the two camps is whether a CTBT would actually impede proliferation. Treaty opponents see little prospect of North Korea and Iran changing policy were the United States to ratify it. Those who advocate ratification believe that a CTBT would enhance U.S. non-proliferation efforts and increase the pressure on others to join (China, Israel, Egypt, Iran, North Korea, Pakistan, India). *America's Strategic Posture, The Final Report of the Congressional Commission on the Strategic Posture of the United States* (Washington, DC: United States Institute of Peace Press, 2009), 81–87. The Report concludes: "The Commission has no agreed position on whether ratification of the CTBT should proceed."

[42] *America's Strategic Posture,* xii.

[43] Ibid., x.

stability."[44] On the issue of global elimination of nuclear weapons, the Commission concludes that it "would require a fundamental change in geopolitics."[45] Commissioners appear to agree that such transformation is not in the offing.

Nonetheless, we are able to discern Bull's "rudimentary consensus" about "minimal order." Tensions among the commissioners aside, there is agreement that the goals of non-proliferation demand international cooperation and that national security strategies emphasizing the role of nuclear weapons send the wrong message to would-be non-proliferation allies and potential proliferators. Hence the Commission's recommendation of *parallel* efforts demonstrates the rise of proliferation concerns in the calculus of deterrence. Though critics can rightly argue that parallel efforts by definition never meet, and that therefore deterrence and disarmament will remain in opposition, this is to miss the point. "Minimal order" now includes a consensus that the milieu goal of non-proliferation cannot be obtained without a re-visioning of deterrence requirements. While it was sufficient during the Cold War to treat deterrence and proliferation separately *and* reap the benefits of possession and milieu goals, the new security environment raises the cost of possession goals. Reliance on nuclear weapons no longer produces desired global stability. This recognition recasts the relationship between possession goals and milieu goals and raises questions about the extent to which one now constitutes the other. In their third essay on the elimination of nuclear weapons, Shultz et al. recognize this new connection between deterrence and proliferation, arguing that maintaining an effective deterrent and reducing the dangers of proliferation and nuclear terrorism are "not mutually exclusive imperatives."[46] In short, possession goals and milieu goals no longer reinforce one another to create a system of international order that generates stability for those who set the rules and those who are expected to live by them. Merely keeping down the number of proliferators, and reducing the potential for terrorists to gain access to nuclear technology will not yield a sustainable security order. These are strategies of denial, of telling others what they are not permitted to seek; they lack a cooperative element, essential for successful milieu goals. The issue now is how to build a new security order.

---

[44] Ibid., 67.

[45] Ibid., 16.

[46] Perhaps reflecting their own hesitation on a fast-track approach to nuclear disarmament, the authors remind their readers/supporters that "Providing for this nation's defense will always take precedence over all other priorities." Shultz et al., "How to Protect our Nuclear Deterrent," *The Wall Street Journal*, 19 January 2010, accessed on the website of *The Wall Street Journal Online* at http://online.wsj.com/article/SB10001424052748704152804574628344282735008.html, 5 February 2010.

OPPORTUNITY FOR DISARMAMENT?

Reflecting on half a century of arms control experience, Lawrence Freedman concludes that "real breakthroughs in theorizing about nuclear disarmament" were achieved decades ago and new theorizing must amount to more than "dusting down" old proposals.[47] What emerged at the beginning of the nuclear age, he argues, was what was possible; arms control was more modest than disarmament but its very modesty, in the absence of more-comprehensive alternative options, also made it a desirable security choice. Freedman attributes the success of arms control to its working "with the grain of international relations." Arms control, in other words, made few demands; it regulated relations between states and, unlike disarmament, did not aim to transform them. Back on the international agenda, arms control initiatives ultimately leading to disarmament must, once again, take their cues from "the grain of international relations."[48] Freedman is convinced that any other approach will quickly stall. To him, new nuclear disarmament theorizing is not about improving traditional disarmament visions but the manner in which we conceptualize the conflicting demands of national security and international governance. In this sense, Wolfers's and Bull's observations about possession goals and milieu goals are of enduring relevance and speak directly to the task of refashioning international order today.

If, as argued here, proliferation concerns in the new security environment shape the calculus of deterrence, long-standing divisions between regulative and transformative arms control begin to erode and new theorizing is possible. Emphasis on deterrence and U.S.–Russian arms control no longer produce an environment in which their bilateral benefits yield milieu goals. Though they maintain a relationship of mutual deterrence, the absence of hostilities dramatically reduces the milieu value of mutual deterrence. Working with "the grain of international relations" now must reflect the increasing disutility of privileging nuclear deterrence and a recognition that possession goals without milieu goals render the former progressively less viable; the threat of nuclear proliferation offers only marginal returns on additional investment in traditional nuclear arsenals. Likewise, working with "the grain of international relations" means transformative arms control must be attentive to the power differentials that inevitably exist in the state system. Milieu goals are great power goals; they have to serve the interests of those powers willing and able to shape international relations. Hence, new theorizing must begin by acknowledging that international order is ultimately about striking a bargain between the power to create rules

---

[47] Lawrence Freedman, "A New Theory for Nuclear Disarmament," *Bulletin of the Atomic Scientists* 65 (July–August 2009): 14–30, at 16.

[48] Ibid., 22.

and the manner in which these rules are formulated and adhered to. Does this mean that more can now be achieved than during previous years of theorizing?

Re-conceptualizing the demands for national security and international governance has to start from Wolfers's assumption that both must be satisfied if the resulting international order is to endure. First and foremost, this means that efforts to determine the role of nuclear weapons in twenty-first century security must part company with the prevailing practice of conducting two separate conversations, namely one on deterrence requirements and another on proliferation threats. Instead, we need to shift focus to a *security* conversation, hence change the nature of the debate itself. Second, this re-conceptualization postulates a shared sense that a stable international order is not about overcoming power differentials, but mitigating their disruptive effects through standards and rules commonly arrived at. Third, re-thinking the role of nuclear weapons must also be an invitation to review their standing vis-à-vis other policy priorities upon which nuclear weapons have a bearing. This would permit a broadening of the traditional arms control agenda and would make regional security assurances and alliance commitments integral to questions of international order and the future of nuclear weapons. Fourth, since it was the milieu goal of avoiding nuclear annihilation through arms control cooperation that legitimated the possession goal of nuclear weapons during the Cold War, a new security order must legitimate nuclear weapons in national arsenals in terms of how well national arsenals contribute to the overall goals of sustainable world order. This would demand a reassessment of numbers and types of nuclear weapons in national arsenals as well as their purposes. To reclaim milieu goals through the possession of nuclear weapons, nuclear weapons states must credibly demonstrate security benefits accruing to the international community. Under any new bargain between national security and international governance, an answer to the question of who benefits must speak to the international community as a whole. In Freedman's assessment, the role of a *strategy* of disarmament in tackling any of these complex problems is at best ambiguous. A legitimate new security order is not about numbers of weapons but about conciliating conflicting interests and aspirations, the very conundrum Bull saw no ready escape from.

In this context, the Obama administration's 2010 Nuclear Posture Review (NPR) makes an important contribution; it is a first attempt to conceptualize a roadmap for security in the twenty-first century. It links *national* security to American *international* security interests and establishes a functional relationship between possession goals and milieu goals.[49] It recognizes the declining utility of large nuclear arsenals in the pursuit of international security objectives. U.S. nuclear forces can therefore become smaller, and conventional capabilities can take on tasks previously assigned to nuclear weapons. A smaller nuclear arsenal signals reduced reliance on nuclear weapons in U.S. strategy as well as meeting America's NPT obligations. At the same time, the NPR pledges to maintain "safe, secure, and effective nuclear forces" while nuclear weapons continue to exist.[50] To this effect, the administration commits to invest in extending the lifetime of nuclear weapons and modernizing the nuclear infrastructure. In addition, the NPR gives an unequivocal negative security guarantee to non-nuclear weapons states that are members of the NPT and abide by its rules: the administration pledges not to engage in nuclear testing and to pursue Senate ratification of the CTBT.

Though disappointing to those expecting a commitment to nuclear no-first-use and bolder arms control steps, the real value of the NPR lies not in its ambition but in its modesty. Its focus is on developing a perspective on nuclear weapons that repositions the United States vis-à-vis the international community. To manage the threat of nuclear proliferation, the United States needs allies, not more nuclear weapons; hence, the document is devoid of references to American nuclear preponderance and assertions of nuclear utility. Rather, emphasis is placed on demonstrable progress toward U.S. NPT disarmament obligations, reduced reliance on nuclear weapons, the "extreme circumstances" under which the United States would consider nuclear use, the goal of *eventual* no-first-use, and the singling out of states noncompliant with NPT rules.[51] Nuclear weapons, the document suggests, are a burden, not an asset, and tolerating their existence in U.S. national arsenals is legitimate only "to defend the vital interests of the United States or its allies and partners."[52] Departing from past practice, the traditional regulative function of arms control is now embedded in a transformative arms control agenda.

The NPR makes clear that nuclear proliferation is not in the interest of the international community and that proliferators will find themselves isolated and confronted by an anti-proliferation coalition led by the United States. By assembling an anti-proliferation coalition, the United States is able to strengthen non-proliferation norms and connect its own arms con-

---

[49] "The Nuclear Posture Review Report," April 2010 (Washington, DC: Department of Defense, 6 April 2010).

[50] Ibid., v.

[51] Ibid., 16.

[52] Ibid., ix.

trol efforts with a broadly supported consensus on the undesirability of nuclear proliferation. The NPR resists going for broke and instead emphasizes steps and measures that can reasonably be expected to work over the medium term. Thus the NPR speaks of the elimination of nuclear weapons worldwide as a distinct policy goal only to the extent that this goal gives *direction* to U.S. arms control efforts whose *purpose* must remain the security of the United States and its allies and partners. The NPR carefully avoids sacrificing credibility for visionary boldness, reflecting the "rudimentary consensus" on the relationship between regulative and transformative arms control. In short, the NPR is working with "the grain of international relations," aiming at what is possible in areas in which consensus can be nurtured. This is no small feat. After decades of bifurcation between possession goals and milieu goals, we see the beginning of a redefinition of possession goals, recognizing that milieu goals are not merely great-power management tools; it is the global security environment shaping the very nature of possession goals.

CONCLUSION

Bull concluded his 1976 essay on a conservative note. "For so long as international society continues to contain a hierarchy of military power, the present one or some other, it does not seem likely that order can be preserved without rules that reflect these priorities."[53]

Nuclear weapons are a major factor in this hierarchy and the prevailing international order. Though new challenges have emerged in the shape of new actors, complex interdependence, globalization, and renewed attention to the desirability of a more-equitable international order, radical transformation of international order is not on the horizon. Notably, however, this paper has shown that the rules that reflect the priorities of international order have evolved. The price of possession goals has led to decreasing returns on milieu goals. Hence, Booth and Wheeler's argument that "while we should not minimize the strength of the obstacles to denuclearization, neither should we ignore the sociological reality that the rigidity in the situation is in part because of the rigidity in our thinking" no longer holds.[54] This paper has identified a significant decline in the "rigidity of thinking." To cope with a new security environment, structures of governance need to emerge that redefine the scope of arms control, the level of cooperation required, and the sustained engagement of major powers. Milieu goals *have* asserted themselves, and a compelling case can be made for a new balance between possession goals and milieu goals. Hence, we witness not a stepped-up

---

[53] Bull, "Arms Control," 16.
[54] Booth and Wheeler, "Beyond Nuclearism," 54.

search for possession goals but broad-ranging efforts of cooperation.[55] For those who reject the existing "hierarchy of military power," such cooperation is but a token of greater transformation yet to be delivered. For others, the imperfections of any system of international order continue to demand caution lest our ability to nurture a consensus on minimal order is eroded by the unpredictable outcome of bolder steps.[56]

As we consider the future of the President's goal of nuclear weapons elimination, four issues are likely to play a critical role. First, there is the problem of how to nurture the delicate domestic balance the President has forged. The NPR shows that the administration has taken innovative steps to conciliate possession and milieu goals in the new security environment while trying to reassure both the arms control and the deterrence communities. There is nothing in the NPR that cannot be supported by both deterrence and disarmament advocates.[57] Strategic belief systems have not been put to the test. That challenge is looming in the future, when negotiations on numbers and types of nuclear weapons are more consequential than the reductions in the New START Treaty. American leadership and its willingness to seek cooperation on issues of international security can rely on broad domestic support only for as long as it can satisfy opposing camps. The New START ratification politics have revealed the fragility of the domestic consensus not merely on issues of arms control and disarmament but on presidential credibility in international negotiations.[58]

Second, U.S. commitment alone, even if sustained, cannot craft an enduring new balance between possession goals and milieu goals. From the

[55] United Nations, 2010 Review Conference of the Parties to the Treaty on the Non-Proliferation of Nuclear Weapons, Final Document, NPT/CONF.2010/50, vol. I (New York: United Nations, 2010), accessed on the website of the *United Nations* at http://www.un.org/ga/search/view_doc.asp?symbol=NPT/CONF.2010/50%20(VOL.I), 20 June 2010. Also see the renewed commitment to securing nuclear materials at the Nuclear Security Summit, 12–13 April 2010, Washington, DC, accessed on the website of the *White House* at http://www.whitehouse.gov/the-press-office/press-conference-president-nuclear-security-summit, 14 April 2010. Testimony by Secretary Clinton and Secretary Gates to the U.S. Senate Foreign Relations Committee in support of the New Start Treaty clearly shows the connection the administration makes between national security policy and international security governance. Accessed on the website of the United States Senate at http://foreign.senate.gov/imo/media/doc/ClintonTestimony100518a.pdf and at http://foreign.senate.gov/imo/media/doc/GatesTestimony100518a.pdf, 20 June 2010.

[56] Bold steps are not necessarily detrimental to security. Adler and Barnett conclude their study of security communities with the reminder that "to understand security requires the fundamental recognition that policymakers have the ability to act upon the world with new knowledge and new understandings about how to organize security." Adler and Barnett, *Security Communities*, 438.

[57] "U.S. Nuclear Posture Review Priorities," Council on Foreign Relations, 6 April, 2010, accessed on the website of the Council on Foreign Relations at http://www.cfr.org/publication/21841/us-nuclear-posture-news-priorities.html, 20 May 2010.

[58] "Obama Pushes for Senate Vote on New Arms Treaty," *The Washington Post*, 18 November 2010, accessed on the website of *The Washington Post* at http://www.washingtonpost.com/wp-dyn/content/article/2010/11/17/AR2010111701598, 18 November 2010; Henry A. Kissinger, George P. Shultz, James Baker III, Lawrence S. Eagleburger, and Colin L. Powell, "The Republican Case for Ratifying New START," *The Washington Post*, 2 December 2010, accessed on the website of *The Washington Post* at http://www.washingtonpost.com/wp-dyn/content/article/2010/12/01/AR2010120104598, 2 December 2010.

perspective of international order, there is an inherent tension between possession goals and milieu goals. By their very nature, possession goals are about hierarchy. The dilemma is that in an anarchic international system, one cannot get milieu goals for all without possession goals for some. What has changed is the price tag for claiming possession goals without attending to milieu goals. The United States has begun to reassess the price it is willing to pay for possession goals in order to make its milieu goals more effective and attractive. There is little evidence of other nuclear powers willing to act on this logic.[59] If the United States fails to engage other nuclear powers in re-evaluating the role of nuclear weapons in international security, the domestic consensus could quickly unravel.[60]

Third, U.S. leadership in arms control is challenged internationally. The very same security environment that is reshuffling the relationship between national nuclear arsenals and proliferation concerns also demands that milieu goals themselves cease to reflect preferred visions of governance. To be sure, reduced American reliance on nuclear weapons and sustained advocacy of non-proliferation cooperation can have important milieu effects. From a perspective of world order, however, these effects continue to represent American-crafted or, at a minimum, American-led Western milieu goals. For those who do not share these goals, they appear as just another form of dominance. In a world of rising powers, others will demand voice in how rules of governance are created and implemented. It is therefore paramount that creating sustainable milieu goals for a new security order must include rule-making power for others. This makes a twenty-first century security order a collective challenge and qualifies the role of American leadership. The United States can lead, but only with due regard to the input of other players. More than buying into a new security order, others will demand a seat at the table.

---

[59] Kingston Reif, "Nuclear Weapons: The Modernization Myth," *Bulletin of the Atomic Scientists*, 8 December 2009, web edition accessed at http://www.thebulletin.org/web-edition/features/nuclear-weapons-the-modernization-myth.html, 10 March 2010. Reif makes the case that the nuclear modernization programs of other nations do not threaten U.S. deterrence capabilities; hence, the United States can indeed reduce reliance on nuclear weapons without sacrificing deterrent effects.

[60] Domestic consensus on President Obama's nuclear policy is delicate, as was evident in the debates prior to its release. "US to Make Stopping Nuclear Terror Key Aim," *The New York Times*, 19 December 2009, accessed on the website of *The New York Times* at http://www.nytimes.com/2009/12/19/us/politcs/19nuke.html, 20 December 2009; "Obama Presses Review of Nuclear Strategy," *The Boston Globe*, 3 January 2010, accessed on the website of *The Boston Globe* at http://www.boston.com/news/nation/articles/2010/01/03/obama_presses-review, 4 January 2010; "Obama's Nuclear-free Vision Mired in Debate," *The Los Angeles Times*, 4 January 2010, accessed on the website of *The Los Angeles Times* at http://www.latimes.com/news/nation-and-world/la-na-obama-nuclear4-2010jan04,0,1799502.story, 6 January 2010; "What's Holding up the Nuclear Posture Review?" *The Weekly Standard*, 6 January 2010, accessed on the website of *The Weekly Standard* at http://www.weeklystandard.com/print/blogs/what%E2%80%99s-holding-nuclear-posture, 10 January 2010; "Nuclear Weapons Review Put Off," *The Washington Times*, 7 January 2010, accessed on the website of *The Washington Times* at http://www.washingtontimes.com/news/2010/jan/07/nuclear-weapons-review, 10 January 2010.

Progress toward nuclear weapon elimination is a test of rule-making power and how that power is shared. It follows logically that a new theory of disarmament is also a new theory of international order. This will become obvious in arms control endeavors including entry into force of the CTBT, negotiations over tactical nuclear weapons in Europe, a fissile material production ban, a sanction regime for NPT violators, ballistic missile defenses, and nuclear arms reductions beyond U.S.–Russian bilateral negotiations; the degree to which any of these measures progresses testifies to national and collective abilities to design a new international order. Hence, the Obama administration's inclusion of nuclear disarmament and the ultimate elimination of nuclear weapons in its policy agenda represents perhaps the most-potent challenge to America's rulemaking power. For disarmament to be pursued, the United States must accept others asserting a say in shaping the rules of governance. Responding to the proliferation challenge and the declining utility of nuclear weapons, the administration re-evaluated its nuclear posture and took a prudent first step. Consensus on future steps will be harder to forge, more difficult to maintain, and more consequential for U.S. leadership.

Fourth and finally, while major states have an incentive to reduce the cost of possession goals, that is, reduce reliance on nuclear weapons in their own strategies to foster support for non-proliferation, the goal of disarmament remains distant. The imperfections of the international system reflect that the relationship between possession goals and milieu goals is complex. Arms control and disarmament steps in pursuit of ultimate nuclear weapon elimination highlight this complexity and impede the emergence of a compelling and transformative elimination logic. As the arsenals of the United States and Russia decline, the existing dispersal of declared and latent nuclear capability elsewhere becomes more prominent, challenging the domestic consensus in both countries to go further despite the continued need for non-proliferation governance structures. Moreover, the extent to which states currently possessing nuclear weapons or planning to do so in the future are willing to adopt disarmament as a milieu goal is unclear. North Korea, India, Pakistan, Israel, Iran and a host of radical non-state actors may not be persuaded that a world without nuclear weapons is preferable, irrespective of who is leading the effort.

Together these observations strongly suggest that though the need for international security milieu goals is increasingly pressing, their realization is far from assured. The rising heterogeneity of international relations that compels states to cooperate and redefine the relationship between national security and international order generates obstacles to cooperation. Nuclear weapons, deeply embedded in the structure of the international system, reflect these obstacles as endemic imperfections. As a milieu goal, their elimination makes sense; but only if the resulting imperfections along the way and the conditions at the point of destination create a global order preferable to that of today. It is in the trading of relative imperfections that disarmament as an approach to world order has to prove its mettle.

Friends Don't Let Friends Proliferate

SCOTT HELFSTEIN

MANY OF US RECALL THE POPULAR SLOGAN, "Friends don't let friends drive drunk." The 1990 slogan was released as a follow-up to the Ad Council and the National Highway Traffic Safety Administration's advertising campaign against drunk driving launched in 1983.[1] The popular slogan pushed the idea that friends had responsibility for one another's behavior. The slogan relied on two mechanisms: that friends should have more leverage to influence each other's actions, and that friends would serve as designated drivers, foregoing the opportunity to drink. According to the Ad Council, the campaign worked. Close to 80 percent of respondents said they prevented a friend from driving drunk, and 25 percent reported that they stopped drinking and driving.[2] Between 1990 and 1991, alcohol-related driving deaths dropped by 10 percent. The simple fact is that the advertising campaign was correct; friends either were willing to use whatever influence they had or took responsibility for the security of others to prevent this dangerous behavior.

Historical evidence suggests that the power of friendship extends beyond drunk driving and even personal relationships. States, it turns out, are subject to similar behavioral patterns. Allied and friendly states usually have greater influence or leverage than do other states. Empirical research on sanctions shows that they are most effective when the sanction sender is an

---

[1] "Drunk Driving Prevention (1983–present)," accessed at http://www.adcouncil.org/default.aspx? Id=137, 15 March 2009.
[2] "What is a Designated Driver Program?" accessed at http://www.nhtsa.dot.gov/people/injury/alcohol/ DesignatedDriver/, 15 March 2009.

SCOTT HELFSTEIN is an Adjunct Scholar at the Modern War Institute at the United States Military Academy at West Point and Senior Fellow at the Center for Cyber and Homeland Security at The George Washington University. He has published on national security issues in leading scholarly journals and has provided policy advice to the U.S. Department of Defense and U.S. State Department.

ally or friend of the target state.[3] The explanation for this finding is that allied states, or those with friendly relations and high levels of economic interdependence, can inflict damage by sanctioning the target. Conversely, sets of states with poor relations and low levels of interdependence are often unaffected and uninfluenced by sanctions. Friends and allies have leverage that can be used to influence behavior, whereas sanctions imposed by states that have poor relations with the target are less likely to bring about the desired policy shifts.

This empirical finding on the effectiveness of sanctions extends to nuclear proliferation. Sanctions that are aimed at changing the nuclear policies of a target are most, perhaps even only, effective when the two states are allies or friends. According to the commonly used data of Gary Clyde Hufbauer, Jeffrey J. Schott, and Kimberly Ann Elliott on international sanctions (the HSE dataset), 18 countries were sanctioned for nuclear activities from 1914 to 2007; only 6 of those cases are coded as partial or complete successes, and there were strong preexisting relationships in 5 of 6 cases.[4] The remaining 12 sanction cases are coded as partial or total failures. Given the general findings on the effectiveness of sanctions across issue areas, the relationship between economic sanctions, nuclear policy, and state relationships is hardly surprising. States with leverage over the policies of others have repeatedly taken responsibility and used this influence to curb the nuclear activities of targets. Similar attempts to restrain the proliferation efforts of unallied or unfriendly states have thus far failed. Simply put, in recent years, friends don't let friends proliferate.

This poses something of a problem for states trying to defend nuclear nonproliferation institutions. The goal of these institutions is to limit nuclear proliferation among all states, not just those that are friends or allies. This raises an important question: since history suggests that sanctions are only useful for altering the nuclear policies among a subset of friendly states, what policy tools are available to influence the behavior of unfriendly states? The two common answers to this question are military punishment and economic inducements, both of which are reasonably controversial. Military punishments often refer to targeted bombings or large-scale military campaigns launched with the intention of disarming the proliferating state.

---

[3] See Gary Clyde Hufbauer, Jeffrey J. Schott, and Kimberly Ann Elliott, *Economic Sanctions Reconsidered: History and Current Policy*, 2d ed. (Washington, DC: Institute for International Economics, 1990); A. Cooper Drury, "Revisiting Economic Sanctions Reconsidered," *Journal of Peace Research* 35 (July 1998): 497–509; Daniel W. Drezner, "Bargaining, Enforcement, and Multilateral Sanctions: When Is Cooperation Counterproductive?" *International Organization* 54 (Winter 2003): 73–102; Anne C. Miers and T. Clifton Morgan, "Multilateral Sanctions and Foreign Policy Success: Can Too Many Cooks Spoil the Broth?" *International Interactions* 28 (April 2002): 117–136.
[4] Hufbauer, Schott, and Elliott, *Economic Sanctions Reconsidered*; and dataset from Drury, "Revisiting Economic Sanctions Reconsidered."

Some observers argue that the high costs of military punishments should offer punishing states greater leverage over the target's behavior, but others suggest military force is a blunt instrument that should be reserved for exceptional situations.[5] While military punishment tries to increase the costs of disobedience, inducements focus on increasing the benefits of cooperation. Inducements are also problematic. On one hand, inducements provide positive incentives for states to cease proliferating, but on the other hand, they set a dangerous precedent by signaling the possible benefits of defiance to other states.[6] The optimal mix of inducements and punishments is a conundrum that has plagued nonproliferation initiatives for some time.

Given the difficulties with military punishments and economic inducements, it seems logical to try and escape that theoretical debate by examining policies that have worked in the past. Economic sanctions have effectively constrained the behavior of friendly states in which sanction senders have leverage. The evidence on sanctions may provide some clues for disarmament and continued nonproliferation efforts. Disarmament cases like Libya, South Africa, and Ukraine exhibit similar though more-complicated patterns of relationship and influence. In each of these cases, internal and external forces provided proliferating states the opportunity and incentive to improve their relations with the West, particularly the United States. It would be wrong to assert that these disarming states were friends with the United States at the time of disarmament, but it is clear that they hoped disarmament would help strengthen the relationship. In each case, internal and external dynamics led these states to seek rapprochement or allegiance with the United States for different reasons; however, the desire for improved relations was a common feature.

This suggests that states are willing to alter their behavior or disarm when coerced by friends or trying to win over new friends. This is especially true when improved relations can alter external dynamics and perceived threats. Ukraine valued improved relations with the United States, given the potential threat from Russia. Libya viewed the United States as a significant threat, meaning that bilateral rapprochement improved their perceived security situation. Similar patterns existed in other bilateral cases, such as Argentina and Brazil. Disarmament was only successful as perceived external threats declined and there was a strong possibility for improved relations.

---

[5] In the security community, this debate has largely focused on the use of preemptive force. See George Perkovich, "Bush's Nuclear Revolution A Regime Change in Nonproliferation," *Foreign Affairs* 82 (March–April 2003): 2–12; Symposium, "Is Preemption Necessary?" *The Washington Quarterly* 26 (Spring 2003): 75–145; and Jofi Joseph, "The Exercise of National Sovereignty: The Bush Administration's Approach to Combating Weapons of Mass Destruction Proliferation," *The Nonproliferation Review* 12 (July 2005): 373–387.

[6] On the importance of reputation, see David M. Kreps and Robert Butler Wilson, "Reputation and Imperfect Information," *Journal of Economic Theory* 27 (August 1982): 253–279.

Returning to the drunk driving metaphor above, there are two mechanisms that have successfully rolled back or restrained proliferation in recent history. First, states use leverage over allies and friends to prevent weapons acquisition. Just as friends should use their influence to stop drunk drivers, evidence suggests that allies can use their influence to further nonproliferation initiatives. Second, states can take responsibility for providing a safety net, ensuring the security of others. Similar to the role of the designated driver who takes responsibility for his friend's security, states can provide implicit or explicit security guarantees that reduce the incentives for nuclear weapons. This paper argues that establishment of improved bilateral and multilateral state ties, as unappealing as it may sound in some cases, is the best way to promote nuclear nonproliferation.

The evidence gathered for this paper does not provide any conclusions or insights into states that eschewed nuclear proliferation altogether. The threat of sanction and punishment may be effective at keeping the majority of states from proliferating in the first place, and it is important to note that the data gathered here only look at states sanctioned after pursuing nuclear weapons programs. A rational choice perspective would suggest that these states expected to pay some costs for their actions. This paper, therefore, does not provide conclusions about the general deterrent power of sanctions in regard to nuclear proliferation.

The paper shows that states pursuing nuclear weapons technologies respond to those with whom they share close relations. In some cases, states can exploit a preexisting allegiance. In other cases, significant changes in domestic and international politics may play an important role in setting the stage for successful counterproliferation policies. This analysis suggests that the best way to ensure the success of the nonproliferation regime is to improve bilateral and multilateral relations with those states that pose the biggest proliferation risks. This does not mean only that states should provide concessions to those violating international norms, but it also means that states should not necessarily wait for changes in domestic or international conditions to act. Robert Axelrod argues that parties can break issues apart, negotiating over small things, in order to improve trust and generate a cooperative attitude.[7] The United States was able to move toward Libyan disarmament only after allowing back-channel discussions, and the primary U.S. carrot was a gradual normalization of relations.[8] Such a policy of improving ties, if successful, offers the states supporting nonproliferation initiatives greater leverage over offending states in the future.

---

[7] Robert Axelrod, *The Evolution of Cooperation* (New York: Basic Books, 1984), chap. 7.
[8] Bruce W. Jentleson and Christopher A. Whytock, "Who 'Won' Libya? The Force–Diplomacy Debate and Its Implications for Theory and Policy," *International Security* 30 (Winter 2005/06): 47–86. Some observers might argue that lifting sanctions is a concession, but such an argument is logically difficult to justify.

The next section of this paper addresses the theoretical problems associated with using punishment and inducement in nuclear nonproliferation contexts. In doing so, it shows why sanctions have become the favorite tool of the international community. The subsequent section examines the methodology employed in the comparative study of sanction episodes, and this is followed by an assessment of the success and failure of sanctions. This is followed by a longer exposition of the Ukrainian disarmament. The paper then shows how changes in the international system and domestic politics can help set the stage for compliance and disarmament. It also argues that the conditions that increase the likelihood of disarmament may be engineered, though it may not always be easy or appealing. The paper ends with some concluding thoughts about the current state of nonproliferation institutions, and addresses their resilience to recent events and possible fragility going forward.

THEORY: COERCION, SANCTIONS, AND NUCLEAR PROLIFERATION

The goal of the Nuclear Nonproliferation Treaty (NPT), and of the other agreements that make up the wider nuclear nonproliferation regime, is to contain the spread of nuclear weapons. Skeptics, often realists, have argued that the spread of nuclear weapons may be beneficial, since it lowers the likelihood of war.[9] These same scholars put little faith in the ability to halt the spread of nuclear weapons. Others, particularly supporters of nonproliferation initiatives, have argued that the spread of nuclear weapons does not completely eliminate the possibility of war, and any subsequent major war is likely to be particularly deadly.[10] That group of scholars also points to the risks of accidental war, and more recently, the possibility of nuclear terrorism, to justify maintaining and strengthening the nuclear nonproliferation institution.[11] The realists may be correct in linking the lack of major war during the Cold War with the advent of nuclear weapons, but are wrong to argue that the international institutions and norms were insufficient to limit the spread of these weapons.

Gradually improving or normalizing relations, with the expectation that proliferating states will change their behavior, is not much of a concession.

[9] Kenneth N. Waltz, "The Spread of Nuclear Weapons: More May Be Better," Adelphi Paper No. 171 (London: International Institute for Strategic Studies, 1981); Bruce Bueno de Mesquita and William H. Riker, "An Assessment of the Merits of Selective Nuclear Proliferation," *Journal of Conflict Resolution* 26 (1982): 283–306.

[10] Scott Sagan, "The Perils of Proliferation: Organization Theory, Deterrence Theory, and the Spread of Nuclear Weapons," *International Security* 18 (1994): 66–107; for more on the debate, see Barry R. Schneider, "Nuclear Proliferation and Counter-Proliferation: Policy Issues and Debates," *Mershon International Studies Review* 38 (1994): 209–234; and Scott Sagan and Kenneth N. Waltz, *The Spread of Nuclear Weapons: A Debate* (New York: W. W. Norton & Co., 1995).

[11] Sagan, "The Perils of Proliferation."

Nonproliferation initiatives have proven reasonably successful over the past 30 years, but the policy measures used to uphold these initiatives have been the subject of continued debate.[12] There are two questions that confront policymakers: how best to prevent states from proliferating or defecting from their nonproliferation obligations, and how best to coerce states into compliance after they defect or obtain nuclear weapons. Theoretical work on international institutions has stressed the importance of reciprocity over repeated interaction, usually suggesting that actors choosing to defect be punished.[13] There are two punishments readily available to states trying to uphold nonproliferation institutions, military force and sanctions. Alternatively, one can raise the value of cooperation by offering inducements or concessions that make future defection less appealing.[14] Each of these measures has costs and benefits when applied to the nuclear nonproliferation regime.

Military punishment, whether used to destroy weapons facilities or to change domestic regimes, remains a controversial feature of the nuclear nonproliferation initiatives. To date, there are no cases in which military punishment received unanimous approval by the United Nations. The most obvious examples of military force, the Israeli bombing of the Iraqi Osirak reactor in 1981 and the U.S.-led invasion of Iraq in 2003, were carried out unilaterally or by a small coalition.[15] Supporters of military alternatives argue that the threat of these large punishments should be sufficient to alter nuclear policies, and if it is insufficient to alter the policies, military punishment is the best way to ensure that the undesired behavior is halted.[16]

Unfortunately, both of these arguments miss a crucial relationship between military punishment and the perceived value of nuclear weapons: the higher the likelihood or costs of expected punishment, the greater the incentive to acquire nuclear weapons in the hopes of deterring the use of force. Military punishment is only an effective means of ensuring nonproliferation if the desire for nuclear weapons is independent of the additional threats

---

[12] Lee Feinstein and Ann-Marie Slaughter, "A Duty to Prevent," *Foreign Affairs* 83 (January/February 2004): 136–150; George A. Lopez and David Cortright, "Containing Iraq: Sanctions Worked," *Foreign Affairs* 83 (July/August 2004): 90–103; Ashton B. Carter, "How to Counter WMD," *Foreign Affairs* 83 (September/October 2004): 72–85; Lewis A. Dunn, "Countering Proliferation: Insights from Past 'Wins, Losses, and Draws,'" *The Nonproliferation Review* 13 (November 2006): 479–489; and "Dr. Strangedeal," *The Economist*, 11 March 2006, 9–10.

[13] Robert Axelrod and Robert O. Keohane, "Achieving Cooperation Under Anarchy: Strategies and Institutions," *World Politics* 38 (1985): 226–254; and George W. Downs, David M. Rocke and Peter N. Barsoom, "Is the Good News about Compliance Good News about Cooperation?" *International Organization* 50 (1996): 379–406.

[14] James T. Laney and Jason T. Shaplen, "How to Deal With North Korea," *Foreign Affairs* 82 (March/April 2003): 16.

[15] Whitney Raas and Austin Long, "Osirak Redux? Assessing Israeli Capabilities to Destroy Iranian Nuclear Facilities," *International Security* 31 (Spring 2007): 7–33.

[16] Richard N. Haass, "Regime Change and Its Limits," *Foreign Affairs* 84 (July/August 2005): 66.

stemming from military punishment. In other words, military punishment must be exogenous to perceived threats if this punishment strategy is to deter proliferation or convince proliferators to abandon their weapons programs. If, as is more likely, perceived threats are endogenous to the possibility of military punishment, there is little reason to believe that military punishment is a useful coercive mechanism for deterrence or compellence. Even if military punishment can be effective, calibrating these punishments to achieve desired ends has proven difficult.

Use of military punishment is further complicated by imperfect information. Dual-use materials and secret facilities are making it more difficult to confirm heavy enrichment and weapons development.[17] Positive confirmation of nuclear activities is difficult to attain. Reliance upon assumptions and beliefs to justify military action in the name of nonproliferation is likely to weaken these initiatives in the future. All of this suggests that military punishment, the most severe enforcement mechanism available, is far from perfect and may even exacerbate challenges to the nuclear nonproliferation regime.

An alternative to raising the cost of punishment is raising the benefits of continued or renewed cooperation by offering inducements or concessions. These measures are used to convince states that they are better off adhering to nonproliferation initiatives than they are by seeking or acquiring nuclear weapons.[18] Some of the concessions that have been discussed in previous circumstances are energy assistance, military aid, preferential trade packages, and nonaggression pacts. Supporters argue that measures like energy assistance and nonaggression pacts are cheaper, easier, and more practical than military punishment, making concessions a better tool in the fight against proliferation.[19]

Concessions, however, also have some downsides. The most common complaint is that inducements are ultimately offered to states that have decided to break the rules. By this logic, state defenders of nonproliferation are rewarding the exact behavior they are attempting to deter.[20] A state can invest in nuclear research and attempt to acquire weapons, only to be bribed into stopping this bad behavior with rewards. As counterintuitive as it seems

---

[17] John F. Sopko, "The Changing Proliferation Threat," *Foreign Policy* 105 (Winter 1996–1997): 3–20.
[18] For a discussion about incentives and conditions necessary for cooperation over repeated interaction, see Axelrod, *The Evolution of Cooperation*; James Morrow, *Game Theory for Political Scientists* (Princeton, NJ: Princeton University Press, 1994).
[19] Laney and Shaplen, "How to Deal With North Korea"; Jason W. Davidson and Michael J. Powers, "If You Want It Done Right, Do It Yourself: Explaining British and French Nonproliferation Policy after Iraq," *The Nonproliferation Review* 12 (November 2005): 405–433.
[20] Daniel W. Drezner, "The Trouble With Carrots: Transaction Costs, Conflict Expectations, and Economic Inducements," *Security Studies* 9 (Autumn 1999): 188–218.

to reward the bad behavior of any one state, the reputation concerns compound this problem further.[21] Offering concessions in response to proliferation for any one state might signal other states that they can extract similar inducements should they attempt to acquire weapons. The purchasing of support through inducements undermines the concept of collective security that lies at the heart of the non-proliferation initiative.[22]

Inducements are also complicated by information problems somewhat similar to those that plague military punishments. Above, information constraints made it difficult to determine whether states were actually proliferating and whether they should face military punishment as a result. When applied to concessions, information constraints make it difficult to ensure that the recently induced state has actually terminated all of its nuclear research and weapons development programs.[23] In the absence of such confirmation, defenders of nonproliferation institutions risk offering concessions to states that take the money and run. Proliferators get their inducements while maintaining covert weapons programs, which sends the worst possible signal to other states.

In light of the complicated cost/benefit considerations of military punishment and inducements, it is not surprising that the international community has gravitated to an alternative mechanism to discourage proliferation: sanctions. States that refuse to ratify nonproliferation treaties or defect from their prior obligations are often subject to unilateral or multilateral sanctions. Imposing international sanctions is rarely easy, since sending states may have interests in the target state, but sanctions are the most common way of dealing with those that violate nonproliferation norms.[24] Sanctions may involve economic embargos, trade restrictions, asset freezes, termination of aid, and travel bans. The purpose of imposing sanctions is to make the defiant state recognize that the costs of proliferation outweigh the benefits.

Sanctions are also an imperfect enforcement mechanism. Unlike military punishment which is often swift, sanctions may take a good deal of time before a target feels that costs outweigh benefits. During this time, states may make substantial headway toward acquiring nuclear weapons. The biggest problem with sanctions, however, is the difficulty of calibrating the cost of

---

[21] Kreps and Wilson, "Reputation and Imperfect Information"; Zeev Maoz and Dan S. Felsenthal, "Self-Binding Commitments, the Inducement of Trust, Social Choice, and the Theory of International Cooperation," *International Studies Quarterly* 31 (June 1987): 177–200.

[22] States benefit from nuclear nonproliferation by ensuring that neither they nor their neighbors have nuclear weapons. For a discussion of collective security, see Joseph S. Nye, Jr. *Understanding International Conflicts: An Introduction to Theory and History*. 4th ed. (New York: Longman, 2003).

[23] Ted Galen Carpenter, "Closing the Nuclear Umbrella," *Foreign Affairs* 73 (March/April 1994): 8–13.

[24] It is interesting to note that research shows that unilateral sanctions are often more effective at achieving target acquiescence than multilateral sanctions. See Drezner, "Bargaining, Enforcement, and Multilateral Sanctions"; and Miers and Morgan, "Multilateral Sanctions and Foreign Policy Success."

the sanction with the perceived benefit from proliferation. Proliferators will only abandon their weapons programs when the cost of the sanctions exceeds the benefits from nuclear weapons. This is difficult to achieve. Since nuclear weapons directly impact perceptions of security, and sanctions are usually economic, the two areas do not equate easily. States with significant security concerns may be indifferent to the economic costs of sanctions as long as they have the chance to improve their security situation or gain prestige.

Despite these problems, sanctions are the preferred means for encouraging nonproliferation and punishing those who choose to proliferate. Critics charge that sanctions are ineffectual, but the costs of military punishment and the contradictions of inducements often leave defenders of nonproliferation initiatives with little choice. Unsurprisingly, sanctions have a mixed record of performance. Since economic sanctions have been and for the foreseeable future will be the primary policy tool available to the nuclear nonproliferation regime, it is important to examine the empirical record of sanction success and look for ways to improve performance.

INQUIRY, METHOD, AND SCOPE

This paper uses the empirical evidence from nuclear sanction episodes to draw insights into disarmament cases and policies that are most likely to buttress nonproliferation initiatives into the future. By focusing on sanction episodes, the comparative empirical study assumes a within-sample structure, meaning that only cases involving sanctions are included. Using sanction episodes to gain insight into the forces that constrain proliferation poses two additional questions: why do states start proliferating at all, and what would happen if no sanctions were imposed. The first question is the subject of a comprehensive statistical study examining the correlates of nuclear proliferation.[25] The study finds that nuclear proliferation is associated with a state's external threat level, moderate level of economic development, low level of integration into the global economy, and lack of great-power security guarantees. Since the analysis used a hazard model, it provides insight into why states start proliferating and why they stop.

The second question, what would happen in the absence of sanctions, is difficult to answer in a convincing fashion. Any assessment is counterfactual in nature since interventions did take place. The best one can do is offer a deductive analysis. Any state that chooses to proliferate does so knowing that it may face punishment. If the threat of punishment is sufficiently large, be it military force or economic sanctions, then a credible threat alone will

---

[25] Sonali Singh and Christopher R. Way, "The Correlates of Nuclear Proliferation: A Quantitative Test," *Journal of Conflict Resolution* 48 (December 2004): 859–885.

TABLE 1
Hufbauer, Schott, and Elliott Data on Nuclear Sanctions, 1914–2007

Sender	Target	Year	Outcome	Sanction Cost (% of GNP)	International Cooperation	Prior Relationship
Canada	India	1974	Partial failure	0.00	Minimal	Mediocre
Canada	Pakistan	1974	Partial failure	0.10	Minimal	Mediocre
U.S. & Canada	South Korea	1975	Success	0.00	Minimal	Strong
U.S.	South Africa	1975	Partial failure	0.00	Minimal	Mediocre
U.S.	Taiwan	1976	Success	0.10	None	Strong
Canada	Japan and EC	1977	Partial success	0.00	None	Strong
U.S.	Brazil	1978	Partial failure	0.00	None	Mediocre
U.S.	Argentina	1978	Partial failure	0.00	Minimal	Mediocre
U.S.	India	1978	Partial failure	0.00	Minimal	Mediocre
U.S.	Pakistan	1979	Failure	0.20	Minimal	Mediocre
Australia	France	1983	Failure	0.00	None	Strong
U.S.	Iran	1984	Partial failure	0.70	None	Antagonistic
U.S. & UN	Iraq (destabilization)	1990–1	Failure	NA	None	Antagonistic
U.S. & UN	North Korea	1993[a]	Partial success	0.00	Moderate	Antagonistic
U.S. & UN	North Korea	1993[b]	Failure	0.60	Moderate	Antagonistic
Russia	Ukraine	1993	Partial success	7.10	None	Neutral
Russia	Kazakhstan	1993	Success	4.60	None	Strong
U.S.	India	1998	Failure	0.20	Moderate	Neutral

Source: All coding is taken directly from the Hufbauer, Schott, and Elliott dataset.
Note: Outcome is coded from 1 (failure) to 4 (success). International cooperation is coded from 1 (none) to 4 (significant). Prior relationship is coded from 1 (antagonistic) to 3 (strong).
GNP, gross national product; EC, European Community.
[a]First attempt.
[b]Second attempt.

be sufficient to deter proliferation. At a minimum, it will encourage states to keep programs small to avoid detection. Given the existence of a credible punishment, there must be sufficient incentives motivating proliferation to begin with. In the absence of intervention, it is difficult to imagine that a state already engaging in prohibited activities would unilaterally choose to stop.

Rather than focus on the difference between groups that chose not to proliferate versus those that terminate programs, a problem already addressed, this project focuses on cases of active intervention to find correlates of success. The sanction data used here come from the Hufbauer, Schott, and Elliott sanction study, ranging from 1914 to 2007.[26] Within the period under study, these authors identify 18 cases in which sanctions were used in response to nuclear activities, all of which are found between 1974 and 1998. These cases are shown in Table 1, along with coding for the result, the level of international cooperation, the target's cost of sanctions as a percent of gross national product (GNP), and the prior relationship between sanction sender and target. The variable coding used comes directly from the Hufbauer, Schott, and Elliott data and is unchanged. The sanction result

---

[26] Hufbauer, Schott, and Elliott, *Economic Sanctions Reconsidered*.

was coded from 1 to 4, with 1 representing failure and 4 representing success. Level of international cooperation also ranges from 1 to 4, where 1 represents no cooperation and 4 represents significant cooperation. Finally, the pre-sanction relationship was coded from 1 to 3, where 1 represents antagonistic relations and 3 represents strong prior relations. There were no coding alterations for this study, adding validity to the findings below, since coding was essentially a blind process.

DETERMINANTS OF SUCCESSFUL SANCTIONS

This section looks at the set of cases where sanctions were used to discourage nuclear proliferation. Within the period under study, there are 18 cases in which sanctions were used in response to nuclear activities, all of which are found between 1974 and 1998. This set of cases does not provide an optimistic outlook on the ability of sanctions to curtail undesired nuclear activities. Of the 18 cases, only 3 cases are coded as successes, with 3 additional cases coded as partial successes. This is hardly an overwhelming endorsement for the use of sanctions to control nuclear proliferation. The 3 cases in which sanctions were successful in altering state policies were the sanctions that the United States and Canada imposed on South Korea in 1975, the U.S. sanctions imposed on Taiwan in 1976, and Russian sanctions aimed at Kazakhstan. The partial successes were the Canadian sanctions imposed on the European Community (EC) and Japan in 1977, the first phase of U.S. sanctions aimed at North Korea, and Russian sanctions targeting Ukraine. Of the remaining 12 cases, 7 are considered partial failures and 5 are considered total failures in which sanctions did not alter state policies at all.

What is not evident from the data provided in the Table is that the sanctions imposed in the first 11 cases were very specific to nuclear materials and technology. Only more-recent sanctions included general economic restrictions. For example, Canada terminated nuclear cooperation after India's 1974 "peaceful nuclear explosion," but the Canadians did not suspend all aid, despite threats.[27] U.S. sanctions imposed against South Africa in 1975, Brazil in 1978, and Argentina in 1978 were limited to halting nuclear fuel shipments.[28] These limited measures, largely employed to ensure the peaceful use of nuclear technology, are a far cry from recent attempts to impose international sanctions through the United Nations Security Council.[29]

---

[27] Ibid.

[28] On South Africa, Richard E. Bissell, *South Africa and the United States: The Erosion of an Influence Relationship* (New York: Praeger, 1982); on Argentina and Brazil, Nuclear Regulatory Commission, Office of International, Exports/Imports, *Pending Export Applications Report* (Washington, DC, June 1982).

[29] Colum Lynch, "U.N. Backs Broader Sanctions on Tehran: Security Council Votes to Freeze Some Assets, Ban Arms Exports," *The Washington Post*, 26 March 2007.

One explanation for sanction effectiveness stresses the aggregate costs of the sanction. In economic terms, the target's sanction costs across the majority of cases were negligible. According to the Hufbauer, Schott, and Elliott data, the costs of sanctions as a percentage of target GNP exceeded 0.00 percent in only 8 cases. There is no clear relationship between economic costs and sanction success across the nuclear subset. Economic costs do not explain the success or failure of sanction episodes.

One might imagine that the success of sanctions is determined by the extent of international cooperation, but there is little international cooperation across these cases. There is minimal international cooperation in only 7 of the 11 cases and moderate cooperation in 3 cases. Cooperation becomes more likely in more-recent cases. Of the 7 cases coded as minimal cooperation, 1 case is considered successful, 1 case is considered a failure, and the rest of the cases are coded as minimal failures. Similar results exist for moderate cooperation, where 1 is coded as a partial success and 2 others are failures. There is no clear relationship between nuclear sanctions and international cooperation in the period under study. This is not surprising, since the role of cooperation in sanctions has a dubious empirical track record to start with. Conventional arguments suggest that cooperative or multilateral sanctions should be more costly than unilateral sanctions, and therefore more effective.[30] More-recent work has explained that multilateral sanctions are often negotiated settlements in which the final sanctions are watered down, making them relatively weak.[31] Sustaining the multilateral coalition for a prolonged period of time also becomes difficult, even when sanctions are relatively weak, since the material incentives to trade with the target increase as the sanction is more effective.[32] Given the debates about cooperation and sanctions, it is not surprising that the comparative cases here do not show any clear pattern.

More surprising is the lack of international cooperation across these cases to begin with. It may be hard to believe, given the current security environment, but other than the Canadians, no one publicly raised a hand or blinked an eye after the 1974 Indian nuclear explosion.[33] It is difficult to determine whether the U.S. response in 1974 was driven more by Cold War concerns or indifference over proliferation, but it was probably the former. India was among the first states to join the Non-Aligned Movement, a group of states that refused to ally with or against either of the great-power blocs.

[30] Hufbauer, Schott, and Elliott, *Economic Sanctions Reconsidered*; Drezner, "Bargaining, Enforcement, and Multilateral Sanctions"; and Miers and Morgan, "Multilateral Sanctions and Foreign Policy Success."
[31] Miers and Morgan, "Multilateral Sanctions and Foreign Policy Success"; Susan Hannah Allen, "Determinants of Economic Sanctions Success and Failure," *International Interactions* 31 (2005): 117–138.
[32] Drezner, "Bargaining, Enforcement, and Multilateral Sanctions."
[33] *Asian Recorder*, 24 June 1976.

Despite its non-aligned status, India had good relations with the Soviet Union, and received Soviet military aid.[34] The United States had little leverage over India, and conflict with India might have brought the United States into conflict with the Soviet Union.

The U.S. response to the Indian nuclear explosion was not the only incident in which Cold War politics took precedence over nuclear nonproliferation. In 1976, Pakistan agreed to buy a nuclear reprocessing plant, but France refused to follow through after General Mohammad Zia ul-Haq took power in a military coup.[35] Pakistan responded by secretly constructing an enrichment plant with parts smuggled in from around the world. U.S. intelligence confirmed the plant's existence in 1978, and the United States subsequently discontinued all aid ($80–$85 million) in 1979.[36] The sanctions were short-lived. Concerns about the Soviet invasion of Afghanistan soon trumped those about Pakistan's nuclear status. The United States initiated a covert plan to resist Soviet forces, and Pakistan's intelligence service became the primary tool for arming and aiding the Afghan *mujahadeen* in fighting Soviet forces.[37] By 1980, Pakistan was in the driver's seat. Pakistan rejected a $400 million dollar aid package from the United States because it wanted a larger commitment. The subsequent 1981 aid package, offering $3.2 billion over six years, was accepted.[38] In response to the aid package, Congress strengthened the provisions that called for termination of aid should a state explode a nuclear device.[39] Recognizing the risk of openly admitting its nuclear capabilities, Pakistan continued work in silence and waited until 1998 to announce successful nuclear tests.[40]

The analysis conducted thus far suggests that economic costs and international cooperation do not play major roles in sanction success. Further, realist concerns like those of Cold War politics often undermined efforts to restrict undesired nuclear behavior. The only variable that offers some explanation of sanction success according to the data above is alliance or friendship. Sanctions are more likely to be effective when the sender and the

---

[34] John Lewis Gaddis, *The Cold War: A New History* (New York: Penguin Books, 2005).

[35] Shirin Tahir-Kheli, *The United States and Pakistan: Evolution of Influence Relationship* (New York: Praeger, 1982).

[36] Richard Burt, "Information Bank Abstracts," *The New York Times*, 17 August 1979, 6.

[37] George Friedman, *America's Secret War: Inside the Hidden Worldwide Struggle Between the United States and Its Enemies* (New York: Broadway, 2005).

[38] Bernard Gwertzman, "Pakistan Agrees to a U.S. AID Plan and F-16 Delivery: $3.2 Billion Being Offered," *The New York Times*, 16 September 1981.

[39] Gerald C. Smith and Helena Cobban, "A Blind Eye to Nuclear Nonproliferation," *Foreign Affairs* 68 (July/August 1989): 53–70.

[40] David B. Ottaway, "U.S. Relieves Pakistan of Pledge Against Enriching Uranium," *The Washington Post*, 15 June 1989; William J. Broad, "Explosion Is Detected By U.S. Scientists: The Blast," *The New York Times*, 29 May 1998.

target have a friendly relationship or alliance. In 5 of the 18 cases, the sanction sender and target are coded as friends or allies. In 4 of those 5 cases, sanctions were successful or moderately successful. There has been only 1 case in which sanctions sent by a friend did not influence behavior, Australia's sanctions against France for nuclear testing in the South Pacific. The striking aspect of this empirical finding is that the only 4 cases in which sanctions were either successful or moderately successful were all cases in which the two states were friends or allies. States that have an alliance, or historically have friendly ties, seem to have greater leverage over sanction targets. Put more succinctly, friends don't let friends proliferate.

The first case of successful sanctions in the dataset was the U.S. and Canadian sanctions imposed against South Korea in 1975. South Korea ratified the NPT in 1968, and continued to develop its commercial nuclear program in the ensuing years. The sanctions were imposed after South Korea announced its intention of acquiring a nuclear reprocessing facility from France.[41] The United States and Canada inhibited the sale by tightening the financing terms on the funding package that South Korea planned on using to acquire the facility. The sanctions were imposed in June of 1975, and the South Koreans quickly backed down in January 1976, canceling the planned purchase.[42]

U.S. sanctions were later effective in restricting Taiwan's nuclear activity. In 1976, U.S. nuclear regulatory bodies, with the help of the Central Intelligence Agency, discovered that Taiwan was secretly reprocessing nuclear fuel at Taiwan's Institute for Nuclear Energy Research (TINER).[43] In response to concerns that the reprocessed fuel was being made into weapons-grade material, the United States stalled two reactor license applications and held up fuel shipments to Taiwan.[44] Taiwan's prime minister renounced the desire to acquire a domestic reprocessing capability, and the reactor used for reprocessing at TINER was dismantled before the U.S. inspection team even arrived in 1977. The research reactor was restarted in 1978, subject to U.S. restrictions, but was later shut down permanently in 1988.[45]

The third case of successful sanctions in the dataset, which is coded as partially successful, was imposed by Canada on the EC and Japan in 1977. After India successfully used Canadian-supplied reprocessed fuel in the

[41] David Burnham, "South Korea Drops Plan to Buy A Nuclear Plant From France: Seoul Drops Plans for a Nuclear Plant," *The New York Times*, 30 January 1976.
[42] Ibid.
[43] Edward Schumacher, "Taiwan Seen Reprocessing Nuclear Fuel: Taiwan Said to Be Reprocessing Nuclear Plant Fuel Secretly," *The Washington Post*, 29 August 1976.
[44] Ibid.
[45] Joseph A. Yager, *Nonproliferation and U.S. Foreign Policy* (Washington, DC: Brookings, 1980); R. Jeffrey Smith and Don Oberdorfer, "Taiwan to Close Nuclear Reactor; U.S. Voiced Concern on Spread of Weapons," *The Washington Post*, 24 March 1988.

1974 explosion, Canada moved to improve safeguards on its nuclear exports.[46] Unable to lead a multilateral effort to improve nuclear safeguards, Canada moved unilaterally to restrict the use of its nuclear material by suspending uranium shipments to the EC and Japan.[47] The EC and Canada negotiated a safeguard settlement in 1978 and agreed to a three-year uranium supply contract.[48] Japan and Canada also negotiated more-stringent safeguards in 1978 that permitted fuel shipments to resume, but Japan subsequently shunned plans for a Canadian-built reactor.

The final three cases involve the first phase of U.S. sanctions against North Korea, in which relations were antagonistic. It is interesting to note that the second phase was considered a failure, and North Korea is currently developing nuclear weapons. The final instances of success involve Soviet sanctions targeting former Soviet bloc states, mainly aimed at removing Soviet nuclear weapons stored in other countries.

The common element across these cases is that allies were capable of applying leverage across a range of issue areas, even if the sanctions were limited. The states in these cases did not necessarily share norms about nuclear proliferation at the time. Taiwan was reprocessing fuel to make weapons, and South Korea maintained a clandestine, if sporadic, nuclear weapons research program until 1979.[49] U.S. sanctions against both countries were successful largely because of preexisting security relationships. Both countries relied upon the United States, implicitly (Taiwan) or explicitly (South Korea), for continued security at the time. Canada's partially successful sanctions also support the idea that allies have greater leverage over each other's nuclear activities. Canada's sanctions were more effective in altering the behavior of the EC than that of Japan. At the time sanctions were imposed, the EC and Canada were allies through the North Atlantic Treaty Organization, whereas no formal alliance existed between Canada and Japan. Friendly states have greater leverage to bring to the table.

The one case in which a friend was unable to influence another's behavior was Australia's attempt to halt French nuclear testing in the South Pacific in 1983. France had been conducting nuclear tests in the South Pacific since 1966, and detonated a 70-kilaton device on Mururoa Island in 1983.[50] Australia, contracted to deliver uranium to France until 1988, halted the

---

[46] David Fishlock and Malcolm Rutherford, "U.S. Proposals Will Disrupt Plans, Nuclear States Fear," *The Washington Post*, 3 May 1977.

[47] "Signature of Agreements on Resumption of Canadian Nuclear Supplies to European Community and Japan—Earlier US–Canada Interim Safeguards Agreement," *Keesing's Record of World Events*, vol. 34 (Keesings: Cambridge, UK, May 1978), 28962.

[48] Ibid.

[49] "Nuclear Weapons Programs: South Korea," accessed at http://www.globalsecurity.org/wmd/world/rok/index.html, 15 March 2009.

[50] "A French Nuclear Test Reported in Pacific," *The New York Times*, 27 May 1983.

shipments in protest. France and Australia attempted to negotiate a compromise over the next two years. France refused to halt testing, and Australia would only support future tests if the South Pacific Forum endorsed testing. The South Pacific Forum unanimously upheld its protest against French testing.[51] Finally, amid a weakening economy, Australia lifted the sanction and resumed uranium shipments in 1986.[52] In this case, Australia lacked the leverage necessary to alter French behavior.

Two other cases, coded as partial failures in the time period under study, are also instructive. The United States sanctioned both Brazil and Argentina in 1978. Both countries had invested in nuclear technology since the 1960s, but both countries refused to sign the NPT. Brazil intended to build a self-contained nuclear program with the help of West Germany, but both countries relied on the United States for enriched uranium.[53] In 1978, U.S. President Jimmy Carter signed the Nuclear Non-Proliferation Act (NNPA), which was intended to improve safeguards for nuclear exports and make it more difficult to acquire nuclear weapons.[54] The act barred the shipment of nuclear fuel to states that had rejected full-scope safeguards, Argentina and Brazil among them. The United States stalled requested fuel shipments throughout the late 1970s. Reversing the rigidity of the Carter administration, President Ronald Reagan softened the U.S. stance on nuclear exports. In 1981, Reagan waived Brazil's $3 million dollar penalty owed to the United States, allowing Brazil to turn to alternative fuel suppliers.[55] Reagan continued on this course by approving the sale of a process control system for a heavy water plant in Argentina in 1982 and the sale of German heavy water in 1983.[56] By 1984, it was clear that sanctions tied to the NNPA had been ineffective, perhaps in part because of Reagan's reversal. Argentina announced that it had acquired reprocessing capabilities in 1983, and the United States believed that it had the capability of producing weapons-grade material.[57] In 1984, the United States formally signed an agreement waiving the Brazilian penalty, and offered to repair defective fuel elements in an aging reactor.[58]

[51] "South Pacific," *Keesing's Record of World Events*, vol. 29, December 1983, 32571.
[52] Associated Press, "Australia Lifts Ban on Export of Uranium," 20 August 1986, accessed at www.joc.com, 15 March 2009.
[53] Robert Wesson, *The United States and Brazil: Limits of Influence* (New York: Praeger, 1981); Jackson Diehl, "Ambitious Argentine Nuclear Development Program Hits Snags," *The Washington Post*, 31 August 1982.
[54] Yager, *Nonproliferation and U.S. Foreign Policy*.
[55] Alan Riding, "U.S. and Brazil Sign Pact Resuming Military Ties," *The New York Times*, 7 February 1984.
[56] Milton R. Benjamin, "U.S. Is Allowing Argentina to Buy Critical A-System: U.S. Allows Argentina to Buy System Critical to Nuclear Growth," *The Washington Post*, 19 July 1982; Milton R. Benjamin, "U.S. to Allow Argentina Nuclear Aid: U.S. Authorizes Nuclear Help For Argentina," *The Washington Post*, 18 August 1983.
[57] Milton R. Benjamin, "Argentina Seen Capable Of 4 A-Bombs a Year," *The Washington Post*, 9 December 1983.
[58] Riding, "U.S. and Brazil Sign Pact."

By this account, the nuclear sanctions in 1978 did not meaningfully alter the behavior of either state. It is interesting to note that it was Reagan, perhaps the only nuclear weapons abolitionist to be president, who took a soft line on nuclear exports.[59] While Reagan's decisions may have seemed reckless at the time, his policies actually helped strengthen U.S. leverage over nuclear activities in Argentina and Brazil over the long run. While both countries maintained weapons programs throughout the 1980s, in 1991 Brazil and Argentina entered into the Quadripartite Agreement, along with the International Atomic Energy Agency (IAEA) and the Agência Brasileiro-Argentina de Contabilidade e Contrôle de Materiais Nucleares.[60] The agreement required mutual supervision and IAEA inspections of nuclear facilities and materials. Then in 1993, Argentina ratified the Treaty of Tlatelolco, which called for a nuclear weapons–free zone in South America.[61] Brazil followed, ratifying the treaty in 1994. Finally, Argentina and Brazil acquiesced to international pressure and signed the NPT in 1995 and 1998, respectively.[62] The export restrictions imposed in 1978 had no meaningful impact on state policies at the time, but both countries eventually acceded to international demands when bilateral and U.S. relations became more collegial.

The comparative case analysis shows that sanctions intended to alter nuclear policies can be effective under the right conditions. Sanction senders that tried to exert influence over states with poor or mediocre preexisting relations failed to bring about the desired outcome. Though friendship does not ensure sanction success, it certainly increases the likelihood of success. In most of the case analysis above, friendship was fixed according to the data coding. State relationships, however, are subject to change, as indicated in the analysis of Argentina and Brazil. States may alter their relationships, given changes in domestic or international conditions. More-recent cases of disarmament show that changing conditions may drive states to improve relations, thereby providing leverage that is crucial to altering nuclear policies. The lessons learned from sanction episodes may help to further our knowledge about disarmament. Sanction episodes are different from disarmament cases, but lessons learned in one context may inform policy in the other.

---

[59] John Lewis Gaddis, *The Cold War*.
[60] Jose Goldemberg and Harold A. Feiveson, "Denuclearization in Argentina and Brazil," *Arms Control Today* 24 (March 1994): 10.
[61] Ibid.
[62] "Brazil signs CTBT, NPT," United Press, 13 July 1998; Julio C. Carasales, "The So-Called Proliferators That Wasn't: The Story of Argentina's Nuclear Policy," *The Nonproliferation Review* 6 (Fall 1999): 51.

UKRAINIAN DISARMAMENT

An exhaustive case study of Ukrainian disarmament is beyond the scope of this article, and many other good case histories exist that provide a detailed account of the process.[63] The case is interesting, given its coding in the HSE dataset and the detailed history of disarmament. The Ukraine case is the only one in the nuclear subset of HSE in which sanctions were successful despite a "neutral" preexisting relationship between the target (Ukraine) and the sender (Russia). The more detailed examination of the case below shows that recurrent Russian threats and sanctions were not sufficient to alter Ukraine's behavior early in the process, and in some cases, even contributed to hardened positions and policy reversals. During the process, however, events such as the Tripartite Agreement and the resolution of the Black Sea Fleet issue helped to reduce animosity and foster more cooperative relations. Russia continued to maintain and exploit its energy-based leverage over Ukraine after these agreements, but such threats did not generate Ukrainian backsliding, and ultimately, Ukraine acceded to the NPT.

After the collapse of the Soviet Union, Ukraine quickly moved to separate itself from Russia. In July 1990, Ukraine adopted the Declaration on State Sovereignty, which called for an independent Ukraine with the right to maintain a military.[64] Much of the military resources available to Ukraine had belonged to the Soviets. Approximately 30 percent of the Soviet defense industry was located in the Ukraine, and this accounted for 50 percent of Ukraine's industry.[65] Besides inheriting a sizable defense industry, Ukraine also inherited the third largest nuclear force in the world.[66] Ukraine's subsequent decision to relinquish control of this nuclear arsenal is often referred to as the most important case of nuclear disarmament to date, and it spurred substantial research into understanding the process.[67]

---

[63] See Mitchell Reiss, *Bridled Ambition: Why Countries Constrain Their Nuclear Capabilities* (Baltimore, MD: Johns Hopkins University Press, 1995), 90–129; Kostyantyn Hryshechenko, "Reducing the Nuclear Threat through Joint Efforts: The View from Ukraine," in John M. Shields and William C. Potter, eds., *Dismantling the Cold War: U.S. and NIS Perspectives on the Nunn-Lugar Cooperative Threat Reduction Program* (Cambridge, MA: MIT Press, 1997), 151–165; Glenn Chaftez, Hillel Abramson, and Suzette Grillot, "Role Theory and Foreign Policy: Belarusian and Ukrainian Compliance with the Nuclear Nonproliferation Regime," *Political Psychology* 17 (December 1996): 727–757; Nadia Schadlow, "The Denuclearization of Ukraine: Consolidating Ukrainian Security," in Lubomyr A. Hadja, ed., *Ukraine in the World* (Cambridge, MA: Harvard University Press, 1998), 271–283; Christopher A. Stevens, "Identity Politics and Nuclear Disarmament," *The Nonproliferation Review* 15 (March 2008): 43–70.

[64] Charles F. Furtado, Jr. "Nationalism and Foreign Policy in Ukraine," *Political Science Quarterly* 109 (Spring 1994): 81–104.

[65] "Ukraine Special Weapons," accessed at http://www.globalsecurity.org/wmd/world/ukraine/index.html, 15 March 2009.

[66] Ibid.

[67] See note 66.

Disarmament was supposed to happen in two phases: the removal of tactical nuclear weapons, and removal of strategic nuclear weapons. The actual road to disarmament became more complex as domestic and international forces continually complicated matters. In the July 1990 Statement of Sovereignty, the Ukrainian Parliament (the Rada) declared that Ukraine would relinquish its nuclear capabilities. Subsequently, Ukraine committed to the removal of the nuclear weapons and promised to accede to the NPT as a non–nuclear weapon state during the Alma Ata meeting in December 1991.[68] Ukraine cooperated with Russian removal of tactical nuclear weapons until March 12, when President Leonid Kravchuk announced that Ukraine was going to halt the transfer. At the time, Kravchuk argued that the Russians were not allowing Ukraine monitors to observe the disposal process. Mitchell Reiss argues that "domestic politics, driven by fear and mistrust of Russia, was the overriding motive behind Kravchuk's suspension announcement."[69]

At the same time, more-nationalist elements in the Rada began voicing concern about the time frame and conditions for denuclearization. This marked a change among nationalist elements, who had initially advocated a non-nuclear Ukraine.[70] The nationalist camp was divided between the moderate nationalists, who wanted security guarantees and financial assistance, and the more radical forces that wanted to keep the nuclear weapons indefinitely.[71] Having been a part of the Soviet system, Ukraine's leaders viewed nuclear weapons both as status symbols and as a way to maintain some degree of parity with Russia.[72] These nationalist sentiments partnered with a belief that Ukraine had given away the tactical nuclear weapons without receiving compensation, contributing to widespread skepticism about Kravchuk's disarmament policies.

Kravchuk's concern was that the United States would lose interest in Ukraine after disarmament, leaving it vulnerable to Russia. In April 1992, James Baker threatened that the United States would reduce aid and cancel an upcoming meeting with President Bill Clinton if Ukraine did not reverse its policy on the tactical weapons. Kravchuk conceded, only to find that the Soviets continued to remove the weapons after Ukraine publicly halted the process. This generated further mistrust in advance of the Lisbon meeting on the Strategic Arms Reduction Treaty (START). During the meeting, the United States signed side letters to ensure that the successor states would

---

[68] Reiss, *Bridled Ambition*, 94.
[69] Ibid.
[70] Andrew Wilson, *Ukranian Nationalism in the 1990s: A Minority Faith* (Cambridge, UK: Cambridge University Press, 1997), 188.
[71] Ibid.
[72] Taras Kuzio, *Ukranian Security Policy* (Westport, CT: Praeger, 1995), 112.

transfer nuclear weapons to Russia, but Ukraine disagreed with the proposed time frame for transfer. While Kravchuk committed Ukraine to the NPT, the Rada failed to ratify the NPT and added addendums to the Lisbon agreements effectively halting further disarmament.[73]

Most accounts suggest that two issues generated Ukrainian reluctance to ratify the NPT: security concerns and financial compensation.[74] Security concerns centered on continued disagreements with Russia and the lack of Western security guarantees. Ukraine and Russia were locked in a debate about the fate of the Crimea and the Black Sea Fleet, with both sides laying exclusive claim to the force.[75] This was particularly contentious for both sides. At the same time, Ukraine continued to face mounting financial troubles. The newly formed state experienced considerable inflation and stagnant growth. Economic weakness posed a significant threat to the state and its leadership, and Ukraine relied on Russia for 70 percent of its energy needs. Given animosity over security issues such as the Black Sea Fleet, Russian threats of economic sanctions posed serious risks. Russia's first overt economic threat, terminating below–market price oil sales, came during the summer of 1992 when Ukraine announced the intention of forming its own currency.[76] Russia followed that threat, in February, by announcing that 1993 oil exports to Ukraine would be limited to 15 million tons, approximately one-third of Ukraine's annual needs.[77] Russia also stated that Ukraine needed to make concessions on the Black Sea Fleet, military bases, and gas pipelines if it was to receive subsidized energy supplies.

In spring 1993, the Clinton administration chose to alter its Ukraine strategy.[78] The initial strategy focused on disarmament as a precondition to a more robust relationship, but the new strategy aimed at addressing disarmament, economic development, and security assurances in parallel. Then-Secretary of Defense Les Aspin traveled to Ukraine in June 1993 to lend further support to the new U.S. position. Ukraine announced that it would deactivate 36 of 130 SS-19 missiles that were nearing the end of their useful life. While the new U.S. strategy, which included a pledge of $175 million to facilitate

---

[73] Thomas Bernauer, Stefan Brem, and Roy Suter, "The Denuclearization of Ukraine," in Thomas Bernauer and Dieter Ruloff, eds., *The Politics of Positive Incentives in Arms Control* (Columbia: University of South Carolina Press, 1999), 111–156.

[74] Stephen D. Olynyk, "Ukraine as a Military Power," in Sharon L. Wolchik and Volodymyr Zviglaynich, *Ukraine: The Search for a National Identity* (Lanham, MD: Rowman & Littlefield, 2000), 69–93; Reiss, *Bridled Ambition*, 100–104.

[75] Kuzio, *Ukranian Security Policy*, 92–94.

[76] Fiona Hill and Pamela Jewett, *Back in the USSR: Russia's Intervention in the Internal Affairs of the Former Soviet Republics and the Implications for United States Policy Toward Russia* (Cambridge, MA: Harvard University Strengthening Democratic Institutions Project, 1994), 70–71.

[77] Daniel Drezner, *The Sanctions Paradox: Economic Statecraft in International Relations* (Cambridge, UK: Cambridge University Press, 1999), 199.

[78] Reiss, *Bridled Ambition*, 106.

Ukrainian disarmament, appeared successful, there were also a series of set-backs in the summer of 1993. First, Russian naval officers protested Ukrainian control of the Black Sea Fleet, leading the Russian Parliament to pass a decree claiming exclusive Russian ownership over the force.[79] The Ukrainian Parliament, in July 1993, responded with a resolution that all nuclear weapons within their territorial borders were the exclusive property of Ukraine.[80] Kravchuk supported the Rada's resolution, effectively reversing his policy on START and NPT ratification.[81] The following month, Russia responded to Ukraine's mounting debt by suspending oil shipments to Ukraine for 10 days, making it the first time that Russia actually carried out its threat to halt supplies rather than raise prices.[82] Ukraine responded by siphoning gas in transit to Germany and Italy, and Russia subsequently offered Ukraine a line of credit and resumed energy shipments.

Tension between Ukraine and Russia remained high through the fall of 1993, especially after the Massandra Summit.[83] During the meeting, both parties felt that they had received concessions, but neither side obtained sufficient commitments to avoid reneging. Haggling continued into November when the Ukrainian Parliament acceded to START with a caveat: it would only destroy 42 percent of the weapons on its territory within the given time frame. Russia responded, once again, by threatening to suspend gas shipments.[84]

The January 1994 Trilateral Agreement between Ukraine, Russia, and the United States was a diplomatic breakthrough, and many observers argue that it laid the groundwork for disarmament. The agreement called on Russia to supply $1 billion dollars of enriched uranium for Ukrainian reactors, and called on all three parties to pledge "respect for the independence, sovereignty, and territorial integrity of each nation." According to Nadia Schadlow, the Trilateral Agreement helped stabilize relations between Russia and Ukraine, thereby reducing Ukrainian concerns about its security.[85] It was the first time that Russia had acknowledged Ukrainian sovereignty, and Ukraine had additional insurance since the United States was a signatory as well. The Trilateral Agreement did not mark the end of Russian–Ukrainian tension, but it did help warm relations and played a major role during the final stage of Ukraine's disarmament.

---

[79] Kuzio, *Ukranian Security Policy*, 104–107.
[80] Ibid.
[81] Hill and Jewett, *Back in the USSR*, 78.
[82] Ibid.
[83] Kuzio, *Ukrainian Security Policy*, 116.
[84] Hill and Jewett, *Back in the USSR*, 78; Drezner, *The Sanctions Paradox*, 200.
[85] Schadlow, "The Denuclearization of Ukraine," 281.

The month after the Trilateral Agreement, Russia again threatened to cut off gas supplies.[86] Ukraine responded by threatening to break its nuclear commitment. Then in April 1994, Ukraine agreed to give up its claim to part of the Black Sea Fleet in return for debt relief, finally drawing the contentious issue to a close.[87] In July 1994, Kravchuk lost the presidency to Leonid Kuchma. While Kravchuk had drawn support from the pro-Europe western Ukraine, Kuchma's constituency was composed of eastern Ukrainians, who felt greater kinship to Russia. Kuchma campaigned on an electoral platform that called for the reversal of Kravchuk policies that he considered antagonistic to Russia.[88] Kuchma faced two familiar hurdles to ratification of NPT: shortfalls in the aid supplied by the United States (only a small percentage of the aid reached Ukraine), and better security assurances from Russia, the United States, and Britain.[89] In subsequent months, Kuchma lobbied for the NPT, and the Rada finally ratified it in November 1994.

Traditionally, case studies of the Ukrainian disarmament focus on the positive incentives associated with the Sam Nunn–Richard Lugar plan, domestic politics and nationalist forces in the Ukraine, historical fears of Russia, and the precarious security environment in post-Cold War Eastern Europe. In a contradictory view, Christopher Stevens argues that Ukraine was actually more frightened of the United States than it was of Russia, was always committed to disarmament, and would only execute after it felt more comfortable with its Westward relationships. In either interpretation of events, improving external relations with the East or the West played an important causal role in disarmament. The strong negative incentives provided by Russia and the positive incentives associated with Nunn–Lugar helped pave the way for disarmament, but neither explains the observed behavior. This refutes the alternate hypothesis, that sanctions, or negative incentives, delivered by historically antagonistic states, often lead to disarmament, as evidence suggested it resulted in backsliding. Pressure from friendly states appears to be a more powerful motivator.

FRIENDSHIP, LEVERAGE, AND DISARMAMENT

Changes in international and domestic conditions may drive states to improve interstate relations, and evidence from sanctions suggests that this desire for friendship may provide the leverage necessary to change a state's nuclear policies. In recent years, the United States has tried to take advantage

---

[86] Drezner, *The Sanctions Paradox*, 202.
[87] Ibid.
[88] Adrian Karatnycky, "The Nearest Abroad," in Uri Ra'anan and Kate Martin, eds., *Russia: A Return to Imperialism* (New York: St. Martin's Press), 79; Reiss, *Bridled Ambition*, 120.
[89] Reiss, *Bridled Ambition*, 120.

of changes in international conditions and others' domestic politics to further its nonproliferation interests. Evidence shows, however, that drastic international changes may not always be necessary for nuclear détente. More-subtle forces can be exploited to improve trust and acquire the leverage necessary to coerce change in nuclear policy, often leading to permanent improvements in relations.

Disarmament and accession to the NPT in Argentina and Brazil did not occur in a vacuum. U.S. policies that reduced tensions in the early 1980s helped the process progress, but the end of the Cold War probably improved U.S. and European leverage vis-à-vis nuclear policies. In disarmament cases, it is difficult to assess the relative importance of key causal variables, such as changing international conditions, the mutual reduction of hostile tensions, and domestic considerations.[90] These cases exhibit some of the same characteristics observed in the Ukrainian disarmament.

South Africa faced a unique set of circumstances prior to its disarmament in the early 1990s, but it is worth examining since it is the only state to give up an indigenously developed nuclear capability. South Africa's apartheid government was compelled to develop nuclear weapons by external security concerns, specifically the continued presence of Soviet and Cuban forces fomenting violence in the southern region of Africa.[91] South Africa's insecurity was further magnified by U.S. policies of isolation adopted in response to apartheid. Just as the end of the Cold War facilitated disarmament in Ukraine, it was also a causal factor in South African disarmament. The end of the Cold War brought an end to the external Soviet–Cuban threats that had motivated the nuclear weapons program in the first place.[92] The end of the Cold War also meant that South Africa had greater economic incentives to improve relations with the United States, and disarmament offered one way to accomplish this goal.

The United States and Europe had pressured South Africa to sign and ratify the NPT since the 1970s, but had not been successful. Attempts to impose nuclear sanctions against South Africa in 1975 had little impact on South Africa's nuclear policies. Congress initially imposed the sanctions as a response to apartheid, and President Carter subsequently toughened the U.S. isolation policy toward South Africa.[93] The administrations of Ronald Reagan and George H.W. Bush softened this isolation policy, much as they

---

[90] For a discussion of indiscriminate pluralism, see Paul F. Steinberg, "Causal Assessment in Small-N Policy Studies," *The Policy Studies Journal* 35 (Spring 2007): 181–204.

[91] Frank V. Pabian, "South Africa's Nuclear Weapons Program: Lessons for U.S. Nonproliferation Policy," *The Nonproliferation Review* 2 (Fall 1995): 1–19.

[92] Ibid.

[93] Richard E. Bissell, *South Africa and the United States: The Erosion of Influence* (New York: Praeger, 1982).

had with nuclear sanctions targeting Argentina and Brazil.[94] The Reagan policy of constructive engagement helped set the stage for disarmament. Again, disarmament happened behind a backdrop of gradually improved relations, and in this case, the United States clearly used its increased leverage to pressure South Africa into renouncing nuclear weapons and accepting the NPT.

While reduced tension and improved relations set the stage for disarmament, there were a number of competing elements in South African disarmament, making it difficult to point to any single causal factor. The reduced external threat from the Soviet–Cuban presence is often cited as a major reason for disarmament, but there were also important domestic issues as well. By the early 1990s, it was becoming clear to the ruling Afrikaner elites that the apartheid system was not sustainable.[95] There was little reason to supply any new regime with nuclear weapons, given the uncertainty about future governance and policies. Compounding this concern was the possibility that nuclear weapons could provide the new regime with a deterrent against outside intervention, which would be particularly problematic if the new regime decided to persecute the former ruling minority.[96] Just as there were international and domestic causes for Ukrainian disarmament, the same was true in South Africa. In both cases, domestic demand for weapons was low or dropped over time. The end of the Cold War changed the cost/benefit analysis for keeping the weapons, but it is difficult to argue that these phenomenal instances of disarmament could have taken place without the desire for and possibility of improved relations with the West. In both cases, the United States used its increased leverage to encourage disarmament.

Thus far, this section has argued that improved interstate relations tied to international and domestic changes can offer the opportunity for increased leverage. Libya's decision to dismantle its weapons programs in 2003 shows that disarmament is possible without drastic changes to the international system and domestic conditions. According to Bruce Jentleson and Christopher Whytock, the Libyan case proceeded in three phases: U.S. unilateral sanctions and military force, 1981–1988; multilateral sanctions, 1989–1998; and direct negotiations, 1999–2003.[97] During the first phase, the United States committed to regime change rather than policy change in Libya. The 1986 bombing of Muammar el-Qaddafi's home was not formally

[94] Milton R. Benjamin, "U.S. Flexible On Gray-Area Atom Exports: Administration Becomes Flexible on Gray-Area Nuclear Exports," *The Washington Post*, 8 August 1982.
[95] Helen Purkitt and Stephen Burgess, "Paths to Disarmament: The Rollback of South Africa's Chemical-Biological Warfare and Nuclear Weapons Programs." (paper presented at the annual meeting of the International Studies Association, Chicago, IL, 20–24 February 2001), accessed at http://www.isanet.org/archive/disarm.html, 15 March 2009.
[96] Ibid.
[97] Jentleson and Whytock, "Who 'Won' Libya?"

intended to kill the leader; such targeting was illegal, but the United States probably would have welcomed that outcome.[98] The hardline U.S. policy was adopted in response to Libya's support for international terrorism, the continued involvement of Libyan intelligence and diplomatic personnel in nefarious acts, and Libya's ongoing attempts to acquire weapons of mass destruction.[99] Relations were frozen, hostilities remained high, and isolation had no meaningful impact on policy throughout the first phase.[100]

In the late 1980s and early 1990s, Libya's economy began faltering. Economic woes were magnified when multilateral sanctions were imposed in 1992, resulting in a 30 percent decline in GNP.[101] Subsequent growth remained slow, around 1 percent per year. Poor economic performance weakened Qaddafi's hold on power as domestic unrest increased.[102] The weakened domestic position did not translate into a desire to improve interstate relations. Rather than cut back weapons development efforts in light of the domestic challenges, Libya reinvigorated its efforts to acquire nuclear and chemical weapons in 1995.[103] The domestic challenges were not sufficient to drive Libya to seek rapprochement with the West, thereby denying the leverage needed to roll back the weapons programs.

Britain began direct negotiations with Libya in the late 1990s, and the United States joined these secret discussions in 1999.[104] When the George W. Bush administration took power, they were surprised to find out about the ongoing negotiations. Some members of the administration wanted to abandon the negotiations and return to a policy of isolation and regime change, but negotiations continued under Assistant Secretary of State for Near Eastern Affairs Edward Walker. The United States and Britain focused on two issues during these negotiations: contrition over the Lockerbie plane bombing that killed 270 people, and the rollback of the weapons programs.[105] The weapons issues often took a back seat in the negotiations, since an agreement was politically impossible without contrition for the Lockerbie bombing and a promise to stop supporting terrorism.[106] Libya

---

[98] Chalmers Johnson, *Blowback: The Costs and Consequences of American Empire*, 2d ed. (New York: Holt, 2004).

[99] Ray Takeyh, "The Rogue Who Came In from the Cold," *Foreign Affairs* 80 (May/June 2001): 67–72.

[100] Jentleson and Whytock, "Who 'Won' Libya?"

[101] See United Nations Security Council Resolution 731 for sanction terms, accessed at www.un. org, 15 March 2009.

[102] Takeyh, "The Rogue Who Came In from the Cold."

[103] "NTI Country Profile: Libya," accessed at http://www.nti.org/e_research/profiles/Libya/index.html, 15 March 2009.

[104] Martin S. Indyk and Edward S. Walker, "What Does Libya's Disarmament Teach About Rogue States?" (speech delivered at the Middle East Institute, Washington, DC, 7 April 2004, summarized in a policy briefing by Nicole Petsel), accessed at http://www.mideasti.org/articles/doc192.html, 15 March 2009.

[105] Judith Miller, "From the Shores of Tripoli," *National Interest* 89 (May/June 2007): 26–32.

[106] Jentleson and Whytock, "Who 'Won' Libya?"

also focused on two policy goals: improved economic relations and reassurance that the United States was calling for policy change rather than regime change. While Libya valued improved economic relations and removal of sanctions, it repeatedly sought reassurance that the United States was not seeking regime change.[107]

After five years of direct negotiations and mutual reassurance, Libya took responsibility for the Lockerbie bombing and promised $2.7 billion in reparations for the victims' families. Even more startling was Libya's announcement in December 2003 that it had terminated all of its weapons of mass destruction programs. Libya signed the Chemical Weapons Protocol and the Additional Protocol of the NPT, and IAEA inspectors were invited to verify disarmament. Some observers have argued that the U.S. use of force in Afghanistan and Iraq signaled the willingness to use force, and this had a significant impact on Libya's decisions in 2003.[108] Of course, one could also make the contradictory argument that ongoing military conflicts actually signaled that the U.S. military was overstretched, reducing the possibility of large-scale military action against Libya.

It is impossible to eliminate U.S. use of force as a causal variable in Libyan disarmament, just as a mix of international and domestic factors played a role in the Ukrainian and South African disarmaments. Note that there were no strong preexisting relationships between the United States and the governments of any of the three countries examined above. Each case involved a mix of policies aimed at improving relations, and leveraging changes in external and internal dynamics when available. The preemptive U.S. strategy, combined with Libya's weak economy, almost certainly contributed to Libya's policy change. Unlike cases that coincided with the end of the Cold War, however, there was no major reduction in the external threat and no major internal revolution. Instead, the Libyan disarmament was carefully engineered. The United States and Britain improved relations with Libya, and ultimately used the leverage that came with congenial relations. In this regard, Libya appears to be a blueprint for future attempts at nuclear disarmament. All the United States offered was normalized relations and the lifting of sanctions, and this was conditional on Libyan cooperation. There were no drastic concessions that could damage the United States' international reputation, and there was no need for forcible disarmament.

---

[107] Ibid.
[108] President George W. Bush and members of his administration have made this argument. See Tod Lindberg, "A Policy of Prevention: The Administration's Strategy against WMD Is Working," *The Washington Times*, 30 December 2003; Adam Roberts, "The 'War on Terror' in Historical Perspective," *Survival* 47 (Summer 2005): 101–130.

CONCLUDING THOUGHTS

Defying many expectations and predictions, the nuclear nonproliferation regime has proven resilient to the recent challenges. The collapse of the Soviet Union resulted in a stockpile of weapons and materials that could have fallen into the wrong hands. Transnational non-state actors have actively sought nuclear weapons, but their efforts have been thwarted thus far. The changing power structure in Asia has led some countries to reevaluate their positions toward nuclear weapons, but most states have concluded that pursuing nuclear weapons runs contrary to their national interests. Perhaps the greatest feat of the nuclear nonproliferation institutions was withstanding the U.S. invasion of Iraq, carried out under the pretense of disarmament. Many countries could have withdrawn from their nonproliferation commitments, as North Korea did, fearing that their treaty obligations might be used as a pretext for invasion and regime change. Instead, most states have upheld their obligations and reaffirmed their commitment to nonproliferation initiatives.

The historical success of nuclear nonproliferation initiatives does not ensure continued success in the future. The nuclear nonproliferation institutions face threats from states inside and outside. Signatories of the NPT that invest in nuclear weapons programs, such as Iran and Syria, pose a serious threat. If states within the regime are allowed to acquire weapons while claiming to uphold their obligations, then other states may be compelled to follow. Nuclear states that have chosen to remain outside of the NPT, such as India and Pakistan, also present complicated problems for supporters of nonproliferation. Ignoring their nuclear capabilities is akin to burying one's head in the sand, but acknowledging and accepting their nuclear status also risks sending the wrong signals. On one hand, it seems as though nonproliferation institutions should evolve to meet these threats. On the other hand, changes to nonproliferation institutions may weaken the historically successful initiatives.

Given the previous success of and continued threats to the nuclear nonproliferation regime, it is important to create nonproliferation policies based on empirical assessment rather than political expedience or conventional theories of coercion. The empirical analysis here shows that the common element across successful sanction cases is friendly relations. Sanctions have successfully altered undesired nuclear polices when the sender and target have had strong preexisting relations. All of the primary cases of disarmament happened in the context of gradually improving relations. Both strong preexisting and steadily improving relations offer leverage that can be used to restrict nuclear activities. The aggregate data on sanctions, and recent disarmament history, confirm the hypothesis that friends don't let friends proliferate.

States have leverage over the nuclear policies of friends and allies, but non-proliferation and disarmament initiatives have not been effective in attempts to influence the behavior of a hostile state. When states have had the leverage that is associated with good relations, they have displayed a willingness to use it. In cases where strong prior relations did not exist, such as Libya, there are benefits for cultivating them. Russia has taken this approach with Iran in recent years. Given Iran's status as a historical competitor in the Caucasus, Russia has little interest in a nuclear-armed Iran in the future. This is magnified by the fact that Iranian weapons would have the capability to reach Russia well before they could reach the United States. Russia's nuclear assistance, however, makes Iran dependent on Russian fuel supply. This may provide Moscow with some degree of leverage over Iranian policy.

The India Lobby and the Nuclear Agreement with India

DINSHAW MISTRY

IN JULY 2005, REVERSING DECADES OF U.S. nuclear nonproliferation policy, President George W. Bush announced a commitment to attaining "full civilian nuclear energy cooperation and trade with India."[1] In November 2006, Congress passed the Henry J. Hyde United States–India Peaceful Atomic Energy Cooperation Act and, in October 2008, approved the necessary follow-on legislation, to formally permit civilian nuclear trade with India. The nuclear agreement with India was a major U.S. foreign policy initiative, and Indian Americans strongly lobbied Congress to approve this agreement. To some, this advocacy effort heralded the emergence of Indian Americans as a leading ethnic lobby that could substantially influence future U.S. foreign policy.[2]

Scholarship on ethnic-group lobbying would suggest that the Indian American effort would not have been successful. Ethnic lobbying is generally successful if the ethnic group has substantial voting power, if the opposition is weak, and if the ethnic group is well organized for foreign policy lobbying. Yet, Indian Americans did not have a large amount of voting power. Moreover, they faced significant opposition from an entrenched nonproliferation lobby. And Indian Americans were not well organized—there was no dominant association that united the dozens of very distinct Indian American

---

[1] The White House, "Joint Statement Between President George W. Bush and Prime Minister Manmohan Singh," Office of the Press Secretary, The White House, Washington, DC, 18 July 2005.
[2] See, for example, John Newhouse, "Diplomacy, Inc.," *Foreign Affairs* 88 (May/June 2009): 73–92; Jason Kirk, "Indian Americans and the U.S.–India Nuclear Agreement: Consolidation of an Ethnic Lobby?" *Foreign Policy Analysis* 4 (May 2008): 275–330.

DINSHAW MISTRY is professor of political science and Asian studies at the University of Cincinnati. He has written extensively on nuclear proliferation and South Asian security affairs in journals such as *International Security*, *Security Studies*, *Asian Survey*, *World Policy Journal*, *Current History*, and *Arms Control Today*.

professional and cultural groups across the United States. How, in these circumstances, did the Indian American effort prevail? This article argues that the mechanism of working through a broader coalition considerably augmented Indian American activism. The breadth of the advocacy coalition, its ability to draw upon the resources of well-endowed constituencies (Indian Americans and business), and the professional expertise within the coalition helped the effort to advance nuclear agreement through Congress.

This article begins by surveying the literature on Indian Americans. It goes on to examine the legislative evolution of the nuclear agreement with India. It then discusses the extent to which different lobbying mechanisms applied to the Indian American effort for the nuclear agreement. Thereafter, it analyzes the most-relevant mechanism—that of lobbying through a broader coalition. It specifies the structure of the "India lobby" that advocated for the nuclear agreement, and the efforts and activities of this lobby. The article concludes by clarifying its empirical contributions and its relevance to the broader literature on ethnic-group lobbying.

ETHNIC LOBBIES AND INDIAN AMERICANS

Ethnic lobbies are defined as "political organizations established along cultural, ethnic, religious, or racial lines," that seek to address issues of concern to the ethnic group.[3] In the area of foreign policy, they may ally with non-ethnic organizations as part of a broader country-focused lobby. For example, the term "Israel lobby," comprising both ethnic-based organizations (various Jewish-American groups) and non-ethnic organizations, has been defined as "a loose coalition of individuals and organizations that actively work to shape U.S. foreign policy in a pro-Israel direction."[4] Similarly, an India lobby actively worked to influence Congress on the nuclear agreement.

Scholarship on Indian American political activism has charted important characteristics of the Indian American community, such as its relatively high income levels; its size, which, while small, has grown in the 2000s and 2010s (the Indian American population increased from 1.7 million in 2000 to 2.6 million in 2007); and its political party affiliations (while most Indian Americans are Democrats, a substantial minority are Republicans). It has also traced the evolution of the Indian American community and its patterns of organization.[5]

---

[3] Thomas Ambrosio, *Ethnic Identity Groups and U.S. Foreign Policy* (Westport, CT: Praeger, 2002), 2.
[4] Stephen Walt and John Mearsheimer, *The Israel Lobby and U.S. Foreign Policy* (New York, NY: Farrar, Strous, and Giroux, 2003), 112.
[5] For the diaspora, see Sandhya Shukla, *India Abroad: Diasporic Cultures of Postwar America and England* (Princeton, NJ: Princeton University Press, 2003); for early analyses of political activism, see Robert Hathaway, "Unfinished Passage: India, Indian Americans, and the U.S. Congress," *The Washington Quarterly* 24 (Spring 2001): 21–34; Devesh Kapur, "Firm Opinions, Infirm Facts," *Seminar* 538 (June 2004): 32–35; Arthur Rubinoff, "The Diaspora as a Factor in US–India Relations," *Asian Affairs* 32 (Fall 2005): 169–187.

The first generation of Indian Americans formed organizations along professional and cultural lines, but was not active in foreign policy. While two early professional organizations—the American Association of Physicians of Indian Origin (AAPI, founded in 1984), and the Asian American Hotel Owners Association (AAHOA, founded in 1989)—were politically active, they were concerned with domestic issues rather than with foreign policy. Also, due to differing agendas, cultural and linguistic differences, and very different conceptions of their identity, the efforts of various Indian American organizations rarely overlapped.[6]

In the 1990s, there was a gradual increase in Indian American political activism, especially among the younger generation. The House of Representatives established an India Caucus in 1993, after a dialogue between members of Congress and the Indian American Forum for Political Education (IAFPE). At this time, IAFPE was concerned about the State Department's somewhat critical views on India. In the 2000s, Indian Americans became even more politically active, partly because of their growing numbers, and also because of their concern over prevailing policy issues.[7] The U.S.–India Political Action Committee (USINPAC) was formed in 2002 to lobby Congress on these issues. USINPAC and dozens of other Indian American professional and cultural associations across the United States lobbied for the nuclear agreement.

THE NUCLEAR AGREEMENT AND ITS LEGISLATIVE PASSAGE

The civilian nuclear agreement with India was a major foreign policy initiative for the Bush administration. It aimed to remove longstanding U.S.–India differences over India's nuclear program, and to thereby boost the U.S. strategic partnership with India. It also had economic and environmental dimensions: it offered a clean source of energy for India's growing economy, and provided civilian nuclear export opportunities for U.S. firms. Still, the initiative undermined U.S. nuclear nonproliferation policy and the global nonproliferation regime by giving India an exemption from the critical full-scope safeguards rule. This rule, embedded in U.S. law and international Nuclear Suppliers Group (NSG) guidelines, banned civilian nuclear trade with countries that had not signed the nuclear nonproliferation treaty and placed all their nuclear facilities under safeguards. For this reason, Con-

---

[6] Prema Kurien, "Who Speaks for Indian Americans? Religion, Ethnicity, and Political Formation," *American Quarterly* 59 (September 2007): 759–783.

[7] These included "war on terror" rhetoric that many feared would contribute to hate crimes; Washington's continued alliance with Pakistan and its designation of Pakistan as a major non-NATO ally; and public furor in the United States over information technology outsourcing, which Indian Americans feared could lead to xenophobic rhetoric and discrimination. Joshua Kurlantzick, "Vote Getters," *The New Republic*, 26 May 2004.

gress, influenced by nonproliferation interest groups, sought substantial nuclear restraints from India before considering any legislation to exempt it from the full-scope safeguards rule.[8]

From October 2005 to 2 March 2006, the Bush administration and India's government negotiated such restraints, involving the separation of India's civilian and military nuclear facilities. Thereafter, on 9 March, the administration submitted proposed legislation that entailed a one-step congressional approval process. Once Congress approved this legislation, the legally binding Section 123 Agreement for U.S.–India nuclear cooperation, that could have imposed additional nonproliferation-enhancing conditions on India, and which the Bush administration had yet to negotiate, would become effective without a second congressional vote of approval. This agreement would go into effect automatically unless Congress passed a resolution of disapproval, though the President could veto such disapproval, and Congress could only override the veto with a two-thirds vote that would be difficult to attain.

Congress did not advance the one-step bill and instead opted to act on the nuclear agreement in two steps. It would first vote on legislation supporting the principle of nuclear cooperation with India. Thereafter, once the Section 123 Agreement with India was completed, it would vote again to approve that agreement, but on a fast-track process similar to that used in trade agreements, which permitted no changes to the agreement.

The two-step process commenced in late June, when Representatives Henry Hyde, chair of the House International Relations Committee (HIRC), and Tom Lantos, ranking minority member in the HIRC, introduced HR 5682 in the House. Senator Richard Lugar, chair of the Senate Foreign Relations Committee (SFRC), introduced a different bill, S 3709, in the Senate. These bills had stronger nonproliferation provisions than those in the Bush administration's March bill.

On 27 June, the HIRC approved HR 5682. On 26 July, the entire House considered HR 5682 with additional nonproliferation-enhancing amendments. Some were accepted, but the three main amendments, introduced by Representatives Brad Sherman, Howard Berman, and Edward Markey, were defeated by votes of 155–268, 183–241, and 192–235. The House then passed its bill 359–68.

On 29 June, the SFRC approved S 3709. S 3709 was then held up for several months. On 16 November, the Senate eventually voted on the bill and also considered 10 amendments. Some were accepted, but the four main nonproliferation-enhancing amendments, introduced by Senators Jeff

---

[8] Paul Kerr, *U.S. Nuclear Cooperation with India: Issues for Congress* (Washington, DC: Congressional Research Service, November, 2008).

Bingaman, Bryon Dorgan, Russell Feingold, and Barbara Boxer, were defeated by votes of 26–73, 27–71, 25–71, and 38–59. The Senate then passed its bill 85-12-3. The House and Senate bills were next reconciled in a conference bill (the Hyde Act). On 18 December, President Bush signed the Hyde Act, but issued a signing statement declaring that many items of concern to India would be advisory and not binding on the administration.

The Bush administration next negotiated the legally binding Section 123 Agreement with India, which was completed in July 2007. Indian domestic politics then held up the nuclear agreement until July 2008, after which the NSG approved nuclear cooperation with India on 6 September 2008. It was only then, with time running out on the congressional calendar, that the Bush administration approached Congress with second-step legislation to approve the Section 123 Agreement. The House approved this legislation, HR 7081, on 27 September by a vote of 298-117, and the Senate approved it on 1 October by a vote of 86-13. On 8 October, President Bush signed the legislation.

To summarize, the Bush administration spent a considerable amount of time and effort in engaging Congress on the nuclear agreement. The India lobby augmented the administration's efforts.

THE MECHANISMS OF INDIAN AMERICAN INFLUENCE

How did Indian Americans lobby Congress on the nuclear agreement? In general, ethnic groups seek to influence foreign policy in ways similar to those of other interest groups, but also in certain unique ways.[9]

John Mearsheimer and Stephen Walt, studying the Israel lobby, observed that this lobby derives its influence in six ways: through the lobby's voting power, its financial strength and electoral contributions, its organizational strength, the absence of strong competition, its domination of public discourse, and because Jewish Americans hold positions of power. Tony Smith, in his study of ethnic lobbying, noted that ethnic groups gain policy influence through voting power, financial contributions, and organizational strengths.[10]

Examining the above mechanisms of influence, some were entirely absent from the Indian American lobbying effort, while others made modest rather than huge contributions. First, the issue of weak competition did not

---

[9] For interest groups, see Frank Baumgartner and Beth Leech, *Basic Interests: The Importance of Groups in Politics and in Political Science* (Princeton, NJ: Princeton University Press, 1998); for a discussion of ethnic group lobbies as interest groups, see Allan Cigler and Burdett Loomis, eds., *Interest Group Politics* (Washington, DC: CQ Press, 2007).

[10] Tony Smith, *Foreign Attachments: The Power of Ethnic Groups in the Making of American Foreign Policy* (Cambridge, MA: Harvard University Press, 2000), 94.

apply—the India lobby faced significant competition from a strong nonproliferation lobby. Second, in terms of domination of public discourse, while the India lobby drew upon strategic affairs experts to support its case, these experts did not dominate discourse (a major daily, *The New York Times*, very strongly opposed the nuclear agreement). Third, there were no Indian Americans pushing the nuclear agreement from high positions of political power (such as a senior member of the National Security Council, an assistant secretary of state, or a congressman or senior congressional staffer). Although a few Indian Americans worked on the civilian nuclear agreement at the mid-levels of the National Security Council, the State Department, and among congressional staff, they only handled routine technical and legislative aspects of the agreement. At a different level, a leading Indian American strategist, Ashley Tellis, who served as adviser to the U.S. ambassador to India from 2001 to 2003, helped conceptualize the nuclear agreement; he also authored a significant report in June 2005 outlining the case for the agreement.[11] Still, Tellis left the administration by mid-2005 and was less involved in the post-2005 lobbying effort. Overall, there was no senior Indian American presence within the executive and legislative branches of government that advocated for and advanced the nuclear agreement through these branches.

Two other mechanisms were present in the Indian American effort—financial contributions and voting power. The magnitude of Indian American influence through their financial contributions to members of Congress cannot be accurately determined, largely because of data limitations. The actual impact of these financial contributions on congressional votes is likely to have been small. On this point, while it is difficult to determine the total amount of Indian American funding to all members of Congress, data is available on a more limited sample of 38 representatives receiving USINPAC funding. Among these representatives, 87 percent voted for the House bill in 2006, and 80 percent voted for the House bill in 2008. The other representatives would be expected to vote less favorably on the legislation, all other factors being equal. Confirming this, among such representatives, 84 percent voted for the House bill in 2006 and 71 percent voted for the House bill in 2008. Still, the difference in favorable votes between those receiving USINPAC funding and those not receiving such funding is relatively small—it was just 3 percent in 2006 and 9 percent in 2008.

In terms of voting power, ethnic groups gain influence when they are clustered in (and constitute a large proportion of the population in) some

---

[11] Ashley Tellis, *Atoms for War: U.S.–India Civil Nuclear Cooperation and India's Nuclear Arsenal* (Washington, DC: Carnegie Endowment for International Peace, 2005).

congressional districts, or when they are widely dispersed across many congressional districts.[12] Examining these issues, the clustering effect was negligible because Indian Americans do not exceed 10 percent of the population in any district, and, in 2006, they constituted 5–9 percent in just seven districts. The dispersal effect was somewhat more relevant to Indian American lobbying. Indian Americans constituted 2–5 percent of the population in 32 districts, and 1–2 percent in some 60 districts. This population dispersal enabled the advocacy campaign to viably draw upon Indian Americans in about 100 congressional districts as it pressed Congress on the civilian nuclear agreement. Still, because the percentage of Indian Americans is very small in most districts—it is less than 1 percent of the population in over 300 districts—Indian American voting power alone did not influence a large majority of congressional votes on the nuclear agreement.

The issue of organizational leadership and strength, which is the ability of an ethnic organization to unify an ethnic group around an issue and to undertake a substantial lobbying campaign, warrants closer examination. One dedicated advocacy organization, USINPAC, undertook its own lobbying campaign and did not extensively coordinate its efforts with other Indian American professional groups. Another group, a U.S.–India Friendship Council (USIFC), whose activities are discussed below, was able to bring some established Indian American professional associations (such as AAHOA and AAPI), as well as leading Indian Americans from several states, into the lobbying effort. Yet many Indian Americans remained outside the ambit of activities where other Indian American groups were present. As one Bush administration official noted, because of professional rivalries, some Indian Americans would not join the administration's outreach activities that involved rival Indian American groups.[13] Further, USIFC lacked the expertise and capabilities for large-scale lobbying.

To summarize, several lobbying mechanisms were present in the Indian American effort for the nuclear agreement, but only to a small degree. By themselves, they would not have substantially affected congressional views on the nuclear agreement. It was the mechanism of lobbying through a coalition that considerably enhanced the Indian American effort for the nuclear agreement. This coalition, and the broader India lobby, is next examined.

THE STRUCTURE OF THE INDIA LOBBY

The India lobby that pressed Congress to endorse the civilian nuclear agreement had several components. It comprised Indian Americans, American

---

[12] David Paul and Rachel Anderson Paul, *Ethnic Lobbies and US Foreign Policy* (Boulder, CO: Lynne Rienner Publishers, 2009).

[13] Miranda Kennedy, "How Delhi Buys Influence with the US Government," *The Caravan* 2 (January 2010).

business, strategic affairs experts, a formal "Coalition" of these groups, the Indian government, Indian business, and additional constituencies. The degree of coordination between each component varied, as explained below. The lobby also drew upon synergies with the Bush administration's outreach effort.

A first component comprised Indian American professional and community groups and the broader Indian American population. One such group was USIFC, formed in early 2006 by a North Carolina entrepreneur for the specific purpose of lobbying Congress on the nuclear agreement. Its core membership comprised approximately two dozen Indian Americans such as information technology entrepreneurs, physicians, hoteliers, and other professionals. USIFC hired a small lobbying firm that was already representing two major Indian American professional groups, AAPI and AAHOA, on domestic policy issues. AAPI, AAHOA, and several other Indian American groups were thereby drawn into the lobbying efforts of USIFC and of a broader coalition. Other groups such as USINPAC and the Indian American Security Leadership Council (a group formed in 2006, having ties with the Washington-area public relations firm Bonner and Associates) undertook additional lobbying.

Second, American business lobbied for the nuclear agreement through established associations such as the U.S.–India Business Council (USIBC) and the Contractors International Group on Nuclear Liability (CIGNL); through the professional firms hired by USIBC and CIGNL; and through the additional efforts of major American corporations. Given its limited personnel resources, USIBC hired three professional firms to assist with its lobbying effort. One was Vickery International/Stonebridge, headed by a former assistant secretary of commerce having extensive experience with India. This firm focused on overall strategy and on reaching out to Indian Americans, and organized the Coalition for the Partnership with India (discussed below). A second, Patton Boggs, focused on Capitol Hill, and its India-related efforts were headed by Graham Wisner, brother of former ambassador to India Frank Wisner. A third, the Litchfield Group, worked on messaging. American corporations working most closely with USIBC were part of the core strategy group in the Coalition for the Partnership with India.[14] They included the two firms considering nuclear reactor sales to India (General Electric [GE] and Westinghouse); and defense firms interested in strategic trade (such as Boeing, Raytheon, and Lockheed Martin). These American defense and high-technology firms promoted the nuclear agreement because they sought access to the Indian defense market; they wanted the

---

[14] Raymond Vickery, *The Eagle and the Elephant: Strategic Aspects of US–India Economic Engagement* (Washington, DC: Johns Hopkins, 2011), 62. Vickery offers an alternative discussion of lobbying that highlights the impact of the Coalition for the Partnership for India, but downplays the impact of other constituents of the India lobby.

United States to lift export control restrictions on India, as this would boost their technology sales to India; they had an interest in India not conducting additional nuclear tests, because such tests would result in sanctions that would disrupt their future exports to India; and the nuclear agreement would help correct the perception in India, stemming from U.S. sanctions imposed after India's 1998 nuclear tests, that the United States was an unreliable arms supplier. Other firms who benefited from improved U.S.–India relations (Ford, the American International Group [AIG], Bechtel, Dow Chemical, Honeywell, Textron, and ITT) also lobbied for the nuclear agreement. Moreover, since its daily operations were conducted from its headquarters at the U.S. Chamber of Commerce, USIBC drew upon the broader resources of the Chamber.

CIGNL had seven members, with General Electric-Hitachi, the U.S. Enrichment Corporation (USEC), and Westinghouse being especially interested in the issue of Indian nuclear liability laws being compatible with international standards.[15] It hired Barbour, Griffith, & Rogers (BGR) in late 2005, and a few other lobbying firms from 2006 to 2008, to lobby for the nuclear agreement. During 2005 and 2006, it focused on lobbying Congress, whereas in 2007 and 2008, it focused on the executive branch.

Third, while sections of the U.S. foreign policy establishment were cautious about the nuclear agreement because it undermined longstanding nuclear nonproliferation policy, some prominent strategic affairs experts supported the agreement.

Fourth, USIBC and its lobbying firms reached out to several Indian American groups and strategic affairs experts to form a "Coalition for the Partnership with India." This single-issue Coalition played a major role in the lobbying campaign, but was dissolved after Congress approved the nuclear agreement.

Fifth, India's government, through the Indian embassy, hired two professional firms to lobby for the nuclear agreement. These were the Republican-leaning BGR, whose India practice was headed by former ambassador to India Robert Blackwill (though Blackwill himself was barred from lobbying for one year after he left government, and therefore remained outside the lobbying effort for much of 2006), and the Democrat-leaning Venable LLP.

Sixth, Indian business, through the Confederation of Indian Industry (CII) and the Federation of Indian Chambers of Commerce and Industry (FICCI), actively promoted the nuclear agreement. While much of their efforts took place in India, these groups were also active in the United States, in part through joint events with USIBC.

---

[15] Andrew Levin, "US-India Nuclear Deal: Business Interests and US Foreign Policy," Institute for the Study of Diplomacy, Georgetown University, 12 May 2011.

THE MAJOR ACTIVITIES OF THE INDIA LOBBY
The Coalition for the Partnership with India

The Coalition for the Partnership with India recognized that the Bush administration was primarily responsible for advancing legislation through
Congress. It considered itself to be playing a supporting role, rather than the
primary role, in moving the civilian nuclear initiative forward.[16] Its efforts
had several dimensions.

First, the Coalition's core group (USIBC, its professional lobbying firms,
and participants from American corporations and Indian American groups)
met regularly, often weekly, to coordinate their efforts. Administration officials such as Undersecretary of State Nicholas Burns also briefed them, typically monthly, about the administration's position.

Second, the Coalition developed a public policy communications strategy having a message, target recipients, and messengers. Its primary message to Congress was similar to the case made by the administration. It argued that the civilian nuclear agreement offered major strategic, energy, and
environmental benefits; its nonproliferation drawbacks (of undermining
the full-scope safeguards rule) were offset by nonproliferation benefits (of
India's separating its civilian and military facilities and placing the civilian
facilities under safeguards); and that the strategic benefits would be lost and
U.S.–India relations would suffer if Congress rejected the agreement.

The recipients of its message were key congressional leaders—the ranking members from both parties in the SFRC and HIRC (Representatives
Hyde and Lantos and Senators Lugar and Joseph Biden); other important
members of these committees; the majority and minority leadership in the
House and Senate; and key members of the India Caucus. The Coalition was
sensitive to the issues of concern to particular representatives and senators.
For example, it recognized that Senator Paul Sarbanes was more concerned
with nonproliferation than with corporate interests; that Senator Barbara
Boxer was critical of India's ties with Iran; and that two-thirds of the physicians in the district represented by Representative Steny Hoyer (minority
whip in the House) were Indian Americans.[17] The Coalition also recognized
that Republicans were more likely to support the Bush administration and
it therefore focused slightly more on persuading Democrats. Overall, its lobbying effort was bipartisan and it reached out to both parties. This helped
maintain the credibility of the lobbying effort when the leadership of congressional committees changed from Republican to Democrat in 2007.

---

[16] This section is drawn from author interviews undertaken on 18 November 2009, and 10 March, 9 July, 26
July, 6 August, and 12 August 2010, in Washington, DC. Since all interviews were off-the-record, the sources
are not cited.

[17] Steve Mufson, "New Energy on India," *The Washington Post*, 18 July 2006.

In terms of the messengers, the Coalition brought all its three constituencies—business, Indian Americans, and strategic affairs experts—to meetings with senators and representatives. This reinforced the message to Congress that the nuclear agreement was not driven by the interests of just a single constituency.

Third, the Coalition's major activity was to arrange several dozen meetings with the key lawmakers noted above. In each meeting, the Coalition was represented by a business leader (often the CEO of a major corporation such as GE, Boeing, Ford, Federal Express, AIG, and Lockheed Martin); a prominent Indian American; and a defense or foreign affairs expert.

The Coalition also lobbied in other ways. It recruited strategic affairs experts to the lobbying effort; distributed a March 2006 letter by 23 experts on Capitol Hill; helped draft op-eds and letters for some experts; and organized a joint letter from its three constituencies to the Senate on 16 September 2006 (this letter was signed by 5 business organizations, 28 firms, 9 Indian American organizations, and over 20 foreign policy experts, illustrating the breadth of the Coalition).[18] The Coalition also professionalized the lobbying efforts of Indian American groups, most of whom were not experienced in lobbying, and it gave Indian Americans talking points for their meetings with lawmakers.

Another significant Coalition event took place on 2 May 2006, when USIFC recruited 150 prominent Indian Americans to visit Washington. In the morning, this group attended a White House briefing on the nuclear agreement (this enabled the White House outreach office to meet face-to-face with a wider audience of Indian Americans, beyond just their leadership, and to build relationships with them). The group then attended a lunch hosted by USIBC, where Indian Americans met their business counterparts. In the afternoon, Indian Americans, joined by business leaders and strategic affairs experts, met with members of Congress from their respective states and home districts. This event illustrates the manner in which the Coalition brought together Indian Americans, business, and strategic affairs experts, as well as the synergies between the Coalition and the Bush administration.

Indian American Groups

Indian American groups lobbied for the nuclear agreement in numerous ways. Some of these groups coordinated their efforts with each other and with business and strategic affairs experts, while also lobbying in their individual capacities, but some were more independent in their lobbying activi-

---

[18] Sridhar Krishnaswami, "Senators Urged to Pass Nuke Bill," 16 September 2006, available at http://in.rediff.com/news/2006/sep/16ndeal.htm.

ties. Typical Indian American lobbying efforts included placing advertisements in major dailies, sending letters to members of Congress, holding informational events, hosting fundraisers and receptions, and having private meetings with key members of Congress.[19]

USIFC was involved in several of the above activities. For example, on 5 April 2006, it placed an advertisement in *The Washington Post* titled "An Appeal to the United States Congress." The appeal was supported by six Indian American organizations—AAPI, AAHOA, IAFPE, Alumni of the Indian Institute of Technology, Federation of Indian Associations Tri-State Area, and National Organization of Indian Associations. On 18 June, USIFC sent a follow-up letter to members of Congress that highlighted the breadth of Indian American interest in the nuclear agreement. It noted that "the national organizations who join us in this letter have a combined constituency of over 150,000 Americans of Indian descent who are active on this issue." USIFC also held fundraisers. For example, on 27 June, two IT entrepreneurs hosted a fundraiser for Senator Biden under the auspices of USIFC.[20] And, on 12 September, USIFC hosted a reception for senators urging them to bring legislation on the nuclear agreement to a vote.

USINPAC undertook a range of lobbying activities. Its major event in 2005 was a reception on 8 November, hosted with Representative Eni Faleomaeaga (the ranking member of the House subcommittee on Asia and the Pacific), and attended by several members of Congress. At this event, Representative Lantos delivered an open letter to India's ambassador affirming his commitment to the nuclear agreement. USINPAC's other main effort in 2005 was to persuade Congress to include pro-India witnesses in congressional hearings.

In 2006, USINPAC held major events in April, May, and June. On 10 April, it hosted an event with Undersecretary Burns, 20 members of Congress, and the Indian American community. On 18 May, it held a lobbying day on Capitol Hill, and met the congressional leadership including Speaker of the House Dennis Hastert, ranking HIRC member Tom Lantos, ranking member of the House Ways and Means Committee Charles Rangel, and the chief of staff for House majority leader John Boehner. That day, recognizing the importance of the issue, Speaker Hastert held a private meeting with the USINPAC chairman and Representatives Chris Cannon and Eni Faleoma-

---

[19] These are the typical activities in outside lobbying, where groups mobilize citizens outside the policy community to contact their legislative representatives, thereby demonstrating to them that an issue is salient to voters, and that the interest group can make the issue even more salient. See Ken Kollman, *Outside Lobbying: Public Opinion and Interest Group Strategies* (Princeton, NJ: Princeton University Press, 1998).

[20] Aziz Haniffa, "N-Deal Vital Strategic Diplomatic Initiative: Senator," rediff.com, 29 June 2006.

vaega (co-chairs of the Congressional Task Force on U.S.–India Trade Relations), to discuss ways to advance civil nuclear legislation.[21] On 21 June, ahead of the mark-up of legislation in the House and Senate, USINPAC co-hosted a press conference with the Congressional Task Force on U.S.–India Trade Relations, the U.S.–India Business Alliance, and Undersecretary Nicholas Burns. Again, several members of Congress attended the event.

USINPAC also held fundraisers for members of the House, such as Representatives Ileana Ros-Lehtinen (co-chair of the India Caucus) and Frank Pallone (founder and past chair of the India Caucus), and for three key senators (Senators John Cornyn [co-chair of the Friends of India group in the Senate], Christopher Bond, and Joseph Biden).

In terms of its political contributions, among members of the House, USINPAC contributed $51,200 to 20 Democrats and $58,549 to 21 Republicans during the 2006 cycle.[22] Among Senators, it contributed $3,650 to four Democrats (Senators Evan Bayh, Ben Cardin, Edward Kennedy, and Mary Landrieu) and $9,100 to five Republicans (Senators Lamar Alexander, Lindsey Graham, John Kyle, John Cornyn, and Richard Lugar). During the 2008 electoral cycle, among members of the House, it contributed $51,800 to Democrats and $9,000 to Republicans, and, among Senators, contributed $9,800 to Democrats.

Other Indian American groups pursued additional activities. For example, AAPI and AAHOA held a joint reception on 10 July 2006, where Secretary of State Rice was the keynote speaker. Further, community publications and websites such as *India Abroad* and *News India* extensively covered drafts of the nuclear legislation, and also named individual members of Congress who had expressed support for or opposition to the bills.[23]

Finally (often at the suggestion of Indian American groups or the Coalition for the Partnership with India), Indian Americans lobbied representatives and senators from their home districts and states. Such lobbying succeeded in getting several representatives to cosponsor the March 2006 legislation—the number of cosponsors in the House increased from 8 on April 30 to 41 by mid-June, including 16 (mostly Republicans) from Texas, 4 Democrats from New York, 3 Democrats from Illinois, and 2 Democrats from Ohio.

Thus, in Ohio, Indian Americans lobbied Representative Sherrod Brown, who was holding out against, but eventually cosponsored, the March

---

[21] USINPAC, "USINPAC Meets with House Leadership to Advance US-India Civil Nuclear Agreement," Press Release, 18 May 2006.
[22] Information obtained by author from a database hosted by the Center for Responsive Politics, http://www.opensecrets.org/pacs/index.php.
[23] Kirk, "Indian Americans and the U.S.-India Nuclear Agreement"; Walter Andersen, "The Indian American Community Comes into its Political Own," *India Abroad*, 1 September 2006, A12.

2006 legislation. In Texas, Indian Americans were particularly active in lobbying their representatives in May and June.[24] The large number of cosponsors from Texas is notable, compared to the fact that there was only one cosponsor each from New Jersey and California, states with high Indian American populations. To take some other examples, in Nevada, an Indian American doctor from Las Vegas lobbied Senator John Ensign in September; late that month, Ensign dropped his hold on the Senate bill.[25] In Mississippi, in early May, a prominent Indian American doctor met with Senators Trent Lott and Thad Cochran (they announced their support for the agreement soon thereafter), and Indian Americans also urged House members from Mississippi to support the agreement.[26] In Florida, a doctor on the USINPAC Leadership Committee met with several members of Congress, including Representative Michael Bilirakis and Senator Mel Martinez. And Indian Americans focused considerable effort on lawmakers from the New York metropolitan region, which had the highest concentration of Indian Americans in the United States.[27] Indian Americans also asserted that it was time for members of Congress to give back to their community.[28]

USIBC and American Business

USIBC and American business pursued several initiatives for the nuclear agreement. Their activities included holding gala events, sending letters from business leaders to Congress, and making economic arguments for the nuclear agreement.

For example, a USIBC gala event on 22 June 2006 included a keynote address by Vice President Richard Cheney and a speech by Senator Biden. Here, Biden publicly endorsed the nuclear agreement, and this influenced several Democrats in the Senate to also support the agreement. It is also worth noting that prominent Indian Americans attended this event, and a USIFC leader organized Senator Biden's participation, illustrating the close links between Indian Americans and business.

To take another example, USIBC drew upon the U.S. Chamber of Commerce. On 21 March, the Chamber's president sent letters to representatives and senators urging them to support the nuclear agreement. In September, when the bill was tabled in the Senate, the Chamber sent another letter urging senators to vote on the legislation.

To take a third example, on 5 April, the chief executives of major U.S. firms (such as AES Corporation, Dow Chemical, Honeywell, McGraw-Hill,

---

[24] Hari Sharma, "U.S.–India Nuclear Deal: The Carrot and the Rod," *The South Asian*, 16 July 2006.
[25] Aziz Haniffa, "N-Bill Could Be Taken Up in Senate on Friday," rediff.com, 20 September 2006.
[26] USINPAC, "Key Members of Congress to Support Civil Nuclear Agreement," Press Release, 5 May 2006.
[27] Mike McIntire, "Indian Americans Test Their Clout in Atom Pact," *The New York Times*, 5 June 2006.
[28] Lalit Jha, "Critical Mass," *Indian Express*, 2 July 2006.

J.P. Morgan Chase, Parsons Brinckeroff, and Xerox) sent a letter to members of Congress endorsing the nuclear agreement. The letter noted that the agreement would "foster technological innovation and the creation of commercial opportunities bringing prosperity to millions."[29]

To take a fourth example, in December 2006, just after Congress passed the Hyde Act, USIBC, in partnership with CII, assisted in taking to India the largest American business development mission in the history of the U.S. government. The group comprised 258 executives from 200 firms, including 30 from 14 firms in the nuclear sector.[30]

The above examples highlight a key aspect of business lobbying, which went beyond the strategic argument made by the Bush administration: business argued that strong political ties with India would generate economic returns for American firms.[31] It noted that nuclear cooperation with India would create thousands of jobs for U.S. vendors. American business initially made the argument that if U.S. vendors obtained contracts for just two civilian nuclear reactors in India, this would create 3,000–5,000 new direct jobs and 10,000–15,000 indirect jobs in the United States. Eventually, it outlined larger economic opportunities, noting that "India's nuclear-energy market—estimated to require $100 billion in foreign direct investment—will open for U.S. companies, which till now has been a closed sector, creating a potential 270,000 American jobs in high-technology engineering and manufacturing over the next decade."[32] And, on defense issues, American firms made the case that improved ties with India would give Boeing and Lockheed Martin a better chance at obtaining a $10 billion contract to sell 126 fighter planes to the Indian Air Force.[33]

In summary, USIBC undertook an extensive lobbying effort for American business. Illustrating the breadth of its endeavors, it had talked to or held meetings with some 40 major companies by July 2006, in the period before the House vote.[34] Further, some U.S. corporations, beyond their efforts with USIBC, lobbied Congress in their individual capacities. These included McDermott International, the Shaw Group, United Technologies, the Chamber of Commerce, USEC, New York Life Insurance, Northrop Grumman, Nuclear Energy Institute, Raytheon, Bechtel, Boeing, Chevron, Westinghouse, General Electric, and Honeywell.[35]

---

[29] "United We Stand for N-Deal: American CEOs," *Indian Express*, 5 April 2006.
[30] A.N. Prasad, "Is the Nuclear Deal about Big Business," rediff.com, 15 July 2008.
[31] Subrata Ghoshroy, *The US–India Nuclear Deal: Triumph of the Business Lobby* (Cambridge, MA: MIT Center for International Studies, 2006).
[32] US–India Business Council, Press Release, Washington, DC, 17 November 2006.
[33] Mira Kamdar, "Forget the Israel Lobby: The Hill's Next Big Player is Made in India," *The Washington Post*, 30 September 2007.
[34] Mufson, "New Energy on India."
[35] Information obtained by the author from a database hosted by the Center for Responsive Politics.

Strategic Affairs Experts

A number of strategic affairs experts endorsed the nuclear agreement, albeit some with caution. Thus, on 10 March 2006, 23 eminent scholars, diplomats, and former policymakers wrote a letter to Congress favoring the nuclear agreement; they outlined its positive strategic, economic, energy, and environmental aspects, and they allayed nonproliferation concerns. Experts also commented favorably on the nuclear agreement in congressional testimony and in the press.

It should also be noted that congressional leaders on nonproliferation, including Republicans such as Senator Lugar, held back their support for the nuclear agreement until they had thoroughly consulted and heard from experts. In the end, they were significantly influenced by the endorsement from nonproliferation experts such as director of the International Atomic Energy Agency (IAEA) Mohammed El Baradei; defense and foreign affairs experts with experience in nonproliferation such as Frank Wisner (who once served as a special envoy on nonproliferation) and Ashton Carter; and senior former members of the cabinet such as former defense secretaries William Perry and William Cohen and former secretary of state Henry Kissinger.

Additional Constituencies

The advocacy coalition drew upon additional constituencies to make its case with Congress. For example, in July 2006, one Indian American group, the Indian American Security Leadership Council (IASLC), recruited eight national veterans groups to endorse the nuclear agreement.[36] Also, in November, the IASLC ran a full-page advertisement in *Roll Call*, signed by veterans' organizations, urging Congress to pass nuclear legislation without tough amendments.[37] To take another example, on 18 May 2006, the American Jewish Committee sent a letter to Congress endorsing the nuclear agreement.

The Indian Embassy and Lobbying Firms

The Indian embassy and India's ambassador to the United States met with and reached out to dozens of members of Congress to secure their support for the nuclear agreement. The lobbying firms hired by the Indian embassy, BGR and Venable, pursued additional extensive efforts.[38] BGR's lobbying effort from late 2005 to 2008 involved some 150 meetings and communications with Bush administration and State department officials, and 360 with congressional staffers and members of Congress. Most of these took

---

[36] Ted McKenna, "Indian American Group Promotes Nuclear Trade," *PR Week*, 27 July 2006.
[37] "And Now, the Vote," *Outlook India*, 14 November 2006.
[38] Information in this section is obtained by the author from a database hosted by the Department of Justice under the Foreign Agents Registration Act, at www.fara.gov.

place from March to December 2006, when Hyde Act legislation was making its way through Congress. In the House, it extensively reached out to five Republicans—Representatives Ros-Lehtinen, Hyde, Dan Burton, Ed Royce, and Joe Wilson (all members of the HIRC; Wilson was also past chair of the India Caucus)—and two Democrats—Representatives Howard Berman and Steny Hoyer. In the Senate, it largely focused on leading Republicans—Senators Lincoln Chafee, Chuck Hagel, Lamar Alexander, Richard Lugar, and Mel Martinez (all members of the SFRC) and Senators John Cornyn, John McCain, and Jon Kyl (who were part of the Republican leadership).

Venable's lobbying activities involved over 400 meetings and communications, including just under 50 with Bush administration and State Department officials, and 370 with members of Congress and congressional staff. Again, most of these occurred between March and December 2006. In the House, it interacted with five Republicans—Representatives Hyde, Ros-Lehtinen, Boehner (the majority leader), Lewis, and Pryce. It worked more extensively with 13 Democrats—Representatives Ackerman (co-chair of the India Caucus), Berman, Crowley, Lantos, Rangel, Faleomavaga, Napolitano, Abercrombie, Brown, Cardoza, Delahunt, Lee, and Waxman. In the Senate, it reached out to key Republicans (Senators Chafee, Cornyn, McCain, Lott, Crapo, Dole, Domenici, Isakson, and Vitter). More significantly, it held several meetings with leading Democrats (Senators Biden, Kennedy, Reed, Reid, Baucus, Dodd, and Levin), and it also met fewer times with some other Democrats (for example, in April 2006, it met Senators Akaka, Bingaman, Dorgan, who still eventually voted against the Hyde Act, as well as Senator Mikulski).

It should also be noted that for the most part, BGR and Venable's lobbying activities did not significantly overlap. Illustrating this, among members of the House International Relations Committee, BGR met with 7 members of Congress and Venable met with 16, though only 3 members of Congress met with both firms. Among members of the Senate Foreign Relations Committee, BGR met 8 senators and Venable met with 20, though only 3 senators met with both firms.[39]

Indian Business

Indian business groups such as CII and FICCI promoted the nuclear agreement in India as well as in the United States. CII's contributions began in the period before the nuclear agreement, when it helped advance U.S.–India relations through numerous business-to-business and government-to-business events. Among these, it hosted track-II dialogues with the Aspen Group

---

[39] This information is obtained by the author from a database hosted by the Department of Justice under the Foreign Agents Registration Act, at www.fara.gov.

that began in 2002. During the 2005 dialogue, participants outlined a framework for civilian nuclear cooperation. It also sponsored congressional trips to India; from 2000 to February 2005, 18 members of Congress and 58 congressional staffers visited India on such trips.[40] These relationship-building initiatives created a greater awareness of India in Congress and in the U.S. strategic community, and thereby contributed indirectly to the success of the nuclear agreement.

These efforts continued in the period 2005–2008, when CII promoted exchanges between Indian Members of Parliament and U.S. members of Congress; these made the members of Congress aware of the importance of the nuclear agreement for U.S.–India relations. Also, as noted above, it partnered with USIBC in bringing U.S. business delegations to India. The business-to-government interaction during such initiatives was also important; Indian government officials met U.S. business leaders and informed them about the significance of the nuclear agreement, and, in turn, U.S. business leaders lobbied for the agreement in the United States.

Synergies with the Bush Administration

The advocacy coalition and Bush administration drew upon mutual synergies in their efforts to persuade Congress. Some of their reinforcing activities, such as the 2 May 2006 event, have been noted above. The Bush administration also interacted with the advocacy coalition in other ways.

First, the White House outreach office held regular, often weekly, conference calls with 10–20 officials from the main Indian American groups.[41] These initiatives kept Indian Americans informed of the administration's efforts. They also helped counter the stand taken by members of Congress who, in their conversations with Indian Americans, noted that the administration was not sufficiently engaging Congress on the nuclear agreement.

Second, administration officials regularly participated in events hosted by Indian American groups and American business. Appearances by Secretary of State Rice, Undersecretary Burns, and other officials energized these groups' members to become more involved in the lobbying effort. In the end, the administration's outreach effort was successful in building relationships with Indian Americans. This helped when the passage of the Hyde Act was delayed until the lame-duck session of Congress in late 2006. It again helped in late 2008, when time constraints were the main concern for the advocates of the nuclear agreement. In these situations, the administration was able to engage Indian American groups, especially because of its stronger relations

---

[40] Farah Stockman, "Trade Plan Would Allow Nuclear Sales to India," *Boston Globe*, 3 July 2006; and Center for Public Integrity, *Power Trips: How Private Travel Sponsors Gain Special Access to Congress* (Washington, DC: Center for Public Integrity, 2006).

[41] Miranda Kennedy, "How Delhi Buys Influence with the US Government."

with them. They, in turn, pressed Congress to advance the civilian nuclear legislation.

To summarize, each component of the India lobby undertook a range of activities to advance the civilian nuclear agreement. The lobbying activities during 2006, discussed above, were essentially replicated in August and September 2008, when the Bush administration sought to advance second-step legislation through Congress.

This breadth of activity was complemented by the strengths within the lobby. These strengths included the fairly vast financial and personnel resources of Indian Americans and business; endorsement from recognized foreign policy experts; the professional, legal, and public relations lobbying expertise within the coalition; and its organizational effectiveness in coordinating the activities of Indian Americans, business, and strategic affairs experts. Thus, the breadth of the India lobby, and the strong capabilities and expertise within the lobby, helped in advancing the nuclear agreement through Congress.

THE IMPACT OF THE INDIA LOBBY
Quantitative Assessments of the Congressional Vote
To what extent did lobbying by interest groups influence the actual votes of members of Congress? To what extent did other mechanisms influence congressional votes? Five hypotheses offer basic assessments of these issues.

The first (H1) tests the impact of lobbying by examining the votes of members of Congress who were directly lobbied by the main lobbying organizations—BGR, Venable, and USINPAC. The second (H2) tests the impact of Indian American voting power by examining the votes of members of Congress in districts having the highest percentages of Indian Americans.[42] The third (H3) tests the impact of financial contributions by examining the votes of members of Congress receiving funding from USINPAC. The magnitude of these contributions was not large, because USINPAC was restricted by law from contributing more than $4,000 to a candidate. Still, members of Congress receiving USINPAC funding would be expected to vote favorably on India-related issues. The fourth and fifth test the impact of relationship-building activities. Thus, H4 examines the votes of members of Congress who were members of the India Caucus in the House, and the equivalent "Friends of India" group in the Senate. These members of Congress were most involved with—and thereby built relationships with—India-related groups in the years prior to the nuclear agreement. H5 examines

---

[42] Here, 37 Congressional districts where Indian Americans comprised more than 2% of the population are included in the analysis. For the Senate, the 9 states having the highest Indian American percentage of the population are included in the analysis.

the votes of members of Congress who participated, or had their staff participate, in trips to India sponsored by CII in the period 2000–2005. Thus, the following five hypotheses can be tested on the main amendments and bills. These tests examine the votes *against* the amendments and the votes *for* the actual bills, because voting against the amendments is the equivalent of supporting a pro-India policy, and voting for the bills is the equivalent of supporting a pro-India policy.

H1: The percentage of pro-India votes among 70 representatives and 37 senators who were directly lobbied by BGR, Venable, and USINPAC is more than the percentage among those who were not directly lobbied by these firms.

H2: The percentage of pro-India votes among 37 representatives and 18 senators from districts and states having a proportionally higher Indian American population is more than the percentage among those from other districts and states.

H3: The percentage of pro-India votes among 38 representatives and 9 senators receiving funding from USINPAC is more than the percentage among those not receiving USINPAC funding.

H4: The percentage of pro-India votes among 182 representatives and 35 senators who were members of the India Caucus is more than the percentage among those who were not members of the Caucus.

H5: The percentage of pro-India votes among 40 representatives and 14 senators who participated (and whose staff participated) in CII-sponsored trips to India is more than the percentage among other representatives and senators.

The votes of representatives and senators are shown in Tables 1 and 2, and the results of the above hypothesis tests are shown in Tables 3 and 4. Three basic observations follow from this analysis.

First, among all representatives and senators, very large majorities favored the final bills: 84 percent favored the 2006 House bill, 72 percent favored the 2008 House bill, 88 percent favored the 2006 Senate bill, and 87 percent favored the 2008 Senate bill. However, smaller majorities voted against the amendments to these bills (see Tables 1 and 2). In short, while most representatives and senators favored the nuclear agreement and the strategic partnership with India, a substantial number were still sensitive to nonproliferation concerns and sought to incorporate these in amendments.

Second, many Democrats took a free vote on the amendments to affirm their nonproliferation credentials. (In the House, Democrats had a free vote in 2006 because they knew that the House legislation would eventually be changed by the Senate. In the Senate, Democrats also had free vote because,

TABLE 1
House Votes on Amendments and Bills

Representatives with the Following Criteria	Vote (Yes or No)	Sherman Amd.	Berman Amd.	Markey Amd.	HR 5682/S 3709 Vote, 2006	HR 7081 Vote, 2008
Lobbied by BGR,	Y	21	24	24	62	44
Venable, USINPAC	N	48	44	46	8	10
	Percent Y	30	35	34	89	81
High Indian American population	Y	17	20	18	30	30
(at least 2 percent) in district	N	20	17	19	7	9
	Percent Y	46	54	49	81	77
Member of India caucus	Y	78	89	93	154	121
	N	104	93	90	29	40
	Percent Y	43	49	51	84	75
Received USINPAC contribution	Y	16	18	16	33	28
	N	22	20	22	5	7
	Percent Y	*42*	*47*	*42*	*87*	*80*
Participated in CII trip to India	Y	19	21	22	33	31
	N	21	19	18	7	8
	Percent Y	*48*	*53*	*55*	*83*	*79*
Democrat	Y	130	146	170	140	119
	N	67	52	29	59	106
	Percent Y	*66*	*74*	*85*	*70*	*53*
Republican	Y	25	37	22	219	179
	N	201	189	206	9	10
	Percent Y	*11*	*16*	*10*	*96*	*95*
Total	Y	155	183	192	359	298
	N	268	241	235	68	118
	Percent Y	*37*	*43*	*45*	*84*	*72*

Source: Data compiled by author from records on congressional votes and author research on lobbying activities.
Note: Voting "No" on the amendments and "Yes" on the final bills (HR 5682 and HR 7081) is considered to be a pro-India approach.

given the Republican majority, Democratic votes alone could not defeat the legislation). The majority of Democrats voted for the amendments to the House and Senate bills (that is, they took a more pro-nonproliferation and less pro-India approach). Thus, 66, 74, and 85 percent of the Democrats voted for the three main amendments to the July 2006 House bill. Also, 58, 58, 56, and 64 percent voted for the four main amendments to the November 2006 Senate bill. In contrast, Republicans voted almost entirely in favor of the administration's preferences.

Thus, party affiliation is a stronger predictor of the congressional vote than any of the mechanisms of influence assessed in the hypotheses.

Third, the majority of the cases *do not support* the five hypotheses assessing the influence of lobbying, voting power, financial contributions, and relationship-building on the congressional vote (this is shown in Tables 3 and 4).

TABLE 2
Senate Votes on Amendments and Bills

Senators with the Following Criteria	Vote (Yes or No)	Bingaman Amd.	Dorgan Amd.	Feingold Amd.	Boxer Amd.	HR 5682/S 3709 Vote, 2006	HR 7081 Vote, 2008
Lobbied by BGR, Venable,	Y	9	9	9	10	32	27
USINPAC	N	28	27	27	27	5	5
	Percent Y	24	25	25	27	86	84
High Indian American	Y	9	11	10	10	16	16
population in state	N	9	7	8	8	2	1
	Percent Y	50	61	56	56	89	94
Member of India Caucus	Y	8	10	9	14	33	33
	N	27	25	26	21	2	3
	Percent Y	23	29	26	40	94	92
Received USINPAC	Y	2	3	2	2	9	10
contribution	N	7	6	7	7	0	0
	Percent Y	22	33	22	22	100	100
Participated in CII	Y	4	5	4	4	13	11
trip to India	N	10	8	9	10	1	2
	Percent Y	29	38	31	29	93	85
Democrat	Y	26	27	25	29	32	37
	N	19	18	19	15	12	12
	Percent Y	58	58	56	64	71	74
Republican	Y	0	0	0	9	53	48
	N	54	53	52	44	0	0
	Percent Y	0	0	0	16	96	100
Total	Y	26	27	25	38	85	86
	N	73	71	71	59	12	13
	Percent Y	26	28	26	39	88	87

Source: Data compiled by author from records on congressional votes and author research on lobbying activities.
Note: Voting "No" on the amendments and "Yes" on the final bills (HR 5682 and HR 7081) is considered to be a pro-India approach.

Specifically, only one hypothesis—H1, assessing lobbying by BGR, Venable, and USINPAC—is supported across almost all the amendments and bills. In the House, this hypothesis is at least weakly supported in all five votes (that is, votes for the three amendments and two bills); among these, it is moderately supported in three of the five votes. In the Senate, the hypothesis is at least weakly supported in four out of six votes, and it is moderately supported in one of these votes.

The other hypotheses are, for the most part, not supported. In the House, the hypothesis on USINPAC contributions is the only one that is supported in the majority of votes; it is at least weakly supported in three out of five votes, of which one shows a moderate level of support. (This hypothesis is also supported for the Senate, but, given the very small number

TABLE 3

Cases Supporting Hypotheses in the House: Difference in Pro-India Voting Percentage between Representatives within and Outside the Relevant Sample

Hypotheses and Sample Tested	n	Sherman Amd. (percent)	Berman Amd. (percent)	Markey Amd. (percent)	HR 5682, 2006 (percent)	HR 7081, 2008 (percent)	Cases Supporting Hypothesis (at Least Weak, Moderate)
H1: Representatives Lobbied - Others	70	7	9	13	5	11	5/5, 3/5
H2: Representatives from High-Percentage Indian American Districts - Others	37					6	1/5, 0/5
H3: Representatives in India Caucus - Others	182					5	1/5, 0/5
H4: Representatives receiving USINPAC contributions - Others	38			3	3	9	3/5, 1/5
H5: Representatives participating in CII trip - Others	40					8	1/5, 1/5

Note: The hypotheses test the difference in percentage of pro-India votes between those covered by a particular mechanism of influence (that is, those Lobbied, in Higher percentage Indian American Districts, in the India Caucus, receiving USINPAC contributions, and participating in a CII trip to India) and all others. Cells showing positive differences are counted as supporting the hypotheses. A hypothesis is considered weakly supported if the difference is 2–8 percent; it is considered moderately supported if the difference is more than 9 percent. For example, on the Sherman amendment, 70 percent of the 70 representatives lobbied had a pro-India vote, whereas 63 percent of the representatives not lobbied had a pro-India vote; the difference between these two samples is 7 percent and this supports H1.

of cases—only 9 senators are counted as receiving USINPAC contributions—this result is not considered in our analysis.) In the Senate, the hypothesis on India Caucus membership is supported in three out of six votes, of which one shows a moderate level of support.

Some qualifications should be noted concerning these first-cut observations. First, in many cases, party affiliation outweighed the mechanisms of influence. Illustrating this, representatives from districts with a high percentage of Indian Americans were also mostly Democrats, and therefore voted for the amendments to the House bill; this accounts for why H2 is not supported in four of the five votes in the House. Second, given the small number of cases, changes in the votes of a very few representatives and senators would change the results in terms of support for the hypotheses. Third, although the above mechanisms of influence did not always translate into pro-India votes, they did help in moving the nuclear agreement through Congress, as discussed below.

TABLE 4

Cases Supporting Hypotheses in the Senate: Difference in Pro-India Voting Percentage between Senators within and Outside the Relevant Sample

Hypotheses and Sample Tested	n	Bingaman Amd. (percent)	Dorgan Amd. (percent)	Feingold Amd. (percent)	Boxer Amd. (percent)	S3709 Vote, 2006 (percent)	HR 7081 Vote, 2008 (percent)	Cases Supporting Hypothesis (At Least Weak, Moderate)
H1: Senators Lobbied - Others	37	3	4	2	20			4/6, 1/6
H2: Senators from High-Percentage Indian American States - Others	18					2	9	2/6, 1/6
H3: Senators in India Caucus - Others	35	5				10	8	3/6, 1/6
H5: Senators participating in CII trip - Others	14				10	5		2/6, 1/6

Note: H4 is not tested in the Senate because of the very small number of senators (9) counted as receiving USINPAC funding.

Qualitative Assessments of the Lobbying Campaign

Five points should be noted in terms of the effectiveness of the lobbying campaign for the nuclear agreement with India. First, the lobbying effort had a mixed impact on advancing legislation through Congress. On the one hand, despite its strong efforts, the India lobby was unable to secure congressional support for the March 2006 one-step bill. On the other hand, the advocacy effort helped advance the alternative bills at critical moments in late 2006 and late 2008, when time was running out on the congressional calendar.

Second, each component of the India lobby had somewhat different effects.[43] Thus, Indian Americans had a relatively greater impact on the House, especially because the House had a large India caucus. Business was relatively more influential in the Senate. Finally, strategic affairs experts played a useful role in influencing representatives and senators—such as Senators Biden and Lugar—who acknowledged but were not hardcore adherents to nonproliferation.[44]

Third, the groups that lobbied—business, Indian Americans, and arms control groups—had motivations that went beyond just influencing Congress. They also sought to convey their activism to their constituents and to create a record of their activities.[45] For example, USIBC's business trips to India were

---

[43] Here, it is hard to determine the legislative outcome if any one component of the lobby (Indian Americans or business or strategic affairs experts) had not participated in the advocacy effort. In such a situation, Congress could have (a) not brought to a vote, (b) rejected, (c) accepted, (d) accepted with some or all of the proposed amendments, or (e) substantially altered, legislation on the nuclear agreement.

[44] Author interview, 9 July 2010.

[45] Author interview, 13 October 2011.

geared not just toward making the case for the nuclear agreement, but also toward its membership. USIBC sought to show its members that it was making connections with India's government so that U.S. firms would not lose out to French and Russian firms in nuclear reactor contracts with India.[46]

Fourth, in terms of shaping the technical details of congressional legislation, nonproliferation groups were more influential than was the India lobby. Some suggestions from arms control groups were incorporated into legislation. Overall, however, the administration was far more influential than arms control groups in shaping the details of the legislation. Administration officials explained to congressional staff that the administration's preferred language on a bill would have the same results as congressional language, and this influenced Congress to accept the administration's position on specific legislative items.

Fifth, in the end, the technical details of legislation and many other aspects of the legislative process were primarily an insider game between the administration and Congress, rather than an outsider game that was pushed by outside lobby groups.[47] The administration had the primary role in negotiating legislation with Congress, and, through its extensive activities discussed above, the India lobby reinforced the administration's efforts to persuade Congress to advance the nuclear agreement.

EMPIRICAL CONTRIBUTIONS

Case studies that facilitate the in-depth contextual understanding of an issue contribute to scholarship in several ways. Most important, they augment and correct limitations in existing discourse on a topic.[48] In a similar manner, this case study fills a major gap in discourse about Indian American lobbying for the civilian nuclear agreement. Existing discourse (the numerous press articles and few scholarly pieces cited in this article) has documented the activities of Indian Americans on the nuclear agreement, but these writings do not comprehensively cover the lobbying effort. Further, many scholars miss the distinction between "Indian Americans" and "the India lobby" (the broader lobbying coalition that included but went much beyond Indian Americans). On a related note, they overstate the role of Indian Americans in the lobbying effort. This article clarifies that Indian Americans were only one component of a broader India lobby. Most significantly, this article has specified that this lobby had several components, that each undertook a range of activities, and that the degree of coordination between the components varied.

---

[46] Author interview, 16 September 2011.
[47] Author interview, 13 October 2011.
[48] Charles Ragin and Howard Becker, *What is a Case? Exploring the Foundations of Social Inquiry* (Cambridge: Cambridge University Press, 1992).

The analysis in this article also offers insights into future Indian American lobbying initiatives. Here, it should be clarified that case studies are not entirely generalizable, and every case has unique aspects. This study has focused on lobbying for a high-profile U.S. foreign policy initiative, and its main characteristics would be most likely to apply to other high-profile policies, rather than to all cases of Indian American lobbying and to all U.S. policies toward India.[49] Possible cases include initiatives to make India a permanent member of the United Nations Security Council; initiatives to strongly tilt U.S. policy toward India and away from Pakistan and China; and efforts to establish a U.S.–India free trade zone in the service sector. Some of the main unknowns in these cases would be the extent to which Indian Americans mobilize; the extent to which the advocacy coalition will draw from the strategic affairs, business, and other constituencies; the strength of the opposition; and changes in Indian American voting power, financial power, and organizational patterns. These factors would determine the extent to which the central features of the India lobby's 2005–2008 effort would apply to future cases.

THEORETICAL CONTRIBUTIONS

Beyond their explanatory richness, case studies enable scholars to test how well different theoretical frameworks apply to the case concerned.[50] Along these lines, this article examined several mechanisms of ethnic group lobbying. It found that some did not apply to this leading case of Indian American lobbying, while others were relevant to a small to moderate degree. It showed that the mechanism of lobbying through a coalition made Indian American activism far more effective.

Such an analysis has implications for additional debates in the ethnic group literature, including debates on ethnic groups and coalitions. While space limitations preclude a thorough examination of these issues, two points may be briefly mentioned.

First, scholars offer competing perspectives on ties between ethnic groups and other constituencies such as business and foreign policy experts (these two constituencies have the most influence in the area of foreign policy), as well as on ethnic group ties with foreign governments.[51] Some observers argue that ethnic groups are an important countervailing force to lobbying by

---

[49] As Lindsay notes, ethnic groups mobilize only when there is a policy around which they can be mobilized, and Indian Americans may mobilize in large numbers only in high-profile cases. James Lindsay, "Getting Uncle Sam's Ear: Will Ethnic Lobbies Cramp America's Foreign Policy Style?" *Brookings Review* 20 (Winter 2002).

[50] Alexander George and Andrew Bennett, *Case Studies and Theory Development in the Social Sciences* (Cambridge, MA: MIT Press, 2005).

[51] Lawrence Jacobs and Benjamin Page, "Who Influences U.S. Foreign Policy?" *American Political Science Review* 99 (February 2005): 107–123; Frank Baumgartner and Beth Leech, *Basic Interests: The Importance of Groups in Politics and in Political Science* (Princeton, NJ: Princeton University Press, 1998).

business and foreign governments, because they offer alternative perspectives on an issue, whereas others note that ethnic groups ally with these constituencies. This case study reveals that the latter perspective is more applicable to Indian American lobbying, with some qualifications. Indian Americans allied strongly with American business and foreign policy experts to make their case. The lobby also interacted with the Indian government, but with some limitations. Thus, the Indian government was actively interested in Indian American mobilization on the civilian nuclear agreement.[52] Also, the Indian embassy routinely informed Indian American groups and the Coalition for the Partnership with India about its position on congressional legislation; it did this in a manner similar to, but much less frequently than, the Bush administration. Still, Indian Americans and the Coalition did not extensively work with the lobbying firms hired by the Indian government. The efforts of the Indian government's lobbyists largely duplicated those of Indian Americans and American business.[53]

Second, the literature is divided on whether coalitions enhance or detract from the lobbying efforts of ethnic groups. One perspective is that coalitions can be detrimental because they reduce group autonomy and are subject to collective action problems. Another perspective is that coalitions enable each constituent to complement the activities of the other, and this increases the effectiveness of the lobbying effort.[54] This case supports the latter perspective. It also reveals that partnering with other constituencies (in this case, business) helped overcome fissures within the ethnic group. As noted previously, because of professional rivalries, Indian American groups were hesitant to team with each other, but they were willing to ally with business and with the broader Coalition for the Partnership with India. This made their efforts far more effective than they would have been if each Indian American group had lobbied separately.

---

[52] For example, in an April 2006 meeting with a congressional delegation in New Delhi, some members of India's ruling party discussed whether India's government should put more effort into mobilizing Indian Americans. United States Embassy, New Delhi, cable, "Codel Hastert and Sonia Gandhi Discuss US-India Ties, Civ-Nuke Agreement," 14 April 2006. Historically, scholars note that "as the Indian-American community grew in numbers, the Indian government tried to use it to influence Congress and the executive branch," though the actual impact of such Indian governmental efforts is unclear. Stephen Cohen, *India: Emerging Power* (Washington, DC: Brookings Institution Press, 2001), 290.

[53] Illustrating this, among members of the House International Relations Committee, all the 7 members lobbied by BGR were also lobbied by USINPAC, whereas 9 of the 16 members lobbied by Venable were also lobbied by USINPAC. Among members of the Senate Foreign Relations Committee, 4 of the 8 members lobbied by BGR were also lobbied by USINPAC, though only 3 of 20 members lobbied by Venable were also lobbied by USINPAC. These data have been compiled by the author from a database hosted by the Department of Justice under the Foreign Agents Registration Act, at www.fara.gov.

[54] Kevin Hula, *Lobbying Together: Interest Group Coalitions in Legislative Politics* (Washington, DC: Georgetown University Press, 1999); Marie Hojnacki, "Interest Groups' Decisions to Join Alliances or Work Alone," *American Journal of Political Science* 41 (January 1997): 61–87.

Finally, this article offers a basis for further research on ethnic group lobbying. Its main points can be compared with additional studies that examine foreign policy lobbying by other ethnic groups.[55] Such studies could identify the principal lobbying mechanisms applying to different ethnic groups. They could also examine whether there were special circumstances behind the coalition for the nuclear agreement with India, and whether any ethnic group lobby can successfully engage in a similar coalition-building strategy.

On this point, some unique circumstances and professional relationships brought together the three constituencies of the India lobby. The ties between Indian business and the Indian government on the one hand, and between Indian business and U.S. business on the other, facilitated interaction between India's government and U.S. business. In turn, India's government provided U.S. business with an incentive to advocate for the nuclear agreement; Indian government officials frequently asserted that as India's ties with the United States improved, American business would have greater investment opportunities in India. And U.S. business, through its professional lobbyists, established links with Indian American groups and with strategic affairs experts to form a broader Coalition for the Partnership with India. Different circumstances and relationships, and differences in the collective action problems and complementarities arising from coalition building, would explain the somewhat different composition and activities of other country lobbies in particular instances of foreign policy advocacy by these lobbies.

To summarize, additional studies could identify the principal lobbying mechanisms, and the characteristics and composition of advocacy coalitions, relevant to other prominent cases of ethnic group lobbying. Such research would enable scholars to better compare and contrast mechanisms of influence across ethnic groups, and to better theorize the different ways in which different ethnic groups influence U.S. foreign policy.*

* The author would like to thank the readers and reviewers of this article for their helpful comments. The author also acknowledges the research assistance of Doug Jackson and the support of the Woodrow Wilson International Center for Scholars, where he wrote much of this article.

---

[55] Scholars have identified Jewish American and Cuban American groups to be the most influential ethnic lobbies in the area of foreign policy. The next seven groups, who are relatively even in terms of their influence, are the Irish, Armenian, Hispanic, Taiwanese, African, Greek, and Indian American communities, whereas the Italian, Mexican, and Polish American communities are also influential. Paul and Paul, *Ethnic Lobbies and U.S. Foreign Policy*, 137.

Japan's Nuclear Hedge: Beyond "Allergy" and Breakout

RICHARD J. SAMUELS
JAMES L. SCHOFF

JAPANESE STRATEGISTS HAVE LONG BEEN ambivalent about nuclear weapons. On the one hand, memories of horrific nuclear attacks on Hiroshima and Nagasaki have sustained antinuclear sentiment and helped justify national policies championing nonproliferation and forgoing an indigenous nuclear arsenal. This "nuclear allergy" has been diagnosed as a genetic condition, and associated institutional and diplomatic constraints on nuclear breakout have been invoked to predict that Japan will find it virtually impossible to reverse course on nuclear weapons.

Japan's non-nuclear bona fides are well established. Until its revision in 2012, Article 2 of Japan's Atomic Energy Basic Law (1955) stated clearly that research, development, and utilization of atomic energy is limited to peaceful purposes.[1] Japan joined the International Atomic Energy Agency (IAEA) in 1957 and has generously supported the agency's work. After considerable debate and delay—and the receipt from the United States of much greater latitude for nuclear fuel handling and reprocessing—Japan ratified the Treaty on the Non-Proliferation of Nuclear Weapons (NPT) in 1976 and

---

[1] The 2012 amendment to the law adds "national security" as one of several reasons nuclear safety should be guaranteed. Although the government and individual lawmakers claim this addition does not conflict with the "peaceful use" of nuclear energy, the revised law is arguably less clear on this point. See, for example, "'National Security' Amendment to Nuclear Law Raises Fears of Military Use," *Asahi Shimbun*, 21 June 2012.

RICHARD J. SAMUELS is Ford International Professor of Political Science and Director of the Center for International Studies at the Massachusetts Institute of Technology. His most recent book is *Special Duty: A History of the Japanese Intelligence Community*.

JAMES L. SCHOFF is a Senior Fellow in the Asia Program at the Carnegie Endowment for International Peace and a former Senior Adviser for East Asia Policy at the U.S. Defense Department. His research focuses on U.S.–Japan relations and regional security.

supported the treaty's indefinite extension in 1995. Japan also ratified the Comprehensive Nuclear Test Ban Treaty in 1997 and was the first to sign the IAEA's Additional Protocol in 1998, allowing a stricter regimen for IAEA inspections of Japanese nuclear facilities.

Consequently, it was surprising to some in 2013 when Japan declined to join 74 other nations that signed a statement in advance of the next NPT review stating that nuclear weapons are inhumane and should not be used under any circumstance.[2] This illuminates the other, more realistic side of Japan's approach to nuclear weapons. The Japanese government does indeed believe that some circumstances might warrant the acquisition and use of nuclear weapons, and the fact that Japan's ability to act on this belief rests solely in the United States' hands is unnerving for certain politicians and bureaucrats in Tokyo.

Amid periodic reviews of the nuclear option in Japan, national policy has consistently depended on the "full range" of U.S. military might to deter nuclear attacks. This policy has been accompanied by frequent reminders to nuclear-armed rivals, as well as to Washington, that preemptive strikes and the use of nuclear weapons can be valid forms of self-defense. Japan has made it clear since the 1950s that it reserves the right (and will maintain the capacity) to develop a nuclear arsenal of its own. This strategy—"lying between nuclear pursuit and nuclear rollback"—is the essence of "the most salient example of nuclear hedging" among global powers.[3] One Japanese analyst has framed Japan's position on nuclear weapons as a balancing act between nuclear approval and nuclear denial.[4]

Over the past four decades, Japan has maintained viable—and deliberately unconcealed—options for the relatively rapid acquisition of nuclear weapons and has justified its decision not to pursue nuclear breakout in many ways. But each time the regional security environment has shifted—such as after China's first nuclear test in 1964, the end of the Cold War, North Korea's nuclear breakout in the 2000s, or the 2010 U.S.–Russia New

---

[2] "Japan Refuses to Back Statement Against A-bombs," *Japan Times*, 26 April 2013. Japan signed a similar statement in October 2013 after some phrases in the April version were changed and new words added to make it more consistent with Japan's "realistic approach" to nuclear disarmament, as opposed to a purely "humanitarian approach." See Yoshiaki Kasuga and Hajimu Takeda, "Japan Finally Backs UN Statement against Use of Nuclear Weapons," *Asahi Shimbun*, 22 October 2013.

[3] Ariel E. Levite, in "Never Say Never Again: Nuclear Reversal Revisited," *International Security* 27 (Winter 2002–2003): 59–88, at 59, 71, introduces and develops this concept. Mike M. Mochizuki, in "Japan Tests the Nuclear Taboo," *Nonproliferation Review* 14 (July 2007): 303–328, calls it "pragmatic pacifism" (306) and argues that "it made sense [for Japan] to retain at least a latent capability to exercise the nuclear option" (311). Llewelyn Hughes, in "Why Japan Will Not Go Nuclear (Yet): International and Domestic Constraints on the Nuclearization of Japan," *International Security* 31 (Spring 2007): 67–96, rejects the term "nuclear hedging" but acknowledges that "the door to independent nuclearization [by Japan] remains ajar" (69) and that "formal barriers to nuclearization are surmountable" (91).

[4] Yuri Kase, "The Costs and Benefits of Japan's Nuclearization: An Insight into the *1968/70 Internal Report*," *Nonproliferation Review* 8 (Summer 2001): 55–68, at 55.

Strategic Arms Reduction Treaty agreement limiting warheads and launchers—Tokyo has reexamined its policy before signaling for (and accepting) U.S. reassurance on extended deterrence.

Early on, U.S. reassurances were a straightforward matter. In the 1960s, U.S. nuclear weapons were dispersed widely around the world. In addition to thousands of nuclear-tipped missiles back home and patrolling the seas, the United States kept nearly 3,000 nuclear weapons "on shore" in the Asia-Pacific region, including some 1,200 on Okinawa, where U.S. strategic bombers were based.[5] This nuclear deterrent cost Japan relatively little: hosting U.S. military bases and providing for its own basic defense. The combination of Japan's unwillingness to contribute fully to its own defense or to the defense of its U.S. ally and Japanese expressions of concern about the reliability of the U.S. nuclear umbrella accentuated Japan's cheap ride on national security.[6]

Reassuring Japan is more challenging today, however, and how Tokyo sorts through its strategic choices is more pertinent than ever. Japan faces new nuclear threats and relative shifts in the regional balance of power. Although more accurate and more potent than before, the U.S. nuclear arsenal is now smaller and less visible, and the "second nuclear age" is ushering in a multipolar and less predictable nuclear landscape.[7] The United States withdrew the last of its land-based nuclear weapons from Asia in 1991 and has reduced its overall nuclear stockpile by about 75 percent since then, and further reductions are being considered.[8] More recently, U.S. reassurance has focused on the capability and flexibility of specific systems, but this has been undercut by Washington's retirement of some that were earlier touted as being mission critical.[9] Bilateral dialogue and closer policy coordination have become more important aspects of reassurance and deterrence for the alliance, but the degree to which this can mitigate rising Japanese concerns about North Korea and China—and for how long—is uncertain.

---

[5] Robert S. Norris, William M. Arkin, and William Burr, "Where They Were," *Bulletin of Atomic Scientists,* November/December 1999, 26–35, at 30. Okinawa was under U.S. administrative control at the time.

[6] On U.S. concerns about a Japanese nuclear breakout in the 1960s, see Francis J. Gavin, *Nuclear Statecraft: History and Strategy in America's Atomic Age* (Ithaca, NY: Cornell University Press, 2012). For an analysis of Japan's cheap ride, see Richard J. Samuels, *Securing Japan: Tokyo's Grand Strategy and the Future of East Asia* (Ithaca, NY: Cornell University Press, 2007). On the connection between extended deterrence and the "irony" of the imbalanced commitments to the alliance, see Barry R. Posen, *Restraint: A New Foundation for U.S. Grand Strategy* (Ithaca, NY: Cornell University Press, 2014).

[7] Keith B. Payne, *Deterrence in the Second Nuclear Age* (Lexington: University Press of Kentucky, 1996).

[8] U.S. Department of Defense, "Fact Sheet: Increasing Transparency in the U.S. Nuclear Weapons Stockpile," 3 May 2010, accessed at http://www.defense.gov/npr/docs/10-05-03_fact_sheet_us_nuclear_transparency_final_w_date.pdf, 3 June 2015; and Scott Wilson, "Obama, in Berlin, Calls for U.S., Russia to Cut Nuclear Warheads," *Washington Post,* 19 June 2013.

[9] For example, the retirement of nuclear-tipped Tomahawk land attack cruise missiles was announced in 2010. See Wade L. Huntley, "Speed Bump on the Road to Global Zero: Nuclear Reductions and Extended Deterrence in East Asia," *Nonproliferation Review* 20 (Summer 2013): 305–328.

Japanese public opinion remains staunchly antinuclear, and Japan would likely be the last country in Northeast Asia to opt for nuclear arms. But while there are many domestic and international constraints on nuclear breakout, there are also signs of a more sophisticated debate in Japan about these issues as the demand for reassurance has escalated. The key questions are how Japan perceives its options, whether and how its calculus could change, and what this would mean for the region and the U.S.–Japan alliance.

To address these questions, we examine the origins and current state of Japan's nuclear hedge and consider how deterrence and reassurance dynamics are evolving in the region. We then explore the prospects and implications for a nuclear breakout by Japan, as well as alternative strategic paths that Japan and the alliance could take. Although Japan's nuclear hedging strategy is likely to continue in the near future, U.S. policymakers (and those throughout the region) should not be sanguine about this strategy continuing indefinitely. Japan's choices ultimately will be determined by how well potential threats can be managed and by the strength of the U.S. commitment to extended deterrence.

JAPAN'S CURRENT POSTURE

The evolution of Japan's nuclear posture owes as much to political circumstances as to a realistic assessment of U.S. capabilities and commitment. Japanese leaders have understood that pursuit of nuclear weapons is politically, diplomatically, and economically impracticable, but they also recognize that an independent nuclear deterrent is unnecessary as long as U.S. guarantees remain credible to potential adversaries. As a result, Japan decided early on to deny itself nuclear weapons and instead hedge against changing circumstances.

Japan's nuclear hedge has two elements. The first involves confirming (and serially reconfirming) the U.S. commitment and capability to use nuclear weapons in defense of Japan. In 1965, for example, Prime Minister Eisaku Sato asked Defense Secretary Robert McNamara to pledge to deploy nuclear weapons against China in the event of war. McNamara and President Lyndon B. Johnson gave that assurance. Similar conversations have followed at various levels of government and the military, always backed by reassuring public statements from Washington. In addition, for decades, the Japanese government turned a blind eye to the possible introduction of U.S. ship- and aircraft-based nuclear weapons during port and base visits in Japan, despite its public pledge to forbid such practices.[10] Beginning in 1976,

---

[10] Martin Fackler, "Japan Says It Allowed U.S. Nuclear Ships to Port," *New York Times*, 9 March 2010; and Norris, Arkin, and Burr, "Where They Were," 31.

each of Japan's National Defense Program Outlines has stated that Japan will depend on U.S. extended deterrence.

The second element involves Japan's maintenance of the foundation for its own nuclear weapons program, should the country ever make that choice. Former Prime Minister Nobusuke Kishi believed that nuclear weapons were absolutely necessary if Japan was to have influence in world affairs, and he instructed his Cabinet Legislation Bureau in 1957 to formally pronounce that Japan's constitution allowed the country to possess nuclear weapons for self-defense.[11] An original member of Japan's Atomic Energy Commission recalled how "we were pressured repeatedly to do basic research on how to make an atomic bomb."[12] Leading politicians have reasserted the constitutionality of nuclear weapons throughout the years, including current and former prime ministers Shinzo Abe and Taro Aso, respectively.[13] In addition, an important policy study by Japan's Ministry of Foreign Affairs (MOFA) noted in 1969 that "regardless of joining the NPT or not, we will keep the economic and technical potential for the production of nuclear weapons, while seeing to it that Japan will not be interfered with in this regard."[14]

Toward this latter end, and despite considerable opposition from within Japan and from the international community, Japan has never wavered from its early commitment to completing the nuclear fuel cycle. This commitment entails the maintenance of vigorous enrichment and reprocessing capabilities, the stockpiling of separated plutonium, and the development of a fast breeder reactor that other nations—most prominently the United States—have long since abandoned as too costly and dangerous. In fact, Japan has the largest nuclear power program of any nonweapons state and is the only one with full-spectrum fuel cycle capabilities.[15] Of course, Japan's nuclear power industry suffered a major blow after the 2011 tsunami-induced meltdowns at plants in Fukushima, and there are many legal, political, and technical restrictions that would make a Japanese nuclear breakout extremely

---

[11] Samuels, *Securing Japan*, 176. Kishi and Foreign Minister Hisanori Yamada reportedly told Douglas MacArthur in 1958 that their government was exploring the nuclear weapons option. See *Kyodo News*, 17 March 2013.

[12] Jacques E.C. Hymans, "Veto Players, Nuclear Energy, and Nonproliferation: Domestic Institutional Barriers to a Japanese Bomb," *International Security* 36 (Fall 2011): 154–189, at 167.

[13] Abe made his comment in a speech at Waseda University in May 2002 when he was deputy chief cabinet secretary, and Aso made the comment in November 2006 when he was foreign minister. The first Abe administration officially clarified this stance in a 2006 statement before the Diet, saying that "even with nuclear weapons, we've understood that possessing them would not necessarily violate the constitution as long as it is kept within [the limits of minimum capabilities necessary for self-defense]." See, for example, "Japan Can Hold Nuclear Arms for Self-Defense: Govt.," Reuters, 14 November 2006.

[14] *Mainichi Daily News,* 2 August 1994; and Taka Daitoku, "The Kishi Doctrine and the Construction of a Virtual Nuclear State in Postwar Japan" (paper presented at the Annual Meeting of the American Historical Association, New Orleans, LA, 5 January 2013).

[15] Nobumasa Akiyama and Kenta Horio, "Can Japan Remain Committed to Nonproliferation?," *Washington Quarterly* 36 (2013): 151–165, at 152. For more on the domestic disputes about Japan's "nuclear back end," see Richard J. Samuels, *3.11: Disaster and Change in Japan* (Ithaca, NY: Cornell University Press, 2013).

difficult. Nonetheless, it has always been important for Japan to keep that option open.

OPENING THE NUCLEAR UMBRELLA

Nestling under the U.S. "nuclear umbrella" was never uncontroversial. Left-wing politicians argued in the mid-1960s that this policy was part of Washington's plan for global domination, and much of the public feared becoming entangled in a nuclear war between superpowers.[16] Some on the political right, seeing reliance on U.S. nuclear weapons as a symbol of Japan's second-tier status, worried about national prestige and pushed for a more overt hedge.[17] Conservative political leaders—including Shigeru Yoshida and Hayato Ikeda in the pragmatic wing of the Liberal Democratic Party (LDP) and revisionists such as Ichiro Hatoyama and Yasuhiro Nakasone—repeatedly called in private for an indigenous nuclear capability.[18]

Inside the bureaucracy, opinions were mixed. MOFA warned in 1959 that Japan should not rule out the possibility of developing nuclear weapons, lest the country lose flexibility in pursuing national security.[19] Later, in 1966, a vice minister of foreign affairs stated publicly that Japan was not protected under the U.S. nuclear umbrella. MOFA immediately issued a "unified viewpoint," introducing one of many awkward locutions the Japanese government uses to describe its national security strategy: it was not accurate to say that Japan was not covered by the nuclear umbrella.[20]

Sato, initially a supporter of Japanese nuclear armament, reversed course when confronted with Washington's strong nonproliferation policy and his own government's internal studies concluding that reliance on extended deterrence was the best way forward.[21] None of the conceivable alternatives—that is, domestic nuclear weapons production, nuclear sharing

---

[16] *Nikkan Jōyaku nado Tokubetsu Iinkai: Nipponkoku to Dai Kan Minkoku to no aida no Kihon Kankei ni Kansuru Jōyaku nado no Teiketsu ni tsuite Shōnin wo Motomeru no Ken* [Proceedings of the Special Committee Considering the Proposed Japan-Korea Treaty], House of Councillors, National Diet of Japan, 3 December 1965.

[17] Daitoku, "Kishi Doctrine," 2.

[18] See Ayako Kusunoki, "The Satō Cabinet and the Making of Japan's Non-Nuclear Policy," *Journal of American-East Asian Relations* 15 (Spring/Winter 2008): 25–50, at 28–29; and Daitoku, "Kishi Doctrine," 3.

[19] "No-Nuke Policy Ruled Out Years before Declaration," *Kyodo News*, 22 December 2008.

[20] Nobumasa Akiyama, "The Socio-Political Roots of Japan's Non-Nuclear Posture," in Benjamin Self and Jeffrey Thompson, eds., *Japan's Nuclear Option: Security, Politics and Policy in the 21st Century* (Washington, DC: Henry L. Stimson Center), 86. For similar Japanese rhetorical gymnastics on defense policy, see Samuels, *Securing Japan*.

[21] Some suggest it is also possible that rather than seriously advocating for nuclear weapons, Sato was instead taking that position in order to extract security guarantees from Washington. See Kusunoki, "The Satō Cabinet," 31; and Michael J. Green and Katsuhisa Furukawa, "Japan: New Nuclear Realism," in Muthiah Alagappa, ed., *The Long Shadow: Nuclear Weapons and Security in 21st Century Asia* (Stanford, CA: Stanford University Press, 2008), 357. Others are less certain. See Kurt M. Campbell and Tsuyoshi Sunohara, "Japan: Thinking the Unthinkable," in Kurt M. Campbell, Robert J. Einhorn, and Mitchell B. Reiss, eds., *The Nuclear Tipping Point: Why States Reconsider Their Nuclear Choices* (Washington, DC:

with the United States, or overtly denying U.S. nuclear protection—was considered viable at that time by most Japanese strategists. Understanding this, and provided with high-level U.S. assurances, in 1967, Sato announced three non-nuclear principles of nonpossession, nonmanufacture, and nonintroduction. A year later he articulated the "four pillars" policy, and in 1970, the government signed the NPT, leaving no doubt about Japan's reliance on the U.S. nuclear umbrella.[22]

One of the four pillars is the three non-nuclear principles, and this pillar is accompanied by three more: (1) promoting nuclear power for peaceful purposes, (2) promoting global nuclear disarmament, and (3) relying on the U.S. nuclear deterrent for protection from the international nuclear threat. The four pillars policy officially opened the nuclear umbrella, and even if it is perceived as leaky by some, this umbrella has remained open ever since. Although the cynical Sato privately called the three principles "nonsense," he was awarded the Nobel Peace Prize in 1974. Ever since, Japanese national policy has recognized the value of maintaining technical capabilities to prevent both the United States and potential adversaries from taking Japan's non-nuclear status for granted. Given Japan's level of technological sophistication, stable civil-military relations, accessible and plentiful plutonium stockpiles, self-contained nuclear fuel cycle, and history of success in "spinning on" commercial technologies, the country's nuclear hedge remains intact and credible.[23]

EXTENDED DETERRENCE 2.0

The U.S.–Japan alliance and its extended deterrent have enabled the nonproliferation policies that help Tokyo signal its intention to refrain from breaking out with its own nuclear arsenal. Another vital factor has been the absence of a consistent existential threat to Japan. Whenever one or both of these factors seem to shift, signs of reconsideration in Tokyo become apparent, and subtle reminders that Japan has other nuclear options are issued to Washington. Japan has long understood how important the nonproliferation objective is to the United States and how to use it for policy leverage.[24]

Brookings Institution Press, 2004), 218–253; and Etel Solingen, *Nuclear Logics: Contrasting Paths in East Asia and the Middle East* (Princeton, NJ: Princeton University Press, 2007), 73.

[22] For more on the Sato turnaround, the three principles, and the four pillars, see Green and Furukawa, "Japan: New Nuclear Realism"; Kusunoki, "The Satō Cabinet"; and Solingen, *Nuclear Logics*.

[23] The U.S. Department of Energy reports that reactor-grade plutonium could be used to produce reliable weapons comparable to those produced using weapons-grade plutonium. See Marvin Miller, "Japan, Nuclear Weapons, and Reactor-Grade Plutonium" (paper presented at the Nuclear Control Institute, Washington, DC, 27 March 2002). For a history of technological "spin on" from commercial to military applications, see Richard J. Samuels, *"Rich Nation, Strong Army": National Security and the Technological Transformation of Japan* (Ithaca, NY: Cornell University Press, 1994).

[24] Green and Furukawa, in "Japan: New Nuclear Realism," focus on this point. See also Richard C. Bush III, Vanda Felbab-Brown, Martin S. Indyk, Michael O'Hanlon, Steven Pifer, and Kenneth M. Pollack,

Primacy of Reassurance

Japanese policymakers often remind their U.S. and regional counterparts (both privately and publicly) about the importance of the U.S. nuclear umbrella and Japan's own ability to go nuclear if necessary. As we have noted, Prime Minister Sato made such a statement in 1964 and 1965, as did Prime Minister Morihiro Hosokawa in 1998, opposition leader Ichiro Ozawa in Beijing in 2002, and Foreign Minister Aso after North Korea's 2006 nuclear test.[25] Additional signals have been sent through Diet interpellations, as well as through unofficial channels and provocative political commentary.[26]

Washington's response to these signals has been consistent. In 2006, U.S. Secretary of State Condoleezza Rice visited Japan and reaffirmed the United States' "will and capability" to meet the "full range of its deterrence and security commitments" in an attempt to reassure Japan that it is still well-protected under the U.S. nuclear umbrella.[27] President Barack Obama offered similar public assurances after North Korea's subsequent tests in 2009 and 2013 when Prime Minister Abe asked him to reconfirm the U.S. commitment to defend Japan with "an unshakeable nuclear umbrella."[28]

For now, reliance on U.S. extended deterrence persists even if discomfort with the status quo is growing. This discomfort stems from different sources. Some Japanese politicians and analysts are worried that a policy designed for a bipolar world order will become less reliable in a multipolar environment filled with regional nuclear powers. Japan could, in this formulation, become "detached" from U.S. strategic thinking.[29] While some seek to prevent this through closer ties with Washington, others chafe under the postwar legal and diplomatic restraints that Japan agreed to live with for the sake of economic development; they would pursue a different postwar relationship with the United States by taking more security and diplomatic matters into their own hands.

"U.S. Nuclear and Extended Deterrence: Considerations and Challenges" (Arms Control Series 3, Brookings Institution, Washington, DC, 2010).

[25] One could also speculate that Japan's December 2008 declassification of the Sato-McNamara notes was another subtle reminder, coming as it did on the heels of the United States' delisting of North Korea as a state sponsor of terrorism, despite the lack of progress on verifying North Korean denuclearization promises.

[26] Although there were no mentions of "extended deterrence" in Diet hearings in 2008, there were 68 in 2009 and 58 in 2010 (accessed at http://kokkai.ndl.go.jp/). There is also a long history of comments by "autonomists" outside government, such as Ikutaro Shimizu, Nisohachi Hyodo, Tadae Takubo, and Terumasa Nakanishi, who have pressed Japan to break away from U.S. security guarantees and develop its own nuclear arsenal. See Matake Kamiya, "Nuclear Japan: Oxymoron or Coming Soon?" *Washington Quarterly* 26 (Winter 2002–3): 63–75, at 66–67; and Furukawa Katsuhisa, "Making Sense of Japan's Nuclear Policy: Arms Control, Extended Deterrence, and the Nuclear Option," in Self and Thompson, *Japan's Nuclear Option*, 111.

[27] "Remarks with Japanese Foreign Minister Taro Aso after Their Meeting," U.S. Department of State, 18 October 2006.

[28] *Sankei Shimbun*, 22 February 2013.

[29] Yukio Satoh, "Agenda for Japan-U.S. Strategic Consultations" (article adapted from a presentation made at the International Symposium on Security Affairs, Tokyo, 18 November 2009).

Yet the Japanese express concern about extended deterrence in contradictory ways. Whereas once they worried about the U.S. commitment when North Korean nuclear weapons could *not* reach the continental United States—that is, that Washington might prioritize proliferation over the medium-range missile threat—now that the prospect of North Korea targeting the U.S. homeland has become more realistic, they express concerns because Pyongyang's nukes *could* reach. For example, a *Sankei Shimbun* editorial suggested that Washington could be "intimidated," quoting a former defense ministry official who opined that "we cannot completely rule out the possibility of Japan's being cut off from U.S. nuclear strategy."[30]

In the case of China, the allies' superiority in conventional forces appears more important than the nuclear balance for now, especially as the U.S. arsenal shrinks. This comes in part from a core challenge of extended deterrence, wherein a deterrence provider seeks to limit a conflict to the region it is protecting in order to avoid an all-out war that might entangle its homeland. Based on this logic, while Washington will do everything it can to prevent the escalation or expansion of an East Asian regional conflict, if the U.S. military cannot dominate conventionally, Washington might default to accommodation rather than resort to nuclear weapons. As one former diplomat explained, "the conventional superiority advantage is critical, because it obviates the whole debate about whether or not Washington would 'sacrifice Los Angeles to save Tokyo' in a nuclear exchange."[31] Consequently, even though nuclear weapons are a major psychological component of extended deterrence (and certainly the most talked about), Japan is also focused on the U.S. projection of conventional power, which is under strain from U.S. budget politics, Chinese military developments, and Japan's unwillingness to invest substantially in its own defense.

The United States' budget problems, coupled with its efforts to reduce nuclear weapons globally, exacerbate a concern some have in Japan over the long-term durability of the U.S. nuclear infrastructure. By some measures, U.S. nuclear capabilities have atrophied over time. The United States has not developed a new warhead in more than 25 years, and it has not tested a weapon since 1992. The U.S. Departments of Defense and Energy stated in 2008 that the United States "is now the *only* nuclear weapons state party to the NPT that does not have the ability to produce a new nuclear warhead."[32]

---

[30] *Sankei Shimbun,* 22 February 2013.
[31] Author's interview with a former MOFA official, 1 August 2007.
[32] U.S. Department of Energy and U.S. Department of Defense, "National Security and Nuclear Weapons in the 21st Century," September 2008. Some argue that because the United States has no need to develop a new warhead or, given the size of its database, to test one, the term "atrophied" is hyperbolic. Others highlight U.S. investments in expensive testing tools—such as the National Ignition Facility—that bolster U.S. confidence in the reliability of its arsenal. Authors' personal communications with Vipin Narang, 9 June 2013, and James Acton, 8 July 2013.

The Obama administration is making some investments to upgrade existing nuclear infrastructure, but Washington will soon face tough and expensive choices about what kind of nuclear deterrent the United States (and its allies) should have in the future.

Some U.S. defense planners believe that when modern security problems are pushed to the higher rungs of a conflict-escalation ladder, the nuclear arsenal inherited from the Cold War will prove to be inappropriate for uses beyond deterring a large-scale nuclear attack against the United States or a close ally. As former deputy secretary of defense John Hamre observed, "the Cold War left us with a massive inventory of [nuclear] weapons we no longer need . . . [and] a shrinking community of nuclear experts hold on [to it] as a security blanket for a future they cannot define."[33]

Recent U.S. administrations have believed that deterrence through conventional weapons is decisively more credible than any existing nuclear alternative. The challenge, however, is that continued U.S. investment in conventional military superiority is precisely what drives weaker states to pursue asymmetric solutions with nuclear weapons (for example, North Korea and Iran) and prompts other major powers to keep pace with their own military investments (for example, China), further worrying regional allies such as Japan. There is no easy balance that truly guarantees security through strength without feeding into a broader security dilemma.

Given the rising profile of these challenges, the United States and Japan began bilateral consultations in 2009 on strategic issues raised by the impending U.S. Nuclear Posture Review (NPR) and Quadrennial Defense Review. For the first time, Japan moved onto the path of officially discussing and even influencing U.S. nuclear strategy and force planning, something to which the United States' NATO partners had long become accustomed. Japan had been unsettled by prior NPRs that unilaterally shifted the U.S. force posture with little consultation.[34] It was concerned that the United States might reach a decision to accommodate North Korea, move toward a "no first use" policy on nuclear arms, or retire nuclear weapons systems, particularly the nuclear Tomahawk cruise missile (TLAM/N), without deploying compensating capabilities.[35]

During this time, Japanese officials reportedly gave American interlocutors a "nonpaper" that described key criteria for sustaining extended deterrence. The paper highlighted reliability (that is, confidence that warheads

[33] John J. Hamre, "Toward a Nuclear Strategy," *Washington Post*, 2 May 2005.

[34] For similar reasons, the United States initiated a dialogue with South Korea around the same time.

[35] For Japanese concerns about "no first use," see Satoh, "Agenda"; and Yukio Satoh, "Kakugunshuku Jidai no Nihon no Anzen Hosho" [Japanese national security in an age of nuclear arms reduction], *Gaiko Forum* (2009): 46–49. For concerns about the TLAM/N, see Hans M. Kristensen, "U.S. Navy Instruction Confirms Retirement of Nuclear Tomahawk Cruise Missile," *FAS Strategic Security blog*, 18 March 2013, accessed at http://fas.org/blogs/security/2013/03/tomahawk/, 3 June 2015.

will function properly), flexibility (holding different targets at risk), responsiveness, discrimination (keeping low-yield options), and the ability to be either stealthy or visible, as warranted by the situation.[36] While there was some doubt at the time about how high up this paper had been approved within the Japanese government, aspects of these criteria continue to be raised by Japanese officials, and the continuation of bilateral consultations on extended deterrence suggests that the allies have plenty to discuss.[37] These criteria appear to reflect real expectations in Japan for extended deterrence that require continued alliance attention.

The success of the bilateral NPR consultations led both sides to want to continue talks, and in March 2011, they "regularized" the Extended Deterrence Dialogue (EDD). The EDD is now a biannual event, with one of the meetings often involving a visit to a deterrence-infrastructure site. In 2013, for example, this included a tour of Naval Base Kitsap in Washington State to see the submarine leg of the nuclear triad and Trident missile facilities.[38] These discussions are not trivial conversations or mere photo opportunities. They are a joint exploration by knowledgeable officials of current and emerging nuclear threats to the alliance, along with possible deterrence strategies.[39]

The site visits are thorough and underscore the fact that U.S. declaratory statements are backed by demonstrable capabilities, with the human capital being among the most important. Site visits make the U.S. nuclear umbrella visible and tangible for Japanese officials and highlight the significant investments that support it. Both countries' principals hope that, over time, the EDD will also enhance deterrence by better integrating nuclear and conventional capabilities within the alliance for a tailored deterrence strategy, especially vis-à-vis North Korea. The EDD also provides Japan with an official channel to share its perceptions about extended deterrence with the United States, which makes the dialogue a useful bellwether for how the Japanese government feels about its nuclear hedge.

The U.S. side reportedly is pleased that the EDD has deepened Japan's understanding of extended deterrence and provided a better appreciation of the role played by conventional forces and missile defense, including high-

---

[36] Hans M. Kristensen, "Japan's Nuclear Secrets," Federation of American Scientists, October 2009, accessed at http://www.fas.org/programs/ssp/nukes/publications1/Sekai2009.pdf, 3 June 2015.

[37] For suggestions that these criteria are not representative of government or citizen views, see Gregory Kulacki, "Japan and America's Nuclear Posture," Union of Concerned Scientists, March 2010, accessed at http://www.ucsusa.org/assets/documents/nwgs/japan-american-nuclear-posture.pdf, 3 June 2015. Japanese officials mentioned these criteria in numerous author interviews between 2010 and 2013.

[38] Kevin Baron, "U.S., Japan Met to Talk Nuclear Deterrence," *Foreign Policy*, 12 April 2013, accessed at http://foreignpolicy.com/2013/04/12/u-s-japan-met-to-talk-nuclear-deterrence/, 3 June 2015.

[39] This is based on interviews with participating U.S. and Japanese officials and military officers in April 2013. The two sides are led by officials from the Japanese Foreign Affairs and Defense ministries and the U.S. State and Defense departments at the deputy director general and deputy assistant secretary levels, respectively.

end missile-tracking radar deployments in Japan.[40] Still, the Japanese side appears to have an appetite for continued dialogue. Security planners in Tokyo acknowledge that discussions are "far deeper than before," but some express concern that Washington will continue to surprise them.[41] Reaffirmation of U.S. commitments and reliability alone is no longer sufficient. The EDD portends a more collaborative form of deterrence that encompasses the full spectrum of conventional and nuclear capabilities possessed by the allies. Japanese strategists who once expressed little more than "sheer and total dependence upon the American deterrent" now understand that assuaging their abandonment fear requires more Japanese involvement in lower (conventional) thresholds of potential conflict, and they seek greater input into Washington's nuclear doctrine and priorities. The EDD will have to balance this carefully.[42]

External Threats

While Washington has some control in addressing the reassurance factor, it faces limits when it comes to threats and threat perceptions. North Korea is a primary concern for Japan, largely because Pyongyang appears to care little about its people and invests heavily in nuclear and missile programs. North Korea's nuclear capability could make the leadership even more reckless. Should the regime face imminent collapse or preemptive attack, it might judge that it has little to lose (and could even forestall outside interference) by striking Japan with a nuclear weapon. There are also questions about whether Pyongyang can maintain effective command and control over these weapons.

Washington's official assessments of North Korea's nuclear capability are written vaguely but express confidence that the North will be able to produce nuclear-tipped missiles in the not too distant future and that their accuracy will improve.[43] To strike Japan, North Korea could use some of its estimated 200 Nodong medium-range ballistic missiles, which have a range of 1,500 kilometers and a payload of one ton. North Korea is also developing a land-based intermediate-range missile (Musudan) that might be able to reach Okinawa and Guam. Although the accuracy of these missiles has been derided in the past, a battery of test launches in July 2006 suggested that

---

[40] Huntley, "Speed Bump on the Road to Global Zero," 16, 21.
[41] Author's interview with a senior defense planner in Japan's Ministry of Defense, Tokyo, 25 March 2013.
[42] Paul J. Saunders, "Extended Deterrence and Security in East Asia: A U.S.-Japan-South Korea Dialogue," Center for the National Interest, January 2012, accessed at http://www.cftni.org/2012-Extended-Deterence-In-East-Asia.pdf, 3 June 2015.
[43] *Christian Science Monitor*, 12 April 2013. Note, though, that inaccuracy can be an even greater threat—for example, if an adversary targets the Sea of Japan but hits an urban center.

North Korea had improved their performance, and in December 2012, it put a satellite into orbit for the first time using a three-stage rocket.[44]

A key problem for extended deterrence is the allies' limited understanding of Pyongyang's strategic calculus and Washington's unexpressed preference to deal with North Korean nuclear threats by conventional methods. There could come a point when Japanese leaders feel that they need more control over the means of response. A 1995 Japan Defense Agency (JDA) report made this point while otherwise dismissing the value of a nuclear option for Japan: "North Korean nuclearization . . . is not an issue that cannot be a condition for discussing the possibility of Japan going nuclear in the future."[45] In other words, the JDA identified North Korea as a threat that could cause Japan to go nuclear.

Compared with North Korea, China's nuclear arsenal and conventional capabilities are much larger and weigh heavily on the minds of Japanese defense planners. The main worry is not simply that China's defense budget has roughly tripled since 2001 to become the world's second largest.[46] Rather, it is the nature of China's military modernization and the relatively quick and substantial investments in capabilities that are aimed at the allies' ability to dominate the skies and seas around East Asia. This strategic force modernization raises the potential costs that U.S. policymakers would need to weigh when considering the option of intervening against Chinese interests on behalf of Japan or Taiwan.

Another long-term problem is that China keeps building new nuclear warheads (about 10 per year). Although official Chinese policy states that China will not use nuclear weapons first—or ever against a non–nuclear weapon state—its intimidation tactics in the maritime and cyber domains have worried some in Japan that these tactics could someday spread to the nuclear realm.[47] The People's Liberation Army, after all, manages one of the world's most active ballistic missile programs. Many of its tactical weapons have enhanced ranges, accuracies, and payloads, and some put Okinawa within range when forward deployed. Upgrades to Chinese missile warheads—including multiple independently targeted reentry vehicles—are en-

---

[44] Yossef Bodansky, "DPRK Strategic Command and Control, Missile Launch Exercise Marks Operational Watershed," *Defense and Foreign Affairs Special Analysis* 24 (July 2006).

[45] Japan Defense Agency, "Concerning the Problem of the Proliferation of Weapons of Mass Destruction," 1995, 34, accessed at http://www.ucsusa.org/assets/documents/nwgs/1995jdastudy.pdf, 3 June 2015.

[46] United States officials estimate that China's actual defense spending was roughly $60 billion in 2001 and that it could be as high as $215 billion in 2012. See U.S. Department of Defense, *Military and Security Developments Involving the People's Republic of China 2013* (Washington, DC: U.S. Department of Defense, 2013), 45.

[47] For China's warhead increase, see the press release for the 2013 SIPRI Yearbook, Stockholm International Peace Research Institute, 3 June 2013, accessed at http://www.sipri.org/media/pressreleases/2013/YBlaunch_2013, 3 June 2015.

hancing Beijing's deterrent and strategic strike capabilities vis-à-vis Japanese and U.S. missile defenses.[48] These slow-moving upgrades to the quality and quantity of Chinese nuclear weapons have some in Tokyo wondering whether Beijing will eventually seek nuclear parity with the United States, something that would require considerable time and investment, as the U.S. arsenal is significantly larger.

Japanese strategists have to ask how much vulnerability the United States is willing to tolerate amid China's strategic modernization and what it is prepared to do on Japan's behalf, if anything, in response to China's moves.[49] Some prominent Japanese analysts suggest that a national nuclear deterrent, even if it were insufficient to deter a force as big as China's in all circumstances, could complicate strategic calculations in Beijing to the extent that China would think twice before threatening to use (or actually using) its own nuclear forces in a regional crisis or conflict.[50] In short, Japan faces its own threats and has its own interests. As Kurt M. Campbell and Tsuyoshi Sunohara suggest, "the persistence of a Japanese-American alliance so robust that it can indefinitely dissuade Japanese leaders from acquiring nuclear weapons cannot be guaranteed."[51]

PROSPECTS AND IMPLICATIONS FOR A NUCLEAR WEAPONS BREAKOUT BY JAPAN

At the moment, the likelihood that Japan would build its own nuclear weapons is low. Constraints are multiple and significant. But they are not fixed, and it is worthwhile to examine the conditions, both internal and external, under which these constraints could loosen and Japan might change course.

Internal Factors

Public opinion. The "nuclear allergy" metaphor was coined in part to describe the Japanese public's aversion to visits by U.S. Navy vessels that might be carrying nuclear weapons.[52] Japanese perceptions were colored not only by the bombs dropped on Hiroshima and Nagasaki in 1945 but also by other incidents, such as in 1954, when a U.S. nuclear test at Bikini Atoll exposed 23 Japanese fishermen to high levels of radiation, eventually killing one and

---

[48] U.S. Department of Defense, *Military and Security Developments Involving the People's Republic of China 2011*, annual report prepared for Congress (Washington, DC: U.S. Department of Defense, 2011), 34.

[49] Brad Roberts, "Nuclear Minimalism," *Arms Control Today* 37 (May 2007).

[50] See the arguments by Hisahiko Okazaki, "Mazu Gijutsutekina Men wo Tsumeyo" [First, we need to examine the technical feasibility of a nuclear option], *Shokun!*, August 2003; and Group Ichigaya, "Kakubusonaki Nippon ni Asu wa Nai" [There is no tomorrow for a Japan without nuclear weapons], *Shokun!*, February 2007.

[51] Campbell and Sunohara, "Japan: Thinking the Unthinkable," 237.

[52] Glenn D. Hook, "The Nuclearization of Language: Nuclear Allergy as Political Metaphor," *Journal of Peace Research* 21 (September 1984): 259–275.

inspiring the *Godzilla* film series that sensationalized the potential danger and unpredictable nature of nuclear weapons.[53]

It was against this backdrop that Prime Minister Sato announced the three non-nuclear principles, a policy that maintains strong public support. As the Cold War wound down, polls showed that more than 75 percent of Japanese respondents still agreed with the three principles, and similar polls in 2006 and 2013 produced the same result. A 1998 Gallup Poll found that only 16 percent of the nation was afraid of being attacked by another country using nuclear weapons, and 89 percent felt no need for Japan to have nuclear weapons.[54] Being a non–nuclear weapons state had, it seemed, become part of Japanese national identity.[55]

The rise of China and the belligerency of North Korea, however, have raised awareness about the U.S. nuclear umbrella: only about 20 percent thought the umbrella was "necessary" in 1995, but almost half thought so in 2010.[56] Still, even when candidates for the national Diet were polled on the issue of Japan developing its own nuclear weapons after two North Korean nuclear tests, more than half did not think such an option should ever be considered; only a third favored keeping this option open for the future, depending on the international situation.[57]

The 2011 Fukushima nuclear accident hardened popular opinion against all things nuclear in Japan and led the government to shut down Japan's nuclear power infrastructure.[58] Despite public opinion and a more independent regulatory system, the current Abe administration and private industry are pushing to revive and sustain the nuclear sector. With little organized political opposition to the conservative, business-friendly LDP government, we have seen Japan's nuclear industry begin to regain its footing. It is already aggressively pursuing development opportunities in Asia, Europe, and the Middle East.

---

[53] Michael Schaller, *Altered States: The United States and Japan since the Occupation* (New York: Oxford University Press, 1997), 71–75.

[54] "Shitsumon to Kaito—Bōei Mondai, Asahi Shimbun Seron Chōsa Shōhō" [Questions and answers on defense issues: Report on *Asahi Shimbun* opinion survey], *Asahi Shimbun*, November 1988; "Hikaku Sangensoku 'Mamorubeki' 8 Wari, 'Kakuhoyu Giron' wa Sanpi Nibun/Yomiuri Shimbun Seron Chōsa" [80% want to keep the three non-nuclear principles: *Yomiuri* opinion poll], *Yomiuri Shimbun*, 21 November 2006; "Asahi Shimbunsha Yūsou Seron Chōsa, Shitsumon to Kaito" [Questions and answers for *Asahi* mail-in survey], *Asahi Shimbun*, 2 May 2013; and "Gallup Japan Poll on the Ownership of Nuclear Weapons and the Threat of Nuclear War," Gallup News Service, 5 June 1999.

[55] Bush et al., "U.S. Nuclear and Extended Deterrence," 33.

[56] "Towareru Anpo, Nichibei Kankei" [Issues and the U.S.–Japan alliance], *Asahi Shimbun*, 11 November 1995; and "Genbaku tōka kara 65nen, Kienu Kaku no Kyōi" [65 years since the atomic bomb was dropped, the nuclear threat remains], NHK Reporting Research and Surveys, October 2010.

[57] "Kurozuappu 2012: Shuinsen Kouhosha Anketo, Hoshu Seneika no Jimin, Kakubusō 'Kento Subekida' 38%" [Close-up 2012: Lower house survey, 38% support consideration of nuclear weapons], *Mainichi Shimbun*, 8 December 2012.

[58] See Samuels, *3.11: Disaster and Change*, chap. 5.

The return to power of the LDP in 2012 and its resounding repeat performance in 2014 are reminders that overwhelming majorities can vote against their polled preferences (while many simply stay at home) and that even democratic governments can act independently of public opinion. The connection of public opinion to policymaking is particularly tenuous with respect to national security. For example, there was considerable opposition to the NPT from the media, business community, and public when Japan signed the treaty in 1970.[59] As we have seen, the decision to forgo an independent nuclear arsenal was based on realist calculations amid U.S. pressure, not on polling data. Campbell and Sunohara's conclusion is correct that "although public sentiment against nuclear weapons remains strong, its ability to fully inhibit the decisions of Japanese leaders should not be exaggerated."[60]

Institutional opposition. Japanese political leaders considering nuclear breakout will face other obstacles besides public opinion, including opposition from an expanding variety of political, bureaucratic, and economic actors. For decades, bureaucratic responsibility for nuclear strategy resided solely in the cabinet, with support from MOFA. Over time, however, the JDA—renamed the Ministry of Defense in 2007—assumed a greater policy role. Nuclear power research and development, which is critical for any potential dual use, was split between the Ministry of International Trade and Industry, now the Ministry of Economy Trade and Industry, and the Science and Technology Agency, which is now part of the Ministry of Education. Each had its own preferences.[61]

In the economic realm, there are those whose interests lie in preserving a purely commercial exploitation of nuclear power.[62] Japan's utilities, the wider business community, bureaucrats charged with promoting economic growth, and politicians with ties to these interests are all powerful actors who would likely oppose a nuclear weapons program. In the event of a nuclear breakout, Japan's electric power industry could be crippled by a loss of access to nuclear fuel and would possibly be required to return current fuel stocks, given that their purchase was predicated on peaceful use. Moreover, large manufacturers such as Hitachi and Mitsubishi could be shut out of

---

[59] George H. Quester, "Japan and the Nuclear Non-Proliferation Treaty," *Asian Survey* 10 (September 1970): 765–778, at 766.
[60] Campbell and Sunohara, "Japan: Thinking the Unthinkable," 242; see also Paul Midford, *Rethinking Japanese Public Opinion and Security* (Stanford, CA: Stanford University Press, 2011).
[61] According to one study, each policy silo acquired an independent veto on nuclear breakout. See Hymans, "Veto Players."
[62] Hughes, "International and Domestic Constraints."

overseas nuclear development projects, and there might be a wider economic backlash against Japanese firms in key markets such as China and South Korea as their governments hype the fear of a remilitarized Japan.[63]

Prefectural governors also have an important vote on what kinds of nuclear-related activities can occur within their jurisdiction. In addition, some influential nonprofit organizations dedicated to preserving Japan's non-nuclear status gained strength following the Fukushima crisis.[64] Proponents of changing the nuclear status quo in Japan would likely face numerous legal and bureaucratic hurdles, including the certainty of drawn-out legal challenges.

Although there is no question that weaponization would be difficult in Japan's contested political system, circumstances can change over time. Japan's robust democratic politics and its determined leadership have repeatedly demonstrated that opposition and veto power are not the same. The Japan–U.S. Security Treaty was ratified in 1960 over violent protests and widespread opposition and now is widely embraced. Japan's Self-Defense Forces, which began as the National Police Reserve during the Korean War, became a robust and lethal military force despite Japan's pacifist constitution and early public opposition. It has never been more widely embraced by the Japanese public than it is at present.

The postwar history of the Japanese military is filled with examples of government restrictions applied, only to be loosened at a later date. This was the case with Japan's acquisition of fighter jets (first denied, then allowed), as well as its acquisition of midair refueling capabilities, legislating an ability to deploy overseas, the use of outer space for defense purposes, and now the possible development of a long-range strike capability.[65] Moreover, while approval for a weapons-related program surely would be even harder to obtain from local officials than approval for nuclear power reactors, it is worth noting that some prefectural governors, such as Issei Nishikawa from Fukui, support nuclear power as the leading employment vehicle in their prefectures. And some governors, such as Shintarō-Ishihara of Tokyo (1999–2012), openly argued for acquiring nuclear weapons. Weaponization work could be done in prefectures with supportive leaders, even if they hosted no reactors.

---

[63] For further analysis of how nuclear plant exports have been central to Japan's "new growth strategy," see Samuels, *3.11: Disaster and Change*.

[64] Samuels, *3.11: Disaster and Change*, chap. 6–7.

[65] The Japanese government has studied and considered acquisition of a long-range conventional strike capability in the past, most notably during the National Defense Program Guideline review of 2004. A similar study was conducted in 2013, although no report was released. Author's interview with Ministry of Defense official, 20 February 2013. For a list of the "salami slicing" of restrictions on the Japanese military, see Samuels, *Securing Japan*.

Finally, even if Japan's plutonium stockpile in Europe is out of reach and much of the separated fuel is controlled by private firms worried about repercussions in international markets, more than enough is held domestically under the aegis of the Japan Atomic Energy Agency (JAEA), a governmental unit. The rest is held by Japan Nuclear Fuel Limited, which is nominally a private firm but one that performs public functions under close government supervision. Even allowing that only two tons of Japan's plutonium stock is both owned by the state (through the JAEA) and present in Japan, and that this might be the only plutonium available for Japanese weapons, this amount alone would be enough to build a large nuclear arsenal of several hundred weapons. In short, it is not clear how much of a constraint contending interests, private ownership of weapons material, and the overseas location of much of Japan's plutonium would actually place on Japan if it were to decide to move from being a latent to an open nuclear weapons state. The motivation is the critical factor, not the obstacles.

Discount Factors

There are four additional constraints that would require leaders to discount the costs of dramatic policy change: (1) the vulnerability of the Japanese population to a first strike, (2) the undermining of Japanese diplomacy, (3) regional instability, and (4) damage to bilateral relations with the United States.

Japan's central vulnerability is its lack of strategic depth. The argument here is straightforward and has often been repeated. The majority of the Japanese population is clustered in a small number of densely populated urban centers. Because a first strike against Tokyo, Osaka, and Nagoya would cripple Japan, nuclear weapons have little military utility.[66] While superficially compelling, this argument is hardly dispositive. It did not prevent Great Britain or Israel, with their similar geodemographic profiles and same primary ally, from developing nuclear arsenals. The Israeli case, in fact, impressed some Japanese with how vulnerability can be discounted in the face of an existential threat.[67] Nor would we expect a strike on New York or Los Angeles to be any less crippling to the U.S. national economy. Moreover, Japan's population density and vulnerability to a first strike—particularly when its arsenal is still limited—could provide a strong motivation to deploy an independent ability to wipe out North Korea's nuclear arsenal preemptively.

---

[66] This was a central argument in every official study of the nuclear weapons option. See, for example, Hughes, "International and Domestic Constraints"; and Mochizuki, "Nuclear Taboo."

[67] Group Ichigaya, "Kakubusō naki Nippon ni Asu wa Nai," *Shokun!*, February 2007.

Second, there is the loss of benefits derived from Japan's diplomatic posture as a non–nuclear weapons state. Legal withdrawal from the NPT is technically very easy—it requires only a 90-day notice to the other parties to the treaty and the United Nations Security Council—but the costs associated with the repudiation of decades of Japanese diplomacy and the nullification of many of the bilateral agreements that undergird the Japanese nuclear power program would require a steep discount by the country's decision makers. Still, many of these leaders are concerned that the nonproliferation regime has been eroding, and Japanese diplomacy is already less strident on this point. Additionally, whether one agrees with this logic or not, supporters of a Japanese indigenous nuclear program have long argued that Japan neutered itself diplomatically by opting out of the nuclear club and that, from a realist perspective, Japan would fortify its diplomacy over the long run by changing its stance.

Third, a nuclear breakout would certainly trigger or accelerate a regional arms race—one that would require a considerably greater investment in defense than postwar Japan has heretofore accepted. If South Korea had not yet broken out, it surely would after a Japanese decision to do so. Koreans have long been suspicious of Japan's nuclear hedging, and the Korean media and its "unnamed" government sources regularly feed the perception that Japan is just a "few screwdriver turns" from a functioning weapon.[68] Even the former ambassador to Japan, Chul-hyun Kwon, explained on the record that "Japan didn't declare having nuclear weapons but they made the raw materials, and they . . . are in fact getting rid of the obstacles one by one as the opportunity offers. In the long term, I guess they are preparing for a nuclear weapon."[69] A Japanese nuclear breakout would not surprise South Korea, but neither would it be met with sympathetic understanding.

China and Russia would likewise respond by repositioning and possibly strengthening their strategic forces, and China in particular would push to isolate Japan diplomatically. Additionally, North Korea could be convinced that its reckless behavior has been rewarded with new alignments in the region. It is understandable, then, that many in Japan see no military benefit to be gained from breakout; instead, they worry that a new, higher-cost round in the extant security dilemma would detract from Japanese national security.[70] But if Japan acted in response to a breakout by South Korea or to

---

[68] See, for example, Tae-Ho Kang and Park Jung Won, "Ilbon Haek-mu-jang ha-myeon Hankookdo 'matdae-eung'" [Counter-action, if Japan nuclear armament], *Hankyoreh*, 19 October 2006.

[69] Sang-Moo Hwang, "Ilbon-eui Haek-mu-jang Chu-jin-kwah Dong-buk-ah Jung-sae" [Sunday consult Japan's nuclear armament and the political conditions on Northeast Asia], KBS News, 1 July 2012.

[70] Kitaoka Shinichi, "Kita no Kaku o Yokushi Suru Tame no Itsutsu no Sentakushi" [Five options to deter North Korea's nuclear weapons], *Chūō Kōron*, December 2006.

significant provocation by other states, then, as Nobumasa Akiyama suggests, "nuclear proliferation in Asia . . . might lower the threshold even for Japan to violate international agreements and treaties."[71]

Fourth, the United States has worked ceaselessly since the 1960s to keep Japan from becoming a nuclear weapons state, arguing that extended deterrence is a nonproliferation tool. According to one confident former Japanese diplomat, "the United States would never allow Japanese nuclear weapons."[72] But what if the drawdown in U.S. budgets and Washington's desire to balance China collide on the Japanese archipelago? What if they meet in the form of a reversal of U.S. policy toward Japanese nuclear armament, especially against a backdrop of an even more dangerous North Korea that threatens to draw the United States into a nuclear war? Given current U.S. budgetary trends, exhaustion from more than a decade of war, and the United States' refusal to act alone during the Arab Spring, it is not farfetched to imagine Washington determining in the future that it can no longer provide regional, much less global, strategic public goods on its own. In other words, it is hardly inconceivable that economic need and existential threat could trump vulnerability in nuclear strategy and overcome political constraint.

Durability of the U.S. Security Umbrella amid New Threats

Despite shifting threat perceptions among Japanese policymakers, Tokyo's level of confidence in U.S. security guarantees remains high as a result of the Obama administration's emphasis on diplomatic and military investments in Asia, Washington's bipartisan emphasis on the importance of alliances, and robust U.S. support for Japan during the tsunami and nuclear disaster in 2011. In the medium term, however, Japanese strategists are closely watching the U.S. response to Sino-Japanese confrontation in the East China Sea over the Senkaku/Diaoyu Islands. For many, this is a representative or test case of the United States' capacity and determination to deter Chinese aggression.[73] Moreover, a nearly 20 percent drop in U.S. defense spending from 2010 to 2015 and congressional resistance to funding base realignment plans in the Asia-Pacific raise doubts for some in Japan about U.S. staying power in the region over the long term.[74] Thus, while there is no imminent loss of confidence, certain trends are unsettling to the leadership in Tokyo.

---

[71] Akiyama, "Socio-Political Roots," 90.

[72] Author's interview with a retired ambassador, Tokyo, 27 March 2013.

[73] Author's interviews with an LDP Diet representative, a retired ambassador, a former senior intelligence official, and an adviser to the prime minister's office, Tokyo, 26–27 March 2013.

[74] Clark A. Murdock, Kelley Sayler, and Ryan A. Crotty, "The Defense Budget's Double Whammy: Drawing Down while Hollowing Out from Within," Center for Strategic and International Studies, 18 October 2012, accessed at http://csis.org/files/publication/121018_Murdoch_DefenseBudget_Commentary.pdf, 3 June 2015.

One of these trends is the decline in the qualitative advantage that the allies have traditionally held over China's armed forces. As one analyst opined, "if the U.S.-China military balance in East Asia reaches parity, then the credibility of the U.S. nuclear umbrella will be gravely shaken."[75] On this view, Chinese and North Korean nuclear force modernization programs will exacerbate the decoupling problem for Japan. But such modernization could also accelerate U.S. rethinking of a possible Japanese breakout. Although a decision by Japan to acquire nuclear weapons may not be in the United States' current interest, Washington's ability and willingness to prevent it would wane over time if China's capabilities were to continue to expand and especially if North Korea's status as a nuclear power were to become a normal part of the strategic environment in Asia. Under such conditions, Japan's desire for nuclear weapons would appear more reasonable and harder to counter.[76]

The United States is taking steps to reassure Japan and shore up deterrence through close consultation and efforts to update plans and capabilities. But if Washington decides to sustain extended deterrence, it will have a tougher time demonstrating consistency and endurance. In years past, the United States' reassurance methods fluctuated, beginning with significant forward presence in the region (both conventional and nuclear) that paved the way for Japan's low-cost strategy of basic defense. When the Cold War ended and U.S. reliance on Japan seemed more equivocal, symbols of the United States' presence and commitment became important, such as the maintenance of force levels in the region of more than 100,000 personnel.[77] When U.S. force levels eventually dropped, Washington emphasized underlying capabilities as the critical factor, and this was also true on the nuclear front—for example, touting the TLAM/N to compensate for lower numbers and then conventional strength and dual-capable aircraft when the TLAM/N was retired.[78] If the allies' conventional advantage over China declines, however, and U.S. defense planners decide that U.S.-based strategic bombers can

---

[75] Nakanishi Terumasa, "'Nippon Kakubuso' no Giron wo Hajimeru Toki" [The start of Japan's nuclear debates], in Nakanishi Terumasa, ed., "Nippon Kakubuso" no Ronten—Kokka Sonritsu no Kiki wo Ikinuku Michi [Debates on "Japan's nuclear armament": How to survive this critical moment in national existence] (Tokyo: PHP, 2006).

[76] Author's personal communication with Thomas Christensen, 15 February 2013.

[77] See Ministry of Foreign Affairs of Japan, "Japan-U.S. Joint Declaration on Security: Alliance for the 21st Century," 17 April 1996, accessed at http://www.mofa.go.jp/region/n-america/us/security/security.html, 3 June 2015.

[78] For repeated emphasis of the role of "unrivaled" U.S. conventional military "preeminence," as well as mention of the option to forward deploy dual-capable aircraft and the potential value of a conventional "prompt global strike" weapon, see U.S. Department of Defense, "Nuclear Posture Review Report," April 2010, 6, 7, 20, 28, accessed at http://www.defense.gov/npr/docs/2010%20nuclear%20posture%20review%20report.pdf, 3 June 2015.

address nuclear threats more efficiently than introducing dual-capable air-craft into the theater, then Washington's "reassurance story" will no doubt need to change again.

ALTERNATIVE STRATEGIC PATHS

To this point, our review of Japan's nuclear weapons options has elided at least four alternative paths to more independent nuclear deterrence for Japan within the alliance framework. The first three involve sharing nuclear weapons that are not of indigenous design and over which Japan would have less than full control. The fourth involves significant enhancement of Japan's conventional strike capabilities. All of these options would require major changes to Japanese defense policy and possibly constitutional reinterpretation or revision.

In the first of the three acquisition scenarios, Japan could opt to buy or lease U.S. weapons. Japanese analysts have raised the possibility of a lease deal with a sunset provision for up to 200 nuclear warheads with cruise missiles. Under the agreement, the United States would retain control over the electronic maps loaded onto the warheads and a right of launch refusal.[79] Although such an approach would still require Japan to cross many of the same legal and diplomatic hurdles that it would face in building its own deterrent, while adding new hurdles for the United States, it would be the quickest and cheapest way for Japan to acquire and maintain nuclear weapons and could be easily reversed if desired. For example, in the event of Korean unification and denuclearization, Japan could simply terminate the lease and return the weapons and infrastructure. Among the many complicating factors, it is hard to imagine the U.S. government providing active support to a Japanese nuclear weapons program if South Korea is emphatically opposed. Presumably, Seoul would have taken a nuclear step first (with some sympathetic understanding from Washington) and would grudgingly accept a Japanese nuclear lease.

The second option could be modeled on the extant arrangement between the United States and the United Kingdom, whereby Britain leases U.S.-made Trident II missiles, codevelops aspects of the submarine platform, and manufactures its own nuclear warhead according to certain U.S. specifications, including the use of some U.S.-made nonnuclear components.[80] This approach would be less reversible and more expensive than the "turnkey" lease method, but it would allow Japan to scale up its nuclear program more

---

[79] Masahiro Matsumura, "Prudence and Realism in Japan's Nuclear Options," Brookings Institution, 10 November 2006, accessed at http://www.brookings.edu/opinions/2006/1110japan_matsumura.aspx, 3 June 2015.

[80] See Jenifer Mackby and Paul Cornish, eds., *U.S.–UK Nuclear Cooperation after 50 Years* (Washington, DC: CSIS Press, 2008).

quickly and somewhat more affordably compared to homegrown options. Either of these approaches, however, assumes a U.S. attitude toward the NPT and the Missile Technology Control Regime that is fundamentally different from its current stance and would be feasible only in the context of a collapse of the global nonproliferation regime. Still, one can imagine how U.S. policymakers could view this kind of approach as preferable to a purely indigenous Japanese effort, not only because it would maintain alliance ties but also because it would provide for a coordinated means of rollback if future conditions permitted.

A third alliance-based option could follow the NATO model of nuclear burden sharing, by which U.S. nuclear weapons are deployed on allied territory under U.S. control until a crisis erupts. At that point, following U.S. authorization, responsibility for the delivery of the weapons devolves to the allied host state.[81] Before then, the ally would participate in command and control arrangements, and its pilots would be trained in nuclear warfighting doctrine. Although such burden-sharing arrangements were more widespread during the Cold War, there remain approximately 150 B-61s deployed at bases controlled by the allied host nations Turkey, Italy, Belgium, the Netherlands, and Germany for delivery by their F-16s or Tornados. The legality of these arrangements, however, has long been disputed under Articles 1 and 2 of the NPT.[82]

Each of these options goes beyond Japan possessing a few bombs but falls short of a fully independent and survivable Japanese nuclear force. All three would, of course, require relaxation of Japan's three nonnuclear principles and the reintroduction of U.S. nuclear weapons to bases on the archipelago. Each would allow more rapid deployment than a purely indigenous deterrent, and each requires U.S. cooperation. Many Japanese analysts who write on nuclear issues, however, advocate greater autonomy. Nisohachi Hyodo, for example, has argued for a force of two submarines roaming separate seas with one missile each, while Kan Ito and Yasuhiro Nakasone recommend "small size" Japanese nuclear weapons.[83] Mitsuo Takai argues, however, that a reliably survivable Japanese nuclear strategy to deal with China or North

[81] See Catherine McArdle Kelleher, "NATO Nuclear Operations," in Ashton B. Carter, John D. Steinbruner, and Charles A. Zraket, eds., *Managing Nuclear Operations* (Washington, DC: Brookings Institution, 1987); Hans M. Kristensen, "U.S. Nuclear Weapons in Europe: A Review of Post-Cold War Policy, Force Levels, and War Planning," Natural Resources Defense Council, February 2005, accessed at http://www.nrdc.org/nuclear/euro/euro.pdf, 3 June 2015; and Thomas Maettig, "Tactical Nuclear Weapons in Germany: Time for Withdrawal?" Nuclear Threat Initiative, 1 March 2008, accessed at http://www.nti.org/analysis/articles/tactical-nuclear-weapons-germany/, 3 June 2015.

[82] Author's personal communication with Owen Cote, 10 June 2013. On the legal questions, see Otfried Nassauer, "Nuclear Sharing in NATO: Is It Legal?," Berlin Information Center for Transatlantic Security, April 2001, accessed at http://www.bits.de/public/articles/sda-05-01.htm, 3 June 2015.

[83] Toshi Yoshihara and James R. Holms, eds., *Strategy in the Second Nuclear Age* (Washington, DC: Georgetown University Press, 2012), 124–125.

Korea would require a much larger force—up to six nuclear submarines with 300 high-yield nuclear warheads—while Takayuki Nishi has suggested that even this might be too small a force to deal with a foe such as China.[84] Either way, this level of militarization would contradict the Japanese Constitution's prohibition of "war potential," as currently interpreted by the government, which makes a distinction based on scale of destructive power.[85] Ultimately, Nishi's consideration of nuclear strategy convinces him that the best approach for Japan remains nuclear abstention coupled with missile defenses, as long as the growth of China's nuclear missile force levels off.

This raises the fourth alternative deterrence strategy, a much-discussed non-nuclear one that would maintain Japan's nuclear hedge but entail a considerable enhancement of its conventional offensive capabilities. As one defense planner has explained, there is much more Japan can do to augment its deterrent short of nuclear weapons breakout.[86] Although Japan's self-imposed ban on the acquisition of long-range strike capabilities has been thinned by successive reinterpretations of the constitution, the Ministry of Defense budget has remained static, and the military has been slow to acquire the carriers, bombers, strike fighters, and ballistic or cruise missiles that would expand Japan's capacity to punish adversaries at a distance.[87] But some Japanese leaders are seriously considering the need to augment U.S. capabilities. One senior military officer invoked a common metaphor: "we have been at our parents' knee [*oya no sune ni kajiru*], but U.S. shins have become thin."[88] He joins a chorus of defense planners who advocate changing the extant alliance model in which the United States is the "sword" and Japan is the "shield" to one in which both countries have offensive capabilities sufficient to deter regional aggression.[89] As Narushige Michishita has reported, "the most widely debated" military option for Japan going forward is the acquisition of strike capabilities for preemptive counterforce operations against hostile bases.[90]

---

[84] Takayuki Nishi, "Nuclear Strategy as a Constraint on Japanese Nuclear Armament" (paper presented at the 52nd Annual Convention of the International Studies Association, Montreal, Canada, 17 March 2011).

[85] Ministry of Defense of Japan, "Defense of Japan 2013," 143 accessed at http://www.mod.go.jp/e/publ/w_paper/pdf/2013/22_Part2_Chapter1_Sec2.pdf, 3 June 2015.

[86] Author's interview with a National Institute for Defense Studies official, Tokyo, 25 March 2013. See also Mochizuki, "Nuclear Taboo," 314. This is consistent with the plans of the Obama administration. See Scott Wilson, "Obama, in Berlin, Calls for U.S., Russia to Cut Nuclear Warheads," *Washington Post*, 19 June 2013.

[87] The Self-Defense Forces have acquired the basics for counterforce conventional strike, including attack fighters, airborne refueling, and joint direct attack munitions that convert gravity bombs into precision-guided munitions. See Narushige Michishita, "Japan's Response to Nuclear North Korea," *Joint U.S.-Korea Academic Studies* 23 (2012): 19–112, at 108.

[88] Author's interview with Japanese military officer, Tokyo, 27 March 2013.

[89] This converging sentiment was heard in multiple interviews with senior officials at the Ministry of Defense and with former MOFA and intelligence officials in Tokyo, 25–27 March 2013.

[90] Michishita, "Japan's Response," 107. He adds that some (unnamed) security specialists think that acquisition of these capabilities could actually undermine the alliance by giving Washington the option of not de-

This "strike capability" movement reached a climax during the drafting of the National Defense Program Guidelines in 2004, when the JDA sought funds to develop long-range, surface-to-surface missile technology.[91] But the LDP's coalition partner, the New Komeito Party, vetoed that proposal and the plan was dropped. The Abe administration put this issue back on the table for consideration in 2013 after South Korea's decision in 2012 to extend the range of its ballistic missile forces to 800 kilometers provided diplomatic cover. Such a shift could enhance Japan's deterrence posture, whether or not it were integrated with U.S. military doctrine in ways that would make deterrence more effective and credible; however, it also risks complicating the regional security dilemma and engendering domestic political blowback. Washington has long pushed for a more militarily capable Japan but is reluctant to weigh in publicly on this sensitive issue, lest the United States be viewed as either encouraging or restraining Japan. On this latter point, in particular, the U.S. side is aware that efforts to dissuade Tokyo from adding strike capacity could be unsuccessful and might accelerate the loss of Japanese confidence in its ally, thereby prompting an even quicker development of independent capabilities.

CONCLUSION

Henry Kissinger has suggested that the logic of war shifted with the introduction of nuclear weapons in ways that are connected directly to issues examined here. He stated that before the nuclear age, "the consequences of abandoning an ally were deemed to be more risky than fulfilling one's obligations. In the Nuclear Age, this rule no longer necessarily held true; abandoning an ally risked *eventual* disaster, but resorting to war at the side of an ally guaranteed *immediate* catastrophe."[92] It is of no little significance that this passage is well known among Japan's strategic elites, many of whom point to the declining credibility of extended deterrence and the fact that nonproliferation norms have also withered.

Campbell and Sunohara, who insist that a Japanese nuclear breakout "would be potentially catastrophic," have warned U.S. leaders and public commentators against raising questions about extended deterrence or encouraging Japan to consider alternatives to its nuclear-hedged status quo:

---

fending Japan. For a 2006 study on this issue by an influential Japanese analyst, see Sugio Takahashi, "Dealing with the Ballistic Missile Threat: Whether Japan Should Have a Strike Capability under Its Exclusively Defense-Oriented Policy," *NIDS Security Reports*, no. 7 (2006): 79–94.

[91] "Draft of Next Midterm Defense Buildup Plan Seeks Missile Research," Kyodo News, 3 December 2004, accessed at http://www.thefreelibrary.com/Draft+of+next+midterm+defense+buildup+plan+seeks+missile+research.-a0126082637, 3 June 2015.

[92] Henry Kissinger, *Diplomacy* (New York: Simon & Schuster, 1994), 608. Note, too, that as secretary of state, Kissinger managed alliance relations successfully and assured allies Washington would come to their aid.

"American leaders and influential commentators both within and outside the government should never signal to the Japanese, even inadvertently, that they actually favor Japan's acquisition of nuclear weapons."[93] But, as we have seen, thoughtful Japanese security specialists have not needed encouragement to cast an unsentimental and realistic eye on the future of extended deterrence. They have needed no prompting to raise questions about Japan's strategic defense and to interrogate U.S. overextension.

Equally thoughtful international security specialists in the United States have begun asking similar questions. Michael J. Mazarr, a professor of national security strategy at the U.S. National War College, is concerned about U.S. "strategic insolvency"—the pursuit of "yesterday's strategy under today's constraints" and the United States' growing inability to manage the gap between its strategic commitments and its national objectives.[94] Barry Posen argues that

> [E]xtended deterrence is a very risky business, and the United States ought to have been glad to shed such commitments after the Cold War ended. Instead, the United States retains extended deterrence commitments in Europe and Asia. . . . Extended deterrence remains a plausible path to one or more nuclear weapons being used either against U.S. forces or the U.S. homeland.[95]

Posen lays out four options for Japan beyond its alliance with the United States. Two are low-probability courses of action: that Japan could find a new nuclear protector or that it could bandwagon with China or other rivals. Echoing some of the strategists explored in this article, Posen observes that a third option would be for Japan to persist with its nuclear hedge, which he says is tantamount to "ignoring the problem" and which one Diet representative called "closing our eyes and whistling past the graveyard."[96] The fourth option, nuclear breakout, is the one that has been explored in this article in its several possible forms.

Like Israel, which has climbed much higher up the nuclear weapons ladder, Japan has assumed what Vipin Narang labels a "catalytic posture," one that "relies on an ambiguous nuclear capability aimed at 'catalyzing' third-party—often U.S.—military or diplomatic assistance to defend the state by threatening to unsheathe its nuclear weapons."[97] To assume this posture,

---

[93] Campbell and Sunohara, "Japan: Thinking the Unthinkable," 219, 246.
[94] Michael J. Mazarr, "The Risks of Ignoring Strategic Insolvency," *Washington Quarterly* 35 (Fall 2012): 7–22, at 8.
[95] Posen, *Restraint*, 97.
[96] Posen, *Restraint*, 102; and author's interview with LDP Diet member, Tokyo, 27 March 2013.
[97] Vipin Narang, "Posturing for Peace? Pakistan's Nuclear Postures and South Asian Stability," *International Security* 34 (Winter 2009–2010): 38–78, at 41.

having assembled nuclear weapons is not even strictly necessary—one simply requires the "ability to assemble a handful of nuclear weapons." Given the availability of a superpower patron and other constraints on more overt change, this posture may continue to serve Japanese security interests well and is Tokyo's most likely choice should it opt to follow Israel. Manipulating the threat of breakout remains a mechanism to keep Washington in the game in East Asia.

Still, we have shown, much remains uncertain in the changing East Asian security environment. North Korea, in particular, is an unpredictable actor and a growing threat to alter Tokyo's calculus. At present, few voices in the Japanese or U.S. strategic communities openly advocate a Japanese nuclear breakout. But given questions about how the emergence of a multipolar nuclear Asia will complicate national and alliance strategies, the possibility cannot be dismissed. Both communities should be aware that current constraints on such a dramatic shift can be stretched, that threat perceptions can change, and that a range of once unthinkable alternatives is available.*

* This article is adapted from Richard J. Samuels and James L. Schoff, "Japan's Nuclear Hedge: Beyond 'Allergy' and Breakout," in Ashley J. Tellis, Abraham M. Denmark, and Travis Tanner, eds., *Strategic Asia 2013–14: Asia in the Second Nuclear Age* (Seattle, WA: National Bureau of Asian Research, 2013), 232–264. The authors are grateful to Mark Bell, Alison Chang, and Kuni Shimoji for their research assistance and to colleagues James Acton, Vipin Narang, and Christopher Twomey for their review of an early draft.

The U.S. Nuclear Umbrella over South Korea: Nuclear Weapons and Extended Deterrence

TERENCE ROEHRIG

FOR MORE THAN 60 YEARS, the United States has maintained an extended deterrence commitment to protect South Korea as part of a system of alliances in East Asia. The guarantee included a mutual security treaty that formalized the U.S. pledge to defend its ally and placed troops along the demilitarized zone (DMZ) as a sign of the U.S. determination to defend South Korea. The U.S. commitment also entailed South Korea's inclusion under the U.S. nuclear umbrella, whereby Washington vowed to use nuclear weapons to deter and, if need be, defeat an attack on the South. The nuclear umbrella included the deployment of tactical nuclear weapons on the peninsula; however, these were removed in 1991.

Despite the longevity of U.S. extended deterrence and the nuclear umbrella in East Asia, there have always been some difficult and troubling aspects of this strategy. An important requirement for successful deterrence is credibility. Would the United States truly be willing to use nuclear weapons in the defense of an ally given the tremendous devastation of those weapons? What if the adversary possessed nuclear weapons that could strike the U.S. homeland or U.S. facilities in the region? Would the United States use nuclear weapons in response to a non-nuclear attack, whether conventional, biological, or chemical? Indeed, some even question whether there *is* a nuclear umbrella.[1]

---

[1] Jeffrey Lewis, "No, the U.S. Doesn't Have Plans to Nuke North Korea," *Foreign Policy*, 17 October 2014, accessed at http://foreignpolicy.com/2014/10/17/no-the-u-s-doesnt-have-plans-to-nuke-north-korea/, 14 May 2017; and Stephan Haggard, "Nuclear Talk: Leon Panetta's Worthy Fights: A Memoir of Leadership in War

---

TERENCE ROEHRIG is Professor of National Security Affairs and the Director of the Asia-Pacific Studies Group at the Naval War College.

These issues raised serious questions about the credibility of the U.S. nuclear umbrella during the Cold War and continue to be concerns today. Despite these credibility questions, South Korean leaders place high value on remaining under the U.S. nuclear umbrella and have exerted great effort to have Washington provide explicit reassurances that the nuclear umbrella remains in place. These issues raise two key questions that are the focus here. What role does the U.S. nuclear umbrella play in South Korean and U.S. security calculations? Why would South Korea and other U.S. allies continue to value and rely on the nuclear umbrella when its credibility is so shaky?

The U.S.-Republic of Korea (ROK) alliance is solid, and there is little doubt the United States would come to South Korea's defense if it were attacked. Washington will continue issuing statements affirming the commitment to use nuclear weapons if necessary to defend South Korea, and the U.S. military will plan and train for the possible use of nuclear weapons. However, in the end, it is highly unlikely that a U.S. president will ever give the directive to use nuclear weapons to defend South Korea because of a number of strategic, operational/military, and moral considerations. Though the Donald J. Trump administration has declared that "all options are on the table" and the President has made several statements and tweeted the possibility of using military force, the likelihood of the United States using nuclear weapons is very low. U.S. nuclear use in Korea would have devastating consequences, and doing so, even in retaliation, would weaken the norms of nuclear use in future conflicts for other states, which is not in anyone's interest. Instead, the United States would rely on conventional options that are far more credible and have similar strategic effects.

The U.S. nuclear umbrella for South Korea will remain in place, as it has become an important part of the regional security architecture that ROK leaders value despite the lingering credibility issues. More importantly, the nuclear umbrella is a political signal for the defense commitment and overall health of the alliance. These elements are not included in standard applications of deterrence theory, yet they are crucial for the security guarantee to South Korea and other U.S. allies. To remove the umbrella would be a critical change to the status quo that could disrupt regional security. Moreover, for the United States, the nuclear umbrella is also an important nonproliferation tool to persuade more states from acquiring nuclear weapons. The U.S. alliance is strong, and Washington will fulfill its commitment to defend South Korea, but it will not use nuclear weapons to do so.

---

and Peace," *North Korea: Witness to Transformation* (blog), 20 November 2014, accessed at http://blogs.piie.com/nk/?p=13644, 14 May 2017.

The remainder of this article will first review the theoretical foundation of extended deterrence, followed by a history of the nuclear umbrella in Korea and an examination of the North Korean threat the umbrella is designed to address. Next, I examine the role of the nuclear umbrella in South Korean security calculations and provide an assessment of the capability, motivations, and credibility of the U.S. nuclear umbrella. The article concludes with a discussion of the implications this case study has for nuclear weapons and extended deterrence.

EXTENDED DETERRENCE THEORY AND THE NUCLEAR UMBRELLA

Deterrence is the use of threats to convince an adversary to refrain from taking an action the defender does not wish it to take. The central tenet of deterrence is a threat issued by the defender to raise the costs of a challenger's actions to the point that the challenger will refrain from taking the unwanted action. The defender must demonstrate that regardless of what the challenger seeks to obtain, the costs of achieving the objective will outweigh the gains. Defenders can seek to deter in two ways: first, by possessing sufficient military capability to deny a victory or pose a long war of attrition,[2] and second, with threats of punishment should the challenger take the unwanted action.[3] Deterrence by punishment forms the core of nuclear deterrence.

Deterrence Situations

Distinctions exist in certain types of deterrence situations that are important for understanding Korea and the U.S. nuclear umbrella because states will act differently depending on the situation. Two sets of deterrence situations are relevant here: primary versus extended deterrence and immediate versus general deterrence.

Primary versus extended deterrence. In primary deterrence, states seek to protect their homeland, while in extended deterrence, a defender is deterring an attack on an ally. For primary deterrence, there is little doubt that a state will defend itself if attacked, but many doubts arise in a situation of extended deterrence. A defender might balk at protecting an ally in a crisis, particularly if the potential costs of doing so are high. Defenders exert great effort to demonstrate their commitment through treaties and alliances, but

[2] Glenn Snyder, *Deterrence and Defense* (Princeton, NJ: Princeton University Press); and John Mearsheimer, *Conventional Deterrence* (Ithaca, NY: Cornell University Press, 1983).

[3] Kenneth Waltz, "Nuclear Myths and Political Realities," *American Political Science Review* 84 (September 1990): 731–745; and Robert Jervis, *The Meaning of the Nuclear Revolution: Statecraft and the Prospect of Armageddon* (Ithaca, NY: Cornell University Press, 1989).

there is always a possibility that the defender will not follow through in a crisis.

Immediate versus general deterrence. Patrick Morgan identifies important differences in deterrence situations that he labels *immediate* and *general* deterrence.[4] Immediate deterrence situations are crises in which the challenger has provided notice either in word or deed that an attack may be forthcoming, prompting the defender to issue specific counterthreats of retaliation to deter the looming assault. In contrast, general deterrence pits two adversaries in a hostile relationship in which either might consider using force against the other if the proper circumstances arose, but there is no immediate danger of an attack. The adversaries build their military capabilities and undertake preparations to defend themselves, but they do not feel the need to issue specific counterthreats. The relationship is relatively stable but with significant enmity and mistrust. Immediate and general deterrence situations are best viewed on a continuum along which a relationship can possess qualities of both immediate and general deterrence. Situations can shift along the continuum, for example, progressing to a crisis that might require counterthreats to deter specific actions before returning to a more stable equilibrium of general deterrence.

The U.S. nuclear umbrella for South Korea has been part of U.S. military preparations that, at most times, resembled a situation of general deterrence. War has not been imminent, and U.S. leaders have not issued specific counterthreats of nuclear retaliation. Instead, Washington has typically issued general statements about South Korea being under the U.S. nuclear umbrella. However, there have been some occasions on which Washington has utilized specific nuclear threats. Although an attack was not imminent, North Korea's six nuclear tests were sufficiently disconcerting to prompt Washington to issue pointed assurances that South Korea remained under the U.S. nuclear umbrella. The spring of 2013 was a particularly tense time on the peninsula following North Korea's December 2012 missile launch, the February 2013 nuclear weapon test, the subsequent United Nations Security Council resolutions, and the worse than normal vitriolic North Korean response. During the annual Key Resolve/Foal Eagle spring exercises that year, the United States made a high-profile demonstration of B-2 and B-52 bombers, which can be used for conventional or nuclear missions, to make a deterrence statement indicating an incremental shift from general toward immediate deterrence. The United States undertook similar actions

---

[4] Patrick M. Morgan, *Deterrence: A Conceptual Analysis,* 2nd ed. (Beverly Hills, CA: Sage Publications, 1983), 27–47.

in the spring of 2016 after the January 2016 nuclear test and again on several occasions throughout 2017 after the plethora of ballistic missile tests and sixth nuclear weapons detonation. Deterrence also works in the other direction, as North Korea seeks to deter the United States and South Korea through its actions and language.

Over the years, deterrence has slid back and forth from general to immediate, but for the most part, strategic deterrence has been stable, with little danger of war breaking out. For example, a 1999 U.S. State Department report by William Perry that reviewed U.S.-North Korea policy noted the tremendous loss of life that would result in another war but that "[u]nder present circumstances . . . deterrence of war on the Korean Peninsula is stable on both sides, in military terms."[5] Although miscalculation is always a possibility, Perry maintained, there is nothing that would suggest to North Korea that a war would not be a disaster for it and that stability will endure. Though the events of 2017 shifted towards immediate deterrence, perhaps farther than had been the case for some time, Perry's assessment is likely to continue in the years ahead.

Credibility

The most challenging problem for deterrence, especially extended deterrence, is credibility. Credibility requires that the defender possess the capability to carry out the threatened retaliation and that it impose sufficient cost to make the challenger refrain from the unwanted action. Finally, the defender must convince the challenger of its resolve to carry out the threat should deterrence fail.[6] These three dimensions of credibility are linked but possess different dynamics. Having the capability to inflict unacceptable harm is the starting point. Without this capability, which is made easier with nuclear weapons, state threats to punish are essentially bluffs. Yet given the precision of today's conventional munitions, even those weapons can have the strategic effects of nuclear weapons. However, the crucial element here is that the challenger must be convinced that the defender possesses the necessary capability. Thus, a defender may still be able to deter with reduced capability so long as the adversary perceives it to be sufficient. Conversely, the challenger may not be convinced even if the defender in fact has the prescribed military capability.

---

[5] William J. Perry, "Review of United States Policy Toward North Korea: Findings and Recommendations," U.S. Department of State, 12 October 1999, 3, accessed at http://nsarchive.gwu.edu/NSAEBB/NSAEBB87/nk20.pdf, 5 June 2017.
[6] William W. Kaufmann, *The Requirements of Deterrence* (Princeton, NJ: Center for International Studies, 1954), 19.

To ameliorate the credibility concerns, defenders have often gone to great lengths to demonstrate that they would indeed come to an ally's defense if attacked. Treaties, alliances, and trade ties along with economic and military aid help demonstrate a defender's commitment to an ally.[7] Yet these assurances can be ignored in a crisis, and there is always a chance that the defender will not follow through on its promise, particularly if a response carries great cost and risk. Thomas Schelling notes that "saying so, unfortunately, does not make it true; and if it is true, saying so does not always make it believed. We evidently do not want war and would only fight if we had to. The problem is to demonstrate that we would have to."[8]

To show its resolve, the United States deployed combat troops to South Korea to help defend the country and act as a trip wire to ensure a U.S. response should deterrence fail. In the first few decades, the United States based two combat divisions close to the DMZ and along the expected invasion routes to the South. Ground troops on the front lines are difficult to remove in a crisis, providing a direct link to the defender's military forces and a signal that the commitment is firm.[9]

Finally, defenders that possess nuclear weapons can reinforce resolve by deploying them to the ally's territory to act as a deterrent or for warfighting if deterrence should fail. In addition or as a discrete measure, the defender can issue statements that the ally is under its nuclear umbrella, indicating that it reserves the right to use nuclear weapons to protect its ally. The presence of nuclear weapons always makes escalation to a nuclear conflict a possibility, particularly if the defender has not provided a "no-first-use" declaration. Thus, even a limited conventional conflict has the potential to escalate to nuclear war.

Certainty of Retaliation

How certain must the threat of retaliation be for deterrence to succeed? Despite a belief by the defender and ally of the absolute certainty of retaliation, the challenger may not be convinced. Moreover, the challenger may conclude that the benefits of an assault are sufficiently high to proceed despite the costs and certainty of retaliation.

Conversely, even in the face of an uncertain or unlikely possibility of retaliation, an adversary may yet be deterred, especially if the costs of retaliation are high and the challenger is unsure that it can control escalation once hostilities commence. Schelling maintains that "it is the essence of a crisis that the participants are not fully in control of events; they take steps and

---

[7] Bruce Russett, "The Calculus of Deterrence," *Journal of Conflict Resolution* 11 (June 1963): 103–109.

[8] Thomas C. Schelling, *Arms and Influence* (New Haven, CT: Yale University Press, 1966), 35.

[9] Terence Roehrig, *From Deterrence to Engagement: The U.S. Defense Commitment to South Korea* (Lanham, MD: Lexington Books, 2006), 179–184.

make decisions that raise or lower the danger, but in a realm of risk and uncertainty." Consequently, Schelling argues, uncertain threats may be credible because "[a] response that carries some risk of war can be plausible, even reasonable, at a time when a final, ultimate decision to *have* a general war would be implausible or unreasonable. A country can threaten to stumble into a war even if it cannot credibly threaten to invite one."[10] Powell points out that there is an important trade-off between wielding power to obtain demands and increasing the risk of escalation. For the challenger, while bringing more power to bear may increase the chances that the defender will back down, it also increases the possible risk that the defender may escalate and events may get out of control, including the use of nuclear weapons.[11] Thus, assessing resolve is a difficult and imprecise process of shifting assessments of costs, benefits, risks, and the defender's resolve.

Depending on the deterrence situation, resolve will have different requirements. During peacetime, it is relatively easy to provide commitments that appear credible. Few costs are apparent when providing security guarantees to any number of allies. However, it is when the situation shifts from general deterrence to a crisis of immediate deterrence that the commitment is tested. The defender now faces a host of serious potential costs that change its earlier cost-benefit calculus. Regarding the nuclear umbrella, it is easy to provide these guarantees to allies in peacetime but far more difficult in a conflict, especially when the threat may be issued to another nuclear-armed state. Moreover, how does a state demonstrate its resolve to use nuclear weapons when none has been in over 70 years.[12]

Other factors also impact the defender's assessment of the costs of upholding its deterrence commitment. First, the capabilities of the adversary are an important element. In a symmetric conflict of relatively equal military power on both sides, particularly if nuclear weapons are involved, coming to an ally's defense could be very costly. Consequently, during the Cold War and U.S. efforts to deter the Soviet Union, the question was asked regularly: would the United States really trade Washington or New York for London or Paris? Washington sought to bridge this credibility gap by deploying tactical nuclear weapons to Europe, but doubts remained. Although debate continues over whether North Korea has the ability to reach the U.S. homeland with nuclear weapons, it is likely to obtain this capability sometime in the future. DPRK (Democratic People's Republic of Korea) nuclear weapons significantly increase the potential costs of any U.S. response to North Korean actions, whether conventional or nuclear, and raise the specter of

---

[10] Schelling, *Arms and Influence*, 97–98.
[11] Robert Powell, "Nuclear Brinkmanship, Limited War, and Military Power," *International Organization* 69 (Summer 2015): 589–626, at 591–592.
[12] Patrick M. Morgan, *Deterrence Now* (Cambridge: Cambridge University Press, 2003), 15.

"decoupling," whereby Washington might hesitate to respond given the costs.[13]

Finally, credibility can also be affected by the defender's reputation and past behavior.[14] Logic would dictate that if the defender has a reputation of not maintaining commitments and backing down in a crisis, enemies and allies will be less inclined to believe in the credibility of future commitments. When studying immediate deterrence cases, Paul Huth found that the "past behavior of the defender in the most recent confrontation with the potential attacker had a significant effect on deterrence outcomes" that "reflects the importance of the interests at stake for the defender."[15] Others have argued it is not reputation or interconnectedness of commitments that determines a state's credibility.[16] Daryl Press contends that "[a] country's credibility, at least during crises, is driven not by its past behavior but rather by power and interests. If a country makes threats that it has the power to carry out—and an interest in doing so—those threats will be believed even if the country has bluffed in the past."[17] In addition, James Fearon argues that "[e]x ante measures of the balance of interests such as alliance ties or geographical contiguity between defender and protégé appear to be related to the failure of immediate deterrent threats."[18] Although scholars disagree, state leaders are often very concerned about reputation and its connection to interests and credibility. The difficulty comes when reputation becomes a goal unto itself and skews larger assessments of the interests at stake.

CREDIBILITY AND THE USE OF NUCLEAR WEAPONS

How credible are threats to use nuclear weapons? Nuclear weapons have been a central element of deterrence for decades, yet they have not been used in a conflict since 1945. States have been reluctant to use nuclear weapons, even when they are facing relatively weak states and have no fear of nuclear retaliation. Despite the hesitance to use nuclear weapons, several states have

---

[13] Brad Roberts, *The Case for U.S. Nuclear Weapons in the Twenty-First Century* (Stanford, CA: Stanford University Press, 2016), 66–67.

[14] See Jonathan Mercer, *Reputation in International Politics* (Ithaca, NY: Cornell University Press, 1996); and Christopher J. Fettweis, "Credibility and the War on Terror," *Political Science Quarterly* 112 (Winter 2007–2008): 607–663.

[15] Paul Huth, "Extended Deterrence and the Outbreak of War," *American Political Science Review* 82 (June 1988): 423–443, at 436–437.

[16] Ted Hopf, *Peripheral Visions: Deterrence Theory and American Foreign Policy in the Third World, 1965–1990* (Ann Arbor: University of Michigan Press, 1995); and Stephen M. Walt, "The Credibility Addiction," *Foreign Policy*, 6 January 2015, accessed at http://foreignpolicy.com/2015/01/06/the-credibility-addiction-us-iraq-afghanistan-unwinnable-war/, 14 May 2017.

[17] Daryl G. Press, *Calculating Credibility: How Leaders Assess Military Threats* (Ithaca, NY: Cornell University Press, 2005), 1.

[18] James D. Fearon, "Signaling versus the Balance of Power and Interests: An Empirical Test of a Crisis Bargaining Model," *Journal of Conflict Resolution* 38 (June 1994): 236–269, at 267.

maintained large nuclear arsenals with detailed war plans and sets of targeting options should they be needed. Throughout the Cold War, and for years after, the United States maintained a first-use posture indicating its willingness to use nuclear weapons first in a conflict rather than wait to retaliate with nuclear weapons. U.S. leaders argued that first use was necessary to offset Soviet conventional strength and obviate the expense of matching the Red Army. In 1972, Secretary of Defense Melvin Laird stated, "Our theater nuclear forces add to the deterrence of theater conventional wars in Europe and Asia; potential opponents cannot be sure that major conventional aggression would not be met with the use of nuclear weapons. The threat of escalation to strategic nuclear war remains a part of successful deterrence at this level."[19]

In the 2010 Nuclear Posture Review (NPR), the Barack Obama administration modified U.S. strategy but stopped short of a no-first-use declaration with the "negative security assurance." Accordingly, the United States would not threaten or use nuclear weapons against non-nuclear states in good standing with their obligations under the Nuclear Non-Proliferation Treaty (NPT). For nuclear weapon states and those not in compliance with the NPT, Washington reserved the right to use nuclear weapons in a narrow range of contingencies, including the use of conventional, chemical, or biological weapons. However, the document noted that while nuclear weapons play a critical role in extended deterrence, "the United States wishes to stress that it would only consider the use of nuclear weapons in extreme circumstances to defend the vital interests of the United States or its allies and partners."[20] U.S. allies in Asia were delighted to not see a no-first-use declaration or that the sole purpose of nuclear weapons was to deter a nuclear attack, but many wondered what was included under "extreme circumstances."

In August 2016, in the closing months of the Obama administration, reports appeared that the president was considering the adoption of a no-first-use policy. The reports sparked considerable debate, and Obama faced stiff opposition within his cabinet.[21] Lewis and Sagan argue that while a no-first-use pledge is useful, it should only be done after careful planning and in consultation with allies. As an interim step, they argue, Obama should have declared that "the United States will not use nuclear weapons against any

---

[19] "Statement of Secretary of Defense Melvin R. Laird before the Senate Armed Services Committee on the FY 1973 Defense Budget and FY 1973–1977 Program," 15 February 1972 (Washington, DC: U.S. Government Printing Office, 1972), 79.

[20] U.S. Department of Defense, "Nuclear Posture Review Report," April 2010, 16, accessed at https://www.defense.gov/Portals/1/features/defenseReviews/NPR/2010_Nuclear_Posture_Review_Report.pdf, 9 October 2017.

[21] Paul Sonne, Gordon Lubold, and Carol E. Lee, "'No First Use' Nuclear Policy Assailed by U.S. Cabinet Officials, Allies," *Wall Street Journal*, 12 August 2016.

target that could be reliably destroyed by conventional means."[22] The Trump administration has begun work on its own NPR and early reports indicate it may recommend development of smaller nuclear weapons to provide the president with a larger set of options. However, for the remainder of the report, it is unclear what will change in this new version.[23]

Despite statements of determination to use nuclear weapons, even if only in extreme circumstances, there are several arguments that raise serious doubts about the credibility of nuclear threats. Traditional realism argued that the hesitation to use nuclear weapons is due to successful deterrence; the possibility of nuclear annihilation made it far too dangerous to risk a nuclear exchange. Yet why have states also been reluctant to use nuclear weapons against adversaries that did not possess nuclear weapons and where nuclear retaliation was not an issue?

One of the answers is the growing norm of the non-use of nuclear weapons.[24] Whether one labels it a taboo or a tradition of non-use, states have been reluctant to use nuclear weapons even against non-nuclear enemies. Nina Tannenwald argues that "a powerful taboo against the use of nuclear weapons has developed in the global system, which, although not (yet) a fully robust prohibition, has stigmatized nuclear weapons as unacceptable weapons—'weapons of mass destruction.'" Consequently, "the effect of this taboo has been to delegitimize nuclear weapons as weapons of war, and to embed deterrence practices in a set of norms . . . that stabilize and restrain the self-help behavior of states."[25] T.V. Paul disputes the label of a taboo but agrees that "the unwillingness to use nuclear weapons can be partially attributed to an informal norm inherent in the tradition of non-use" but must encompass both rational/materialistic and normative/ideational considerations.[26]

There are several factors that explain this restraint. First, leaders have a clear understanding of the destructive power of nuclear weapons.[27] As a result, Stephen Cimbala maintains, leaders become more cautious and seek to

---

[22] Jeffrey G. Lewis and Scott D. Sagan, "The Common-Sense Fix That American Nuclear Policy Needs," *Washington Post,* 24 August 2016, accessed at https://www.washingtonpost.com/opinions/the-common-sense-fix-that-american-nuclear-policy-needs/2016/08/24/b9692dd0-6596-11e6-96c0-37533479f3f5_story.html?utm_term=.369752fa7845, 10 May 2017.

[23] Paul Mcleary, "With Pentagon, State Positions Vacant, Trump Nuclear Review Slows Down," *Foreign Policy,* 15 September 2017, http://foreignpolicy.com/2017/09/15/with-pentagon-state-positions-vacant-trump-nuclear-review-slows-down/.

[24] Nina Tannenwald, *The Nuclear Taboo: The United States and the Non-Use of Nuclear Weapons Since 1945* (Cambridge: Cambridge University Press, 2007); T.V. Paul, *The Tradition of Non-Use of Nuclear Weapons* (Stanford, CA: Stanford University Press, 2009); and Schelling, *The Strategy of Conflict,* 260.

[25] Tannenwald, *The Nuclear Taboo,* 2–3.

[26] Paul, *The Tradition of Non-Use of Nuclear Weapons,* 2–3.

[27] Ibid., 2.

avoid these confrontations because "leaders will be staring into Nietzsche's abyss, and the abyss will be staring back."[28]

Second, states would incur what Paul calls the "reputational costs of nuclear use." Leaders that cross the nuclear threshold for the first time in decades, especially if doing so first in a conflict, would receive a deluge of international condemnation. Leaders, government institutions, and military capabilities are the likely targets of nuclear weapons, yet the indiscriminate nature of nuclear use would cause large-scale casualties among civilian populations who are deemed undeserving of a nuclear holocaust. Thus, Lewis and Sagan argue that "it is hard to imagine a circumstance in which it would be either ethically responsible or strategically wise to use a nuclear weapon when a conventional one would suffice."[29] Consequently, states are self-deterred from using nuclear weapons, particularly against non-nuclear states.[30]

In a study that included public opinion attitudes, Press, Sagan, and Valentino argue that the U.S. public does not possess a "nuclear aversion" and would support nuclear use if it provided a military benefit over conventional weapons. However, the situations in which this would be the case in Korea are few. Moreover, some respondents were concerned about setting a precedent that would make it easier to use nuclear weapons against the United States in the future.[31] While this may lessen some of the domestic political pressure to refrain from using nuclear weapons, it is not clear how much impact it would have on a president's decision to go nuclear.

In addition to these concerns, there are also tactical/military reasons to avoid the use of nuclear weapons. The use of strategic or lower-yield tactical nuclear weapons would contaminate the battle space and make future operations far more difficult. Follow-on ground operations would require that units wear special gear and take numerous other precautions that would cause a very slow advance. The long-term effects on civilian and military personnel of nuclear detonation and the potential impact on neighboring states make even the use of small-yield tactical nuclear weapons problematic. Moreover, states would be very hesitant to escalate because, as Schelling notes, "senior officials, civilian and military, acknowledged and expected that if the nuclear 'threshold' were ever crossed by either side in a war, the other might feel instantly released from inhibitions, and there might be no

---

[28] Stephen J. Cimbala, *Nuclear Strategizing: Deterrence and Reality* (New York: Praeger, 1988), 7.

[29] Lewis and Sagan, "The Common-Sense Fix."

[30] Paul, *The Tradition of Non-Use of Nuclear Weapons*, 25–36.

[31] Daryl G. Press, Scott D. Sagan, and Benjamin A. Valentino, "Atomic Aversion: Experimental Evidence of Taboos, Traditions, and the Non-Use of Nuclear Weapons," *American Political Science Review* 107 (February 2013): 1–19.

telling how far escalation would go."[32] The ability to control the escalation ladder once first use occurs is uncertain, and U.S. leaders should not want to set a precedent for others to escalate in a crisis by doing so itself in anything but the most dire of circumstances. As Scott Sagan notes, U.S. use of nuclear weapons would have a serious impact on nonproliferation because it "would encourage many other states to abandon their ethical inhibitions against developing nuclear weapons and thus would increase the likelihood of future nuclear wars."[33] Paul cautions that "the tradition of non-use is one norm that Washington would be well advised to preserve, for once it is broken, it may not be easy to resurrect it even if future leaders wished to do so."[34] Finally, even if the United States were responding to nuclear first use, Thomas Nichols writes that "it makes no sense to try to reestablish it [nuclear taboo] by violating it *again*."[35]

Although states have refrained from using nuclear weapons in war for years, and pressure to continue this tradition remains, a state may yet use a nuclear weapon, particularly if it believes its existence is threatened. This returns to the core difference between primary and extended deterrence: nuclear threats are more credible in primary than extended deterrence. Thus, Paul argues, "a nuclear state may not use its ultimate capability unless a threshold is crossed, for example, when a vital issue, such as the survival of the state itself, is threatened. . . . Breaking the tradition would elicit the revulsion of generations to come, unless it was for a question of extremely vital importance, such as the physical existence of the nuclear state or its key allies."[36]

THE HISTORY OF NUCLEAR UMBRELLA IN SOUTH KOREA

The nuclear umbrella began as one part of the extended deterrence commitment for South Korea that included the deployment of tactical nuclear weapons with its forces in South Korea.[37] The first U.S. nuclear weapons arrived in South Korea in January 1958 as part of an effort to modernize U.S. forces. Discussions to deploy these weapons began sometime in 1955 and arose in the context of concern for Soviet and Chinese efforts to rearm North Korea after the Korean War, which was a violation of the armistice. U.S. defense officials argued that these arms shipments were altering the

---

[32] Thomas C. Schelling, "The Role of Nuclear Weapons," in L. Benjamin Ederington and Michael J. Mazarr, eds., *Turning Point: The Gulf War and U.S. Military Strategy* (Boulder, CO: Westview Press, 1994), 105– 115, at 106.

[33] Scott D. Sagan, "Realist Perspectives on Ethical Norms and Weapons of Mass Destruction," in Sohail H. Hashmi and Steven P. Lee, eds., *Ethics and Weapons of Mass Destruction: Religious and Secular Perspectives* (Cambridge: Cambridge University Press, 2004),73–95, at 91.

[34] Paul, *The Tradition of Non-Use of Nuclear Weapons*, 212.

[35] Thomas M. Nichols, *No Use: Nuclear Weapons and U.S. National Security* (Philadelphia: Pennsylvania University Press, 2013), 161–162.

[36] Paul, *The Tradition of Non-Use of Nuclear Weapons*, 12.

[37] Roehrig, *From Deterrence to Engagement*, 164–193.

military balance and needed to be addressed.[38] Secretary of State John Foster Dulles challenged this assessment and asked for "publishable evidence" that the violations were occurring before taking action. The Pentagon resisted this request, and according to Donald Stone Macdonald's assessment of State Department archives, "the 'published evidence' was never satisfying"[39] and "the Defense Department was unable to develop a completely convincing brief showing such violations."[40] The determination of communist violations was essential because without it, the United States would have been the one violating the armistice.[41]

U.S. officials also hoped that modernization, including the possibility of nuclear weapons, would provide justification for reducing the size of the ROK military, a force that required heavy U.S. funding given South Korea's struggling economy. During a National Security Council meeting in September 1956, President Dwight Eisenhower lamented that "we were surely spending an awful lot of money in Korea" and that "[ROK president Syngman] Rhee was insisting on too large forces."[42] Dulles argued that nuclear weapons should not be included until Rhee actually reduced his military.[43] Ultimately, Rhee refused to implement any reductions, regardless of the decision on nuclear deployments.

For several months preceding the decision, debate raged in Washington over whether U.S. force modernization in Korea should include nuclear weapons. The State Department was reluctant to include nuclear weapons, believing they were "very conspicuous weapons," would create a propaganda opportunity for North Korea, would generate resentment in the region, and were not worth the political price that would be paid.[44] While Dulles agreed that modernization needed to be a priority, he did not believe it should include nuclear weapons.[45] However, Dulles did recognize that the deployment of nuclear weapons might have a restraining influence on President Rhee. During armistice talks, Rhee expressed his opposition to the agree-

---

[38] "Memorandum of Discussion at the 245th Meeting of the National Security Council," 21 April 1955, *FRUS*, 1955–1957, XXII, part 2, 243–244.
[39] Donald Stone Macdonald, *U.S.-Korean Relations from Liberation to Self-Reliance: The Twenty-Year Record* (Boulder, CO: Westview Press, 1992), 23.
[40] Ibid., 78.
[41] Ibid.
[42] "Memorandum of Discussion at the 297th Meeting of the National Security Council," 20 September 1956, *FRUS*, 1955–1957, XXIII, part 2, 309–310.
[43] "Memorandum of Discussion at the 334th Meeting of the National Security Council," 8 August 1957, *FRUS*, 1955–1957, XXIII, 480–489.
[44] "Memorandum of Discussion at the 326th Meeting of the National Security Council," 13 June 1957, *FRUS*, 1955–1957, XXIII, part 2, 445.
[45] "Memorandum of Discussion at the 318th Meeting of the National Security Council," 4 April 1957, 420–427; and "Memorandum of Discussion at the 326th Meeting of the National Security Council," 13 June 1957, *FRUS*, 1955–1957, XXIII, part 2, 443–454.

ment, believing that hostilities should not end until the peninsula was reunited under his control. Ultimately, Rhee refused to sign the armistice, and U.S. officials feared that he might restart hostilities. Rhee's actions and rhetoric were so disturbing that Washington had a contingency plan in place named Operation Everready to oust him should that become necessary.[46] Nuclear weapons on the peninsula might assist in helping to restrain Rhee's ambitions.

The Pentagon countered that these weapons were absolutely essential to prevent U.S.-ROK forces from being overrun in the early stages of an invasion. With Seoul's proximity to the DMZ, nuclear artillery was necessary to cover the approaches to the capital and prevent this crucial objective from falling early in a conflict. Nuclear weapons would also be an important signal of the U.S. defense commitment to South Korea, allowing Rhee to reduce his troop levels and save the United States money.[47] Peter Hayes also maintains that the U.S. Army was intent on deploying nuclear weapons to South Korea because of budget implications that allowed the army to better compete with the navy and air force for nuclear missions and congressional funding.[48] In the end, Eisenhower approved the deployment of nuclear weapons along with Honest John missiles and 280-millimeter cannons, both dual capable, in NSC 5702/2 in August 1957, the first U.S. nuclear weapons in Korea.

For the U.S. military, the presence of tactical nuclear weapons in South Korea achieved several goals. A 1979 U.S. Defense Department report noted,

> U.S. theater nuclear forces have a symbolic importance that transcends their direct military value. They are the visible evidence of the broader U.S. commitment and of the linkage between our deployed posture and the strategic nuclear forces. . . . [Nuclear weapons] also dramatize to a potential attacker that any conventional attack could set off a chain of nuclear escalation, the consequences of which would be incalculable.[49]

Should deterrence fail, the U.S. Army intended to use nuclear weapons as part of a war-fighting strategy early in a conflict to stop a North Korean assault. Periodically and sometimes in response to specific North Korean actions, the United States sought to enhance deterrence by demonstrating its willingness to use nuclear weapons. For example, in 1976, two U.S. Army

[46] "Memorandum by the Director of the Executive Secretariat to the Secretary of State," 28 October 1953, *FRUS, 1952–1954*, XV, part 2, 1569–1570.
[47] "Memorandum From the Secretary of the Army to the Secretary of Defense," 27 June 1957, *FRUS, 1955–1957*, XXIII, part 2, 464–465.
[48] See Peter Hayes, *Pacific Powderkeg: American Nuclear Dilemmas in Korea* (Lexington, MA: Lexington Books, 1991), 34.
[49] Harold Brown, *Department of Defense: Annual Report, Fiscal Year 1979* (Washington, DC: U.S. Government Printing Office, 1979), 68.

officers were attacked and killed in the Joint Security Area of Panmunjom by a group of North Korean soldiers. In response, the United States brought B-52 bombers from Guam that flew up the peninsula, veering off from North Korea at the last instant. DPRK leaders knew these planes were capable of carrying nuclear weapons, and when the crisis ended, the Defense Department stated the flights would continue, with one to two per month.[50] During the annual spring exercise in 1982, the United States utilized for the first time the Airland Battle doctrine, which simulated the use of nuclear weapons to defend the South during a North Korean invasion.

North Korean leaders were well aware of the U.S. nuclear umbrella and the possibility of U.S. use of nuclear weapons. In addition, North Koreans had clear memories of the pounding they took from conventional bombing during the Korean War. Referring to the 1982 exercises, North Korea declared that "[n]obody can guarantee that this unprecedentedly largescale war exercise staged with many nuclear weapons will not escalate into a full-scale nuclear war against our republic."[51] Over the years, North Korean statements have made many similar references. No doubt, the U.S. nuclear umbrella has been a serious concern for North Korea and an important motive for its nuclear ambitions.

For several years, U.S. officials took a "neither confirm nor deny" position on nuclear weapons in South Korea, although most assumed these weapons were present. However, in 1976, Secretary of Defense James Schlesinger acknowledged their presence publicly, in part to reassure ROK leaders in the wake of Richard Nixon's withdrawal of a combat division and rapprochement with China, neither of which was done in consultation with Seoul. In addition, it also accompanied efforts to dissuade South Korea from acquiring its own nuclear weapons. Later, Washington added other nuclear-tipped missiles, including the Sergeant and the Nike-Hercules along with atomic demolition mines and gravity bombs.[52] Estimates of the number of nuclear weapons deployed to South Korea at any given time ranged from 250 to more than 600 depending on the year.[53]

As time passed, many, including top U.S. military officials began to question the wisdom and utility of basing tactical nuclear weapons in South Korea. The goal of U.S. nuclear weapons was to blunt a North Korean assault, so nuclear forces needed to be forward-deployed close to the DMZ. Yet doing so made these weapons vulnerable to a preemptive strike or being

---

[50] Hayes, *Pacific Powderkeg*, 60.

[51] Byung Chul Koh, *The Foreign Policy Systems of North and South Korea* (Berkeley: University of California Press, 1984), 90.

[52] Bruce Cumings, "The Conflict on the Korean Peninsula," in Yoshikazu Sakamoto, ed., *Asia: Militarization and Regional Conflict* (London: Zed Books, 1988), 105; and Ralph N. Clough, *Deterrence and Defense in Korea: The Role of U.S. Forces* (Washington, DC: Brookings Institution, 1976), 6.

[53] See Hayes, *Pacific Powderkeg*, 102; and Cumings, "The Conflict on the Korean Peninsula," 105.

overrun by North Korean forces during the initial stages of an invasion. If these weapons could not be withdrawn in time, this situation would create a dangerous "use-or-lose" scenario that could cause unintended escalation to nuclear war. Using tactical nuclear weapons had other serious consequences. Detonation on the peninsula would cause severe damage and spew radioactive fallout, endangering South Korean and U.S. military personnel along with South and North Korean civilians. Fallout would also likely drift into China, the Soviet Union, and Japan, causing further nuclear contamination and raising regional tensions. Thus, the use of tactical nuclear weapons was always a dangerous proposition with many serious consequences. By the 1970s, U.S. nuclear weapons had been removed from their forward positions to ones farther south.

By the late 1980s, as the end of the Cold War approached, support for maintaining nuclear weapons at all in South Korea had begun to fade. In 1987, U.S. Forces Korea Commander General Louis Menetrey remarked, "I do not envision any circumstance which . . . would require the use of nuclear weapons."[54] The following year, Lieutenant General John Cushman, the former commander of I Corps that protected the approaches to Seoul, maintained that "nuclear weapons are no longer necessary for the defense of Korea" and that "actual use would be an appalling catastrophe even to the victor."[55] In October 1991, President George H.W. Bush announced that the United States would begin a process to remove all U.S. nuclear weapons from the peninsula. The move was intended in part to coax North Korea into relinquishing its nuclear ambitions and comply with International Atomic Energy Agency inspection requirements. President Bush also hoped that removing U.S. tactical nuclear weapons would nudge President Mikhail Gorbachev to do the same, ensuring that the Soviet arsenal remained safe and secure as the Cold War ended.[56] By December 1991, the removal process was complete, and South Korean president Roh Tae-woo announced, "as I speak, there do not exist any nuclear weapons whatsoever, anywhere in the Republic of Korea."[57]

NORTH KOREA'S NUCLEAR WEAPONS: THE THREAT THAT DRIVES THE NUCLEAR UMBRELLA

For years, North Korea's conventional capabilities were the primary concern for U.S. and ROK defense planners. After the disaster of the Korean War,

---

[54] Fred Hiatt, "U.S.: No Use of A-Arms Envisioned in S. Korea," *Washington Post,* 3 December 1987.

[55] J. McBeth, "Withdrawal Symptoms: Americans Ponder the Removal of Nuclear Weapons," *Far Eastern Economic Review,* 29 September 1988, 35.

[56] Susan J. Koch, *The Presidential Nuclear Initiatives of 1991–1992* (Washington, DC: National Defense University Press, 2012), accessed at http://ndupress.ndu.edu/Portals/68/Documents/casestudies/CSWMD_CaseStudy-5.pdf, 15 May 2017.

[57] James Sterngold, "Seoul Says It Now Has No Nuclear Arms," *New York Times,* 19, December 1991.

Washington and Seoul were determined to deter another conventional assault across the DMZ. As Pyongyang's conventional capabilities grew, extended deterrence and the nuclear umbrella were directed largely toward a North Korean conventional attack. By the 1990s, the DPRK's military capabilities had become more complicated and asymmetric with its growing ballistic missile force, special operations units and, chemical, biological, and nuclear weapons supplementing its significant conventional strength. We now turn to a brief assessment of North Korea's ballistic missile, nuclear, chemical, and biological weapon programs.

Ballistic Missiles

North Korea's ballistic missile force is one of its chief military assets. For several decades, the DPRK has been working on its ballistic missile program, in part through acquisitions from the Soviet Union and work on its own indigenous capability.[58] The North Korean missile force contains approximately 500 short-range Scud missiles that can target the peninsula and 150 to 200 medium-range Nodong missiles that can reach most of Japan and U.S. bases there.[59] North Korea has also developed another short-range missile, the KN-02 or Toksa. The missile is an upgraded Soviet SS-21 that uses solid fuel, an important improvement over the bulk of its liquid-fuel missiles.

North Korea continues work on longer-range systems.[60] The Musudan or Hwasong-10 is an intermediate-range ballistic missile that can reach Guam. The missile has been flight-tested on several occasions, but only one of the tests was considered a possible success.[61] A *New York Times* report speculated that the failures may have been due to U.S. cyberattacks in what have been dubbed "left-of-launch" operations.[62] However, other analysts have raised doubts about the ability to hack into North Korea's missile program.[63]

---

[58] Markus Schiller, "Characterizing the North Korean Missile Threat," RAND, 2012, accessed at http://www.rand.org/pubs/technical_reports/TR1268.html, 15 May 2017.

[59] Greg Thielmann, "Sorting Out the Nuclear and Missile Threats from North Korea," Arms Control Association, 21 May 2013, accessed at https://www.armscontrol.org/threats/Sorting-Out-the-Nuclear-and-Missile-Threats-From-North-Korea, 15 May 2017.

[60] Uzi Rubin, "North Korea's Missile Program: How Far It Has Come, How Far It Needs to Go," *NK News*, 29 May 2017, accessed at https://www.nknews.org/pro/north-koreas-missile-program-how-far-it-has-come-how-far-it-needs-to-go/, 2 June 2017.

[61] David Wright, "Analysis of North Korea's Musudan Missile Test—Part 1," Union of Concerned Scientists, 24 June 2016, accessed at http://allthingsnuclear.org/dwright/analysis-of-north-koreas-musudan-missile-test-part-1, 31 May 2017.

[62] David E. Sanger and William J. Broad, "Trump Inherits a Secret Cyberwar against North Korean Missiles," *New York Times*, 4 March 2017, accessed at https://www.nytimes.com/2017/03/04/world/asia/north-korea-missile-program-sabotage.html?_r=0, 31 May 2017.

[63] Jeffrey Lewis, "Is the United States Really Blowing Up North Korea's Missiles?," *Foreign Policy*, 19 April 2017, accessed at https://foreignpolicy.com/2017/04/19/the-united-states-isnt-hacking-north-koreas-missile-launches/, 31 May 2017.

Flight tests have also occurred for the KN-11/Pukguksong-1, a missile being developed as a submarine-launched ballistic missile. Since 2014, North Korea has conducted several tests of the missile from a ground-based platform, a submerged platform, and a Sinpo-class submarine named for the Sinpo South Shipyard, but with mixed results.[64] Tests have also been conducted for the KN-15 or Pukguksong-2, the land-based, medium-range variant of the KN-11. Another missile that was first revealed during the 15 April 2017, parade to commemorate Kim Il-sung's birthday and flight-tested is the KN-17 or Hwasong-12, a short-to medium-range Scud variant that has fins on the warhead to allow for maneuverability in flight. The KN-17 was initially believed to be an anti-ship missile, but since North Korea does not have the necessary sensors and ISR (intelligence, surveillance, and reconnaissance) for these types of operations, analysts believe this will be more important for improved accuracy in hitting ground targets.[65]

Finally, work also continues on building an intercontinental ballistic missile (ICBM) capable of reaching the United States. In his 2017 New Year's Day speech, Kim Jong-un declared that North Korea was in the "final stage of preparation for the test launch of [an] intercontinental ballistic missile."[66] In July, North Korea conducted two tests of the KN-20 or Hwasong 14, a mobile ICBM, demonstrating further progress in extending the range of its missiles. Though analysts disagree over whether DPRK missiles can reach the continental United States, North Korea continues to advance the capabilities of these systems.

Nuclear, Chemical, and Biological Weapons

North Korea's nuclear weapons program remains the most serious concern for regional stability. Pyongyang has tested on six occasions: October 2006, May 2009, February 2013, twice in 2016, and in September 2017. A 2015 estimate placed North Korea's nuclear arsenal at 10 to 16 weapons from spent fuel produced at the Yongbyon reactor and highly enriched uranium produced at one or possibly two enrichment facilities.[67] A study by David

---

[64] Joseph S. Bermudez, Jr., "North Korea's Ballistic Missile Submarine Program: Full Steam Ahead," 38 North, 5 January 2016, accessed at http://38north.org/2016/01/sinpo010516/, 31 May 2017; and John Schilling, "A New Submarine-Launched Ballistic Missile for North Korea," 38 North, 25 April 2016, accessed at http://38north.org/2016/04/jschilling042516/, 31 May 2017.

[65] Jessie Johnson, "North Korea Hails Test of 'Precision-Guided' Missile as Success, Vows Bigger 'Gift Package' for U.S.," *Japan Times*, 30 May 2017, accessed at http://www.japantimes.co.jp/news/2017/05/30/asia-pacific/north-korea-hails-test-precision-guided-missile-success-vows-bigger-gift-package-u-s/#.WS63PGjyvIU, 31 May 2017.

[66] Kim Jong-un, "2017 New Year's Address," Korean Central News Agency, 2 January 2017, accessed at http://www.ncnk.org/sites/default/files/KJU_2017_New_Years_Address.pdf, 2 June 2017.

[67] Joel Wit and Sun Young Ahn, "North Korea's Nuclear Futures: Technology and Strategy," U.S.-Korea Institute at SAIS, 2015, accessed at http://38north.org/wp-content/uploads/2015/02/NKNF-NK-Nuclear-Futures-Wit-0215.pdf, 31 May 2017.

Albright and Serena Kelleher-Vergantini in June 2016 increased these estimates to 13 to 21 warheads.[68] Even more troublesome, Albright extrapolated data for North Korea's future arsenal and projected three possible scenarios for a stockpile of 20, 50, or 100 nuclear weapons by 2020.[69]

Although North Korea continues working on the various components, it is unclear exactly how far it has progressed toward its goal of developing an effective and reliable nuclear deterrent. In addition, debate continues over whether North Korea has succeeded in miniaturizing a nuclear weapon so that it is sufficiently small to fit on a ballistic missile. In March 2016, Admiral William Gortney, head of NORAD and commander of NORTHCOM, testified before Congress that "while the KN-08 remains untested, modeling suggests it could deliver a nuclear payload to much of the Continental United States."[70] The day before Gortney provided his assessment, Kim Jong-un was pictured next to North Korean scientists and a silver globe that was presumed to be a model of a nuclear warhead.[71] After the September 2017 test, North Korea released another photograph showing Kim Jong-un with what it maintained was a hydrogen warhead that had been weaponized. North Korea has yet to provide definitive evidence of this capability, but assessments have moved toward the conclusion that North Korea has achieved this objective. In any case, it is certain that Pyongyang will strive to reach this goal sometime in the future. Moreover, even if systems are not fully capable, they may be sufficiently close to what Wit and Ahn call "emergency operational capability," which generates some deterrence benefit even if the systems are not fully reliable.[72]

North Korean technicians and scientists face some difficult challenges to ensure that any nuclear weapons system functions as hoped, including modernizing its missile force from liquid to solid fuel, improving the range and accuracy of its ballistic missiles, and developing a survivable, long-range reentry vehicle. North Korea has shown significant progress, but the obstacles are numerous; as Dana Struckman, retired U.S. Air Force colonel and missileer has noted, "building a nuclear weapon and its delivery system, and then keeping them operational for the long term is hard—even harder for

[68] David Albright and Serena Kelleher-Vergantini, "Plutonium, Tritium, and Highly Enriched Uranium Production at the Yongbyong Nuclear Site," Institute for Science and International security, 14 June 2016, accessed at http://isis-online.org/uploads/isis-reports/documents/Pu_HEU_and_tritium_production_at_Yongbyon_June_14_2016_FINAL.pdf, 31 May 2017.

[69] David Albright, "Future Directions in the DPRK's Nuclear Weapons Program: Three Scenarios for 2020," 38 North, 26 February 2015, accessed at http://38north.org/2015/02/dalbright022615/, 4 June 2017.

[70] Admiral William E. Gortney, "Statement before the Senate Armed Services Committee," 10 March 2016, accessed at http://www.northcom.mil?Portals/28?Documents?Gortney_Posture%20Statement_SASC_03-10-16.pdf, 19 April 2017.

[71] "Kim Jong Un Guides Work for Mounting Nuclear Warheads on Ballistic Rockets," KCNA, 9 March 2016.

[72] Wit and Ahn, "North Korea's Nuclear Futures," 9.

those states attempting to do it under the umbrella of international sanctions and monitoring"—"it won't be easy . . . or cheap."[73] The United States, South Korea, and others will never accept North Korea as a nuclear weapons state, and the use of force to eliminate the program is unlikely.[74] The Trump administration has announced on numerous occasions that "all options are on the table" and President Trump has sent several provocative tweets that indicated military options were under serious consideration. Despite the rhetorical battle between Kim Jong-un and Trump, neither side has utilized a military option and the use of military force is dangerous and risky. Thus, for the United States there may be few actions to take short of reinforcing deterrence, increasing sanctions, improving missile defense, maintaining a watchful eye on North Korea's proliferation activities, and making certain that further growth of the DPRK's program is as difficult and expensive as possible.

Finally, North Korea also has a significant chemical and biological weapons program. The DPRK is believed to have 2,500 to 5,000 tons of several chemical agents, including mustard gas, VX, and sarin.[75] These chemical agents are produced indigenously and could be delivered with ballistic missiles, rockets, and artillery.[76] North Korea also possesses a biological weapons program, but less is known about these weapons.

UNDER THE NUCLEAR UMBRELLA: SOUTH KOREAN SECURITY CALCULATIONS

Over the years, South Korea has relied on U.S. nuclear weapons and the nuclear umbrella in its security planning as a deterrent to prevent a repeat of the Korean War. One of the venues for the United States to provide affirmation of the nuclear umbrella is the annual Security Consultative Meeting (SCM) that includes the ROK minister of defense and the U.S. secretary of defense. At the conclusion of this meeting, both parties issue a joint communiqué that reaffirms the principles of the alliance and outlines mutual agreement ona variety of issues. Since 1978, the communiqué has included a specific reference that "Korea is and will continue to be under the U.S. nuclear umbrella."[77] The wording changed little over the next 30 years, although its position within the communiqué shifted based on events.

---

[73] Dana Struckman and Terence Roehrig, "Not So Fast: Pyongyang's Nuclear Weapons Ambitions," *Georgetown Journal of International Affairs*, 20 February 2013, accessed at http://journal.georgetown.edu/not-so-fast-pyongyangs-nuclear-weapons-ambitions-by-dana-struckman-and-terence-roehrig/, 23 March 2017.

[74] Terence Roehrig, "Fixing America's Impossible, Unchangeable North Korea Goals," *The Diplomat*, 7 June 2016, accessed at http://nationalinterest.org/feature/fixing-americas-impossible-unchangeable-north-korean-goals-16495, 25 May 2017.

[75] ROK Ministry of Defense, "Defense White Paper," 2014, 29.

[76] Joseph Bermudez, Jr., "North Korea's Chemical Warfare Capabilities," 38 North, 10 October 2013, accessed at http://38north.org/2013/10/jbermudez101013/, 22 May 2017.

[77] U.S. Department of Defense, "Joint Communique, the 11th ROK-U.S. Security Consultative Meeting," October 1978.

The October 2009 SCM Joint Communiqué between Secretary of Defense Robert Gates and Minster of Defense Kim Tae-young contained an important change in the nuclear umbrella clause. Following North Korea's second test in May 2009, the communiqué "reaffirmed the U.S. commitment to provide extended deterrence for the ROK, using the full range of military capabilities, to include the U.S. nuclear umbrella, conventional strike, and missile defense capabilities."[78] The statement repeated the U.S. commitment but reminded that extended deterrence, while including the nuclear umbrella, need not rely solely on it; missile defense and conventional military strikes are also part of deterring North Korea.

Guarantees of the nuclear umbrella also came occasionally from higher levels. In June 2009, Presidents Barack Obama and Lee Myung-bak held a summit meeting in Washington, DC. As a result of North Korea's May 2009 test, South Korean officials lobbied hard for the summit to include a statement of the U.S. defense commitment, including an explicit reference to the nuclear umbrella. The White House was hesitant to do so given that it ran counter to Obama's speech in Prague that called for a decreased role of nuclear weapons in international security along with their eventual elimination.[79] The administration complied, despite its misgivings, elevating the commitment from a statement between ministers to one between heads of state. Consequently, the Joint Vision of the Alliance issued during the summit reiterated "the continuing commitment of extended deterrence, including the U.S. nuclear umbrella," providing the high level guarantee Seoul desired.[80]

Since North Korea conducted its first nuclear test, ROK analysts and leaders have devoted considerable attention to extended deterrence and the role the U.S. nuclear umbrella plays in South Korean security calculations. The security environment has changed dramatically since the end of the Cold War, requiring increased analysis regarding deterrence, nuclear weapons, and the nuclear umbrella. From these efforts, ROK planners and analysts have articulated several reasons for their belief in the importance of the nuclear umbrella in South Korea's security planning.

First, many analysts believe that the power of nuclear weapons is critical to deterring a nuclear-armed North Korea. During the Cold War, Moscow

---

[78] U.S. Department of Defense, "41st U.S.-ROK Security Consultative Meeting Joint Communiqué," 22 October 2009, accessed at http://www.defense.gov/Releases/Release.aspx?ReleaseID=13072, 14 February 2017.

[79] Office of the Press Secretary, "Remarks By President Barack Obama in Prague as Delivered," 5 April 2009, accessed at https://obamawhitehouse.archives.gov/the-press-office/remarks-president-barack-obama-prague-delivered, 9 October 2017.

[80] "Joint Vision for the Alliance of the United States of America and the Republic of Korea," 16 June 2009, accessed at https://obamawhitehouse.archives.gov/the-press-office/joint-vision-alliance-united-states-america-and-republic-korea, 31 May 2017.

and Washington were rational actors that were well aware of what was at stake and understood the logic of deterrence. Today, many in South Korea have little confidence in the rationality of the Kim Jong-un regime and believe he is willing to tolerate a great deal of risk.[81] To confront these dangers, the power of the U.S. nuclear umbrella provides the needed certainty that aggression would entail serious costs for Pyongyang. As Chang Kwoun Park notes, "In order to deter North Korea's nuclear threat, North Korea must be made to accurately understand that any North Korean provocation will be promptly followed by punishment that will overwhelm them."[82] South Korea lacks the necessary conventional strength to impose such costs, making nuclear weapons and the U.S. nuclear umbrella a necessity for this task.[83]

Second, it must be made clear to North Korea that it has no chance of escalating a conflict to nuclear weapons without paying a severe price from nuclear retaliation. In other words, Pyongyang cannot be allowed to control the escalation ladder in a clash with the South, and the nuclear umbrella adds significant uncertainty to North Korea's calculations that it could do so in a crisis. Moreover, the U.S. nuclear umbrella lets South Korea respond and even escalate with conventional weapons in response to aggression with less fear that North Korea will go nuclear, as doing so would bring nuclear retaliation under the umbrella.[84] Thus, if North Korea were to act as it did in 2010 by sinking a ROK ship or shelling an island, South Korea could retaliate since the nuclear umbrella would counter any North Korean threats to escalate.

Third, some ROK analysts maintain that the nuclear umbrella is less about actual war fighting and more about offsetting the political leverage North Korea might believe it gains from having nuclear weapons. Pyongyang might use its nuclear weapons to intimidate the South for political or economic concessions or possibly to achieve domestic political goals.[85] The nuclear umbrella is necessary to neutralize any perceived political power that North Korea thinks it gains from its nuclear weapons. Signaling the strength of the U.S. commitment to the alliance without the nuclear umbrella would be insufficient to achieve this goal in the minds of many ROK analysts.[86]

---

[81] Author interview, 22 May 2013.
[82] Chang Kwoun Park, "ROK-U.S. Cooperation in Preparation for Hostile Actions by North Korea in Possession of Nuclear Weapons," *Korean Journal of Defense Analysis* 22 (December 2010): 499–513, at 507.
[83] Park Hwee-rhak and Kim Byung-ki, "Time to Balance Deterrence, Offense, and Defense? Rethinking South Korea's Strategy against the North Korean Treat," *Korean Journal of Defense Analysis* 24 (December 2012): 515–532, at 522.
[84] Author interview, 20 May 2013.
[85] Park, "ROK-U.S. Cooperation," 512.
[86] Author interview, 20 May 2013.

Fourth, the U.S. nuclear umbrella also has an important impact on South Korean domestic politics. When the DPRK tests its ballistic missiles and nuclear weapons, ROK leaders feel serious pressure from their citizens to "do something" in response. The U.S. nuclear umbrella furnishes reassurance for the ROK public and gives their leaders political cover that they are in fact responding to the North Korean threat. In addition, the nuclear umbrella spares the country from conducting a formal, contentious debate about acquiring its own nuclear weapons.[87] There are increasing calls, particularly among conservatives, for South Korea to have its own nuclear weapons. Indeed, South Korea sought to build nuclear weapons in the 1970s under Park Chung-hee, fearing a declining U.S. defense commitment, but abandoned the effort after heavy U.S. pressure. More recently, conservative ROK politicians have called for an indigenous nuclear capability, and public opinion surveys have expressed strong support for this option.[88] However, President Moon Jae-in has declared in no uncertain terms that South Korea will not request the return of U.S. tactical nuclear weapons or develop its own.[89] The U.S. nuclear umbrella helps the government resist these demands.

Finally, although ROK analysts acknowledge that nuclear weapons may have limited military utility in dealing with North Korea, the political significance of the nuclear umbrella is crucial. One group of ROK scholars have argued that the nuclear umbrella provides an important sign of the strength of the U.S.-ROK alliance and a critical signal of assurance.[90] Another group of ROK analysts maintains that the nuclear umbrella generates confidence for South Korea, showing a level of commitment to ROK security that goes beyond any provided by conventional forces. The U.S. nuclear umbrella is an important component of the security architecture, and although the United States is unlikely to launch a nuclear strike, the umbrella is more important as a political signal to provide assurance to South Korea of the overall defense commitment.[91] As one defense analyst has noted, the U.S. extended deterrence commitment is a series of connected segments that include political, economic, and military elements. The nuclear umbrella is an essential aspect of the overall extended deterrence commitment, and there would be a gap without it.[92] As a result, the nuclear umbrella is a significant

---

[87] Author interview, 20 June 2012.
[88] Kim Jiyoon and Karl Friedhoff, "The Fallout: South Korean Public Opinion Following North Korea's Third Nuclear Test," Asan Institute for Policy Studies, 24 February 2013, accessed at http://en.asaninst.org/contents/issue-brief-no-46-the-fallout-south-korean-public-opinion-following-north-koreas-third-nuclear-test/, 3 June 2017.
[89] Paula Hancocks and James Griffiths, "No nuclear weapons in South Korea, says President Moon," *CNN*, September 14, 2017, http://www.cnn.com/2017/09/14/asia/south-korea-moon-nuclear/index.html.
[90] Author interview, 4 November 2010.
[91] Author interview, 3 November 2010.
[92] Author interview, 5 November 2010.

part of the alliance that sends a strong indication of U.S. support to ROK leaders and the public, even if the likelihood of using nuclear weapons is low. The nuclear umbrella aids in strengthening the alliance demonstrating the lengths to which the United States will go to defend the South, and, in turn, a robust alliance helps make the nuclear umbrella appear more credible to South Koreans.

THE U.S. NUCLEAR UMBRELLA: CAPABILITIES, MOTIVATIONS, AND CREDIBILITY

The United States has a large nuclear arsenal should it ever decide to exert the nuclear umbrella. Often described as the "triad," one leg consists of Minuteman III ICBMs divided between three air force bases. Each missile carries one warhead with an explosive yield of 300 to 500 kilotons (KT). The second leg is the 14 Ohio-class submarines, the "boomers" that carry 24 Trident II D-5 missiles each, with a yield of 300 to 475 KT per warhead. To comply with the New START Treaty, the ICBM force will be reduced to 400 deployed launchers, and the number of launch tubes on the "boomers" will be decreased to 20 to reach the overall treaty limits of 700 deployed launch vehicles and 1,550 total deployed warheads.[93] Although using one of these two legs is an option for the nuclear umbrella, their destructive power makes it likely that U.S. leaders will refrain from doing so. Delivering a strategic warhead against North Korea would be viewed as disproportionate, and although regional players could be warned prior to launch, sending a ballistic missile into the region is likely to upset Beijing and Moscow and further disrupt regional stability.

Instead, the United States would be far more likely to use the third leg of the triad consisting of B-2 and B-52 bombers. These planes are capable of carrying B-61 gravity bombs or nuclear-tipped AGM-86B air-launched cruise missiles. The B-61 is an adjustable yield bomb and depending on the model can be set to produce a yield ranging from 0.3 to 170 KT. Cruise missiles are armed with W80-1 warheads that also have adjustable yields ranging from 5 to 150 KT.[94] The yields of these weapons, even at their lowest level, remain substantial, and their use would nonetheless constitute nuclear use. The devastation wrought by even a small nuclear weapon would be catastrophic, yet when compared with the use of strategic nuclear weapons, there is a greater likelihood that U.S. leaders would order the use of these

---

[93] U.S. Department of State, Bureau of Arms Control, Verification and Compliance, "New START Treaty Aggregate Numbers of Strategic Offensive Arms," 1 January 2015, accessed at http://www.state.gov/t/avc/rls/235606.htm, 31 May 2017.

[94] Amy Woolf, *Nonstrategic Nuclear Weapons* (Washington, DC: Congressional Research Service, 23 February 2015); and Hans M. Kristensen, "W80-1 Warhead Selected For New Nuclear Cruise Missile," Federation of American Scientists, 10 October 2014, accessed at https://fas.org/blogs/security/2014/10/ w80-1_lrso/, 24 May 2017.

smaller-yield weapons. Finally, bombers have the benefit of being able to be recalled once launched and have a "demonstration" capability that ICBMs do not and is more problematic for submarines. Particularly for extended deterrence, bombers can be flown in ways that reassure an ally and its public while making a statement to an adversary.

Some in South Korea have called for a return of U.S. tactical nuclear weapons to the peninsula. Cheon Seong-whun has argued that the nuclear umbrella is "fragile," and if North Korea develops long-range missiles with nuclear warheads, "there is doubt that the United States could protect Seoul at the risk of nuclear attacks on New York or Los Angeles. The United States should consider redeploying tactical nuclear weapons in South Korea to effectively deter North Korea's nuclear threats."[95] Chong Mong-joon, a member of the ROK National Assembly and primary shareholder of Hyundai Heavy Industries, has also been a strong advocate for returning U.S. nuclear weapons and for South Korea to build its own. Although the return of tactical nuclear weapons was an option under consideration by the Donald Trump administration,[96] it is very unlikely the United States would ever return tactical nuclear weapons to Korea and the Moon administration will not make a request to do so.

The U.S. nuclear umbrella does exist; should the president of the United States choose to do so, the nuclear forces to defend or retaliate for an ally are available. The U.S. military goes to great lengths to train for implementing the nuclear mission should the order come. Thus, when viewing the capability side of the equation, the United States has a credible nuclear option. The difficulty comes with resolve, the other component of credibility, and it is here that there are many reasons why the order to use nuclear weapons to defend South Korea will not and should not come.

RESOLVE AND THE U.S. NUCLEAR UMBRELLA
Successful deterrence is premised on the defender's determination to respond; the defender must demonstrate that it is willing to carry out the threat should deterrence fail. Yet what scenario would prod a U.S. president to use nuclear weapons for the first time since 1945? Short of a direct attack on the United States, there would be enormous pressure on the president to

---

[95] Lee Jong-heon, "Calls for Nuclear Weapons in South Korea," UPI, 21 October 2009, accessed at http://www.upi.com/Top_News/Special/2009/10/21/Calls-for-nuclear-weapons-in-South-Korea/UPI-51191256130461/, 15 April 2017.

[96] William M. Arkin, Cynthia McFadden, Kevin Monahan, and Robert Windrem, "Trump's Options for North Korea Include Placing Nukes in South Korea," NBC News, 7 April 2017, accessed at http://www.nbcnews.com/news/us-news/trump-s-options-north-korea-include-placing-nukes-south-korea-n743571, 31 May 2017.

refrain from escalating a conflict to nuclear weapons. There are several reasons why a U.S. president would think long and hard about using nuclear weapons in Korea and ultimately refrain from doing so.

First, if a crisis came to the point that Washington was considering the use of nuclear weapons, North Korea would have crossed a very serious line, such as a major conventional attack, invasion, or a nuclear first strike. If such an event occurred, it is likely that Washington and Seoul, accompanied by broad international support, would move to end this security problem in a regime change operation. Consequently, ROK and U.S. troops would be deeply engaged and moving into North Korea. The use of nuclear weapons would contaminate the battle space and make follow-up operations exceedingly more difficult. In addition, South Korea would have to deal with the task of cleaning up an irradiated North in the unified Korea that would follow.

Second, the nuclear blast and accompanying short-and long-term effects could have devastating consequences throughout the region. Although the DPRK regime and its military forces would be the target, the indiscriminate nature of nuclear weapons would result in thousands of DPRK civilians being killed in a nuclear strike. To use nuclear weapons simply because Washington said it would or as an act of retaliation has little operational value while carrying huge human, political, and economic costs. Moreover, the fallout and other effects could drift south over Seoul or toward China, Japan, Russia, and others in the region. Referring to a study of nuclear options during the First Gulf War, Colin Powell notes, "The results unnerved me. To do serious damage to just one armored division dispersed in the desert would require a considerable number of small tactical nuclear weapons. . . . If I had had any doubts before about the practicality of nukes on the field of battle, this report clinched them."[97] The geography of Iraq is very different from that of Korea, but the problems Powell raises for nuclear use would also apply.

Third, as scholars have argued concerning the nuclear taboo or tradition of non-use, a U.S. president would be under extreme pressure to avoid escalation and not cross a nuclear firewall that has been in place since the end of World War II. The president would be very reluctant to resort to this option and cross over this long-standing norm. Moreover, using nuclear weapons sets a dangerous precedent that makes it easier for other states to use nuclear weapons in a future conflict. Even if North Korea used nuclear weapons first, using them in retaliation only makes it more difficult to reestablish a firewall that is in the U.S. strategic interest.

Finally, while a nuclear response is highly unlikely, the United States has a multitude of lethal and precise conventional weapons that it would not hesitate to use to defend South Korea. Consequently, a U.S. conventional

---

[97] Colin L. Powell, *My American Journey* (New York: Random House, 1995), 486.

response is far more credible and would have the same devastating strategic effect on North Korea and its leaders as nuclear weapons. Thus, the U.S.-ROK alliance is highly credible, and there is no doubt Washington would come to Seoul's assistance if attacked, but the use of nuclear weapons would almost certainly not be part of the response.

Critics of this argument will maintain that the United States must respond to Pyongyang's use of nuclear weapons in kind because doing otherwise would send a message to other allies that U.S. security guarantees are meaningless, and Washington would never be able to resurrect the nuclear umbrella again. However, the United States has always stated that it has a range of options for responding to any type of conflict in Korea. A forceful U.S. conventional response that leads to regime change in North Korea would not damage U.S. credibility. There is no absolute obligation that the United States must respond with nuclear weapons, only that aggression be met with a robust, appropriate U.S. reply. A powerful U.S. conventional response that has the same strategic effect as nuclear weapons would mitigate any perception in the United States and among its allies or adversaries that U.S. security commitments lack credibility.

An important dimension of the U.S. nuclear umbrella is that Washington has not given a no-first-use guarantee, going only so far as a negative security assurance. While there is merit in the United States providing a no-first-use guarantee, it is likely North Korean leaders would not believe it. Moreover, even if the United States withdrew its nuclear umbrella in a formal declaration, North Korea would never be certain that U.S. leaders would not use nuclear weapons to defend South Korea. So long as the United States retains a nuclear weapons arsenal, a certain degree of ambiguity will remain; North Korea will have little confidence in a U.S. statement not to use nuclear weapons first or a pronouncement that removes South Korea from the nuclear umbrella.[98]

For South Korea and other U.S. allies, the goal of the nuclear umbrella is security and deterrence. The nuclear umbrella demonstrates a commitment to provide the ultimate capability to deter aggression and reassure the ally of its importance to Washington. Yet for the United States, the nuclear umbrella has another important goal: nonproliferation. After every North Korean nuclear weapon test, the United States reassured South Korea of its inclusion under the nuclear umbrella for fear Seoul might consider develop-

---

[98] Patrick Morgan, "Considerations Bearing on a Possible Retraction of the American Nuclear Umbrella over the ROK," Project on Improving Regional Security and Denuclearizing the Korean Peninsula: U.S. Policy Interests and Options, National Committee on North Korea, October 2009, accessed at http://www.ncnk.org/resources/publications/Morgan%20Considerations%20Bearing_on_a_Possible_Retraction_of_the_American_Nuclear_Umbrella.pdf, 31 May 2017.

ing its own nuclear weapons. The 2010 NPR maintains that security relations with allies "can also serve our non-proliferation goals . . . by reassuring non-nuclear allies and partners that their security interests can be protected without their own nuclear capabilities."[99] Once North Korea developed the ability to strike the U.S. homeland with nuclear weapons, ROK leaders feared decoupling because it was now vulnerable to a nuclear attack. One ROK politician remarked after North Korea's fourth nuclear test, "It's time for us to peacefully arm ourselves with nuclear weapons from the perspective of self-defense to fight against North Korea's terror and destruction."[100] As a result, U.S. leaders have worked hard to reassure South Korea to dissuade it from moving in that direction. Thus, Choi and Park argue, "A strong U.S. security commitment and the provision of its nuclear umbrella play the role of a 'bottle cap' that keeps South Korea from thinking it needs to develop nuclear weapons."[101]

South Korea's acquisition of nuclear weapons surprisingly became part of the 2016 U.S. presidential election. During the campaign, Donald Trump indicated that he believed nuclear proliferation was likely and that the acquisition of nuclear weapons by South Korea and Japan would not be such a bad idea.[102] Trump asserted that Seoul and Tokyo were not paying their fair share to support the presence of U.S. forces. If they were unwilling to increase their contributions, the United States would consider withdrawing its forces, and nuclear weapons could compensate for the U.S. departure. The Obama administration spoke out strongly against this course of action, and Trump has since backed away from this suggestion. Despite the stir that Trump caused with his campaign remarks, the U.S. commitment to nonproliferation and the role of the nuclear umbrella in achieving that goal are likely to remain.

IMPLICATIONS: SOUTH KOREA AND THE U.S. NUCLEAR UMBRELLA

Three important implications emerge from this study. First, despite the regular reassurances that South Korea remains under the U.S. nuclear umbrella and the unambiguous capability present for using nuclear weapons,

---

[99] U.S. Department of Defense, "Nuclear Posture Review Report," 31.

[100] Yi Whan-woo, "NK Test Stirs Call for Nuclear Armament," *Korea Times*, 18 January 2016, accessed at http://www.koreatimes.co.kr/www/news/nation/2016/01/180_195722.html, 31 May 2017.

[101] Kang Choi and Joon-sung Park, "South Korea: Fears of Abandonment and Entrapment," in Muthiah Alagappa, ed., *The Long Shadow: Nuclear Weapons in the 21st Century* (Stanford, CA: Stanford University Press, 2008), 390.

[102] "Transcript: Donald Trump Expounds on His Foreign Policy Views," *New York Times*, 26 March 2016, accessed in http://www.nytimes.com/2016/03/27/us/politics/donald-trump-transcript.html?_r=0, 24 April 2017; and "Milwaukee Republican Presidential Town Hall," CNN, 29 March 2016, accessed in http://cnnpressroom. blogs.cnn.com/2016/03/29/full-rush-transcript-donald-trump-cnn-milwaukee-republican-presidential-town-hall/, 26 May 2017.

significant credibility problems remain regarding resolve. Under what circumstances would the United States be willing to use nuclear weapons to defend South Korea? Even in a crisis and without a no-first-use policy in place, a U.S. president would be under tremendous stress for political, moral, and military reasons to refrain from using nuclear weapons and crossing a long-standing fire break. Washington would likely go to great lengths to respond only with conventional weapons, even in the face of North Korean use of chemical or biological weapons, and possibly even nuclear weapons. Using nuclear weapons in a conflict sets a disastrous precedent that is not in the U.S. or anyone else's interest.

Here is the paradox this study has addressed—with these uncertainties, the credibility of the U.S. nuclear umbrella is in great doubt, but allies continue to ask for and rely on the nuclear umbrella. Yet even a guarantee that is largely incredible still has deterrence value, particularly given the overwhelming destructive power of nuclear weapons. As Schelling argues, even uncertain threats can contribute to deterrence. Regarding extended deterrence in Europe, former British secretary of state for defense Denis Healey remarked that "it takes only five per cent credibility of American retaliation to deter the Russians, but ninety-five per cent credibility to reassure the Europeans."[103] Thus, with the high levels of mistrust between Washington and Pyongyang, the nuclear umbrella has an impact on North Korean leaders because they may not be convinced that the United States might not use nuclear weapons. While the credibility of the nuclear umbrella may be questionable from some vantage points, it may not be so from that of the adversary. Enemies and their militaries tend to view these circumstances from a worst-case assessment that the defender may indeed respond so that credibility may be stronger in their eyes than what others might believe. Despite all of the uncertainties, South Korean leaders continue to place a high value on the U.S. nuclear umbrella. Thus, the political and symbolic value of the nuclear umbrella, along with a belief that the credibility of the U.S. guarantee is "good enough," motivates ROK leaders to continue vigorous calls for the nuclear commitment.

Second, despite the credibility questions, the nuclear umbrella continues to have important symbolic effects for South Korea as a sign of the U.S. commitment to defend the country. Again, Healey maintains that "Europe's concern with the credibility of American deterrence is a function of its general confidence in the wisdom and consistency of American leadership rather than changes in the relative military power of the United States and the Soviet Union."[104] To not reaffirm the nuclear umbrella following North Korea's

---

[103] Denis Healey, *The Time of My Life* (New York: W.W. Norton, 1989), 243.
[104] Ibid.

nuclear tests would have been an alteration of the security architecture that would have been difficult for Seoul to accept. Despite the credibility problems, why is the U.S. nuclear umbrella so highly valued by South Korea? Patrick Morgan maintains that "American extended nuclear deterrence *is woven into East Asian international politics and US relations with East Asia*. In the eyes of various governments, it is one of the salient characteristics of a satisfactory status quo."[105] As noted earlier, the nuclear umbrella is viewed by South Korea as a demonstration of the U.S. commitment that bolsters ROK confidence in ways that cannot be achieved with allies and conventional weapons, even though there are significant credibility issues. Although the early statements of the Trump administration have raised some serious questions in the minds of South Koreans concerning the U.S.-ROK alliance, overall, there is confidence in the long-term outlook of the U.S. defense commitment.

While the importance of the nuclear umbrella to ROK security remains, it is only one part of a broader security structure. The 2010 NPR states that "enhancing regional security architectures is a key part of U.S. strategy for strengthening regional deterrence." In addition, "these regional security architectures include effective missile defense, counter-WMD capabilities, conventional power-projection, and integrated command and control all underwritten by strong political commitments."[106] In 2014, Under Secretary for Arms Control and International Security Rose Gottemoeller maintained,

> [E]xtended deterrence is not only about nuclear weapons. Extended deterrence has to do with our complete alliance relationship and that, of course, contains within it a full panoply of weapons systems and everything that goes with weapons systems to make them effective—such as effective command, control, communications, and reconnaissance capabilities. Conventional weapons—and very effective conventional weapons at that—are a core, inherent part of extended deterrence.[107]

A forthcoming Trump NPR is unlikely to change these fundamentals of U.S. extended deterrence. Thus, the nuclear umbrella remains an important component of the regional security architecture but is only one piece of that structure, and an important political statement of reassurance for South Korea, even though the United States is unlikely to ever use these weapons.

Third, for the United States, the nuclear umbrella is in part a guarantee for the security of South Korea, but it is also an important tool for U.S. nonproliferation goals. After the first North Korean nuclear test, U.S. leaders

---

[105] Patrick Morgan, "Considerations Bearing on a Possible," 3.
[106] U.S. Department of Defense, "Nuclear Posture Review Report," 32–33.
[107] Michael Chernin and Sabin Ray, "On the Frontline of U.S. Nuclear Policy with Under Secretary Rose Gottemoeller," *Brown Journal of World Affairs* 21 (Fall/Winter 2014): 253–260, at 255–256.

feared that Seoul might be tempted to pursue a nuclear capability, and calls by conservative elites in South Korea for its own nuclear weapons have grown. Van Jackson, the former Korea lead at the Pentagon, maintains that "in my conversations with experts from Australia, Japan and South Korea over the years, . . . I've concluded that these states are signatories of the Nuclear Nonproliferation Treaty and have not gone nuclear mostly because of the U.S. nuclear umbrella extended to them."[108] U.S. assurances of the nuclear umbrella are important efforts to convince South Korea to continue forgoing nuclear weapons and keeping the NPT regime from deteriorating further. As noted earlier, though the credibility of the nuclear umbrella is low, it has been sufficient to persuade South Korea and other U.S. allies not to go nuclear.

CONCLUSION THE U.S. NUCLEAR UMBRELLA AND THE FUTURE OF THE ALLIANCE

The U.S. nuclear umbrella has been a part of the security architecture in Korea and East Asia more broadly for many years, and it is likely to remain. The nuclear umbrella is real; the United States maintains a large nuclear arsenal that is more than capable of defending South Korea and other allies with nuclear weapons that could inflict terrible damage on any adversary. This part of extended nuclear deterrence is highly credible. It is resolve that remains the problematic element, as it was during the Cold War in Europe and Asia, and it will remain so in the future. It is essential that the reluctance to use nuclear weapons remains. The U.S. defense commitment to South Korea is credible despite some of the early difficulties in relations under the Trump administration. If South Korea were attacked, there is little doubt the United States would be there to protect its ally. However, that response will be with conventional assets, not nuclear weapons. The use of conventional weapons is credible with similar strategic effects on North Korea so that deterrence remains robust. Moreover, even a small chance of nuclear use, given the costs, will have a deterrent effect on North Korea. Washington will continue to provide its nuclear umbrella as an important political signal for the alliance and as part of its nonproliferation policy while also gaining some benefit for its deterrence posture. The credibility problems of the nuclear umbrella will remain, but the U.S. nuclear umbrella will be "good enough" for successful strategic deterrence of North Korea.

---

[108] Van Jackson, "The U.S. Doesn't Need Tactical Nuclear Weapons in Asia," *The Diplomat*, 2 July 2015, accessed at http://thediplomat.com/2015/07/the-us-doesn't-need-tactical-nuclear-weapons-in-asia/, 9 October 2017.

Some would maintain this is an argument for smaller, more useable nuclear weapons to make U.S. nuclear use more palatable.[109] However, even smaller nuclear weapons will encounter the same obstacles and problems noted here and are not the answer. Others would argue that this makes a case for South Korea to acquire its own nuclear capability.[110] Again, there are a host of reasons why this is a bad idea for South Korea and would do little to improve its security.[111] Strategic deterrence is solid in Korea, and Pyongyang knows that any major military operation against the South, to include the use of nuclear weapons, would be tantamount to regime suicide. The more difficult problem in Korea is deterring lower-level DPRK provocations, and ROK nuclear weapons along with U.S. tactical nuclear weapons would do little to address this challenge. In the end, the combined conventional military strength of the U.S.-ROK alliance along with an uncertain nuclear umbrella is more than sufficient to deter a nuclear North Korea.*

* The views expressed in this report are the author's alone and do not represent the official position of the Department of the Navy, the Department of Defense, or the U.S. government. Participation in this study was supported by the Academy of Korean Studies grant funded by the Korean Government (MEST) (AKS2012-AAZ-2101) and administered by the University of Wisconsin-Milwaukee.

---

[109] Keir A. Lieber and Daryl G. Press, "The Nukes We Need," *Foreign Affairs* 88 (November/December 2009): 39–51.

[110] K.J. Kwon, "Under Threat, South Koreans Mull Nuclear Weapons," CNN, 18 March 2013, accessed at http://www.cnn.com/2013/03/18/world/asia/south-korea-nuclear/, 24 May 2017.

[111] Terence Roehrig, "The Case for a Nuclear-Free South," *JoongAng Daily*, 19 June 2014, accessed at http://koreajoongangdaily.joins.com/news/article/article.aspx?aid=2990820, 23 March 2017.

The Role of Villain:
Iran and U.S. Foreign Policy

PAUL R. PILLAR

THE ISLAMIC REPUBLIC OF IRAN HAS BECOME, in two senses, an extraordinary preoccupation of the United States. One sense is that Iran is the subject of a strikingly large proportion of discourse about U.S. foreign policy. American pundits and politicians repeatedly mention Iran, usually with specific reference to its nuclear program, as among the biggest threats the United States faces. Republican nominee Mitt Romney, when asked in the last presidential debate of the 2012 campaign what was the single greatest future threat to U.S. national security, replied "a nuclear Iran."[1] For politicians of both major U.S. political parties, expressions of concern about Iran and of the need to confront it have become a required catechism. The U.S. Congress has spent much time on such expressions and on imposing with lopsided votes ever broader economic sanctions on Iran. Frequent and evidently serious references are made to launching a military attack against Iran, even though such an attack—an act of aggression—would probably mean a war with heavy costs and damage to U.S. interests and probably would stimulate the very development of an Iranian nuclear weapon that it ostensibly would be designed to preclude.[2]

The other extraordinary aspect of this preoccupation is that it is divorced from the actual extent of any threat that Iran poses to U.S. interests. The

---

[1] "Transcript of the Third Presidential Debate," 22 October 2012, accessed at http://www.nytimes.com/2012/10/22/us/politics/transcript-of-the-third-presidential-debate-in-boca-raton-fla.html?pagewanted=all&_r=0, 30 December 2012.

[2] The Iran Project, *Weighing Benefits and Costs of Military Action Against Iran*, accessed at http://www.wilsoncenter.org/sites/default/files/IranReport_091112_FINAL.pdf, 30 December 2012.

PAUL R. PILLAR is a retired CIA officer and nonresident senior fellow at the Center for Security Studies at Georgetown University. His most recent book is *Why America Misunderstands the World: National Experience and Roots of Misperception*.

Islamic Republic, as a matter of capabilities as well as intentions, does not endanger those interests to a degree that corresponds to the intense focus that the subject receives in American debate. The principal sources of the preoccupation are instead to be found in history, politics, and customary American ways of perceiving adversaries.

AN EXAGGERATED DANGER

One of the most-obvious indications of the disconnect between rhetoric and reality on this subject—and specifically on the core concern of a feared Iranian nuclear weapon—is that the Iranian regime, as assessed by the U.S. intelligence community, has not even decided to build such a weapon.[3] The Iranians are interested in nuclear weapons, and some of their past work belies their public assertions that only non-military purposes have entered the thinking about their nuclear program. They have good reasons, however, not to have decided to cross the nuclear weapons threshold and instead to let any future decision about building a bomb be a response to the policies of the West and especially of the United States. The prospect of reaching economically and politically beneficial agreements with the West is a reason never to build a bomb, which any such agreements would rule out. Conversely, if armed hostilities appear more likely, this would be an incentive to try to develop a nuclear weapon, because of its presumed deterrent value.

American alarm about Iran's nuclear program seldom considers the long record that this program, which began in the 1970s under the Shah, has of slow progress, evidently due to technical problems and insufficient Iranian knowledge.[4] Previous Western assessments have overestimated how quickly Iran could become able to build a nuclear weapon.[5] A similar observation can be made about Iran's work, and estimates about that work, on delivery systems and, specifically, ballistic missiles, notwithstanding cooperation for many years between Iran and North Korea on missiles and other defense matters.[6] An Iranian missile with intercontinental range now seems at least several years away, if it ever materializes at all.

Presumptions rather than analysis have characterized American discourse about the consequences if Iran were to acquire a nuclear weapon. It

---

[3] James Risen and Mark Mazzetti, "U.S. Spies See No Iran Moves to Build Bomb," *The New York Times*, 25 February 2012.

[4] On the technical and knowledge deficiencies of the Iranian program, see the comments of former international nuclear inspector Olli Heinonen in Yossi Melman, "Behind the scenes of UN nuclear inspection of Iran," *Haaretz*, 22 October 2010, accessed at http://www.haaretz.com/weekend/week-s-end/behind-the-scenes-of-un-nuclear-inspection-of-iran-1.320599, 31 December 2012.

[5] Jeffrey T. Richelson, *Spying on the Bomb* (New York: W.W. Norton, 2005), 503–517.

[6] Steven A. Hildreth, *Iran's Ballistic Missile and Space Launch Programs* (Washington, DC: Congressional Research Service, 6 December 2012), 35–38.

is widely taken for granted, and repeatedly voiced even by those who disagree among themselves on other aspects of Iran, that the advent of an Iranian nuclear weapon would be a very bad development that would exacerbate instability, or even worse, in the Middle East. Few have challenged this consensus.[7] The consensus, however, is grounded in little more than intuition, augmented by stereotyped images of the Iranian leadership.

Some of the belief that an Iranian nuclear weapon would be a calamity rests on the notion that Iranian leaders are religiously driven radicals who do not think like Western leaders and who cannot be deterred even by the prospect of severe retaliation against their country. The problem with this view is that it simply does not accord with the behavior that Iranian leaders have displayed during the more than three decades of the Islamic Republic's existence. The Iranians have repeatedly demonstrated that they respond to foreign challenges and opportunities with the same considerations of costs and benefits, and of the impact on the interests of their regime, as other leaders do. This has been true even on matters involving Iranian behavior that violated international law or was otherwise objectionable to the West. For example, Iran ended an earlier campaign of assassinating Iranian dissident exiles in Europe when it became apparent that the assassinations were beginning to harm significantly Tehran's relations with European governments. Iranian leaders demonstrated the same carefully calculated way of determining policy even during the most trying experience in the Islamic Republic's history: the eight-year war that began when Saddam Hussein's forces invaded Iran in 1980.[8] The Iranians' prosecution of the war at great cost to themselves demonstrated how fervently they, like most other peoples, resist when their homeland is the target of aggression. The war nonetheless ended when the Iranian supreme leader, Ayatollah Ruhollah Khomeini, "drank the cup of poison," as he put it, in agreeing to a cease-fire when the costs of continuing the war appeared to outweigh any benefits. Khomeini's successors have given every indication of being motivated, as are other leaders, by an interest in maintaining their regime and their power—in this life, not some afterlife. They are subject to the same principles of deterrence as anyone else.

Even many commentators who reject the image of irrational Iranian mullahs subscribe to another part of the conventional wisdom about why an Iranian nuclear weapon supposedly would make the political and security situation in the Middle East markedly worse. This part, which sounds more

---

[7] A conspicuous exception is Kenneth Waltz, "Why Iran Should Get the Bomb," *Foreign Affairs* 91 (July/August 2012): 2–5. For an argument that does not go as far as Waltz in suggesting that an Iranian bomb would be desirable but explains why it would not be a significant threat, see Paul R. Pillar, "We Can Live With a Nuclear Iran," *Washington Monthly* 44 (March/April 2012,): 13–19.

[8] Bruce Riedel, "If Israel Attacks," *The National Interest* 109 (September/October 2010), 6–13, at 11.

sophisticated than the hypothesis about mad mullahs, holds that even if Iran never detonated a nuclear weapon, the mere possession of one would enable it to intimidate other states and otherwise to throw its weight around in harmful ways. Intuitively this seems to make sense. Nuclear weapons are serious business. Shouldn't owning them have a serious impact on what the owner can do in his neighborhood?

Moving from intuition to analysis, however, this part of the conventional wisdom breaks down, too. Possession of nuclear weapons can make a difference in international relations only insofar as the possibility that they will be used somehow enters into the thinking of decision makers. If no one believes that is a possibility, the weapons are merely a very expensive adornment in an ammunition bunker. For possession of a nuclear weapon to make possible Iranian intimidation that is not taking place today would require something that Iranian leaders would like to do but currently are dissuaded from doing because of the prospect of some foreign actor retaliating. The issue in question also would have to be seen as so important to Tehran that it could credibly threaten to escalate the matter to the level of nuclear war—and thereby neutralize the other actor's threat of retaliation—with all of the costs and risks such escalation would entail for Iran itself. One struggles to think of any conceivable issue where these conditions would arise.

Nuclear weapons, given their awesome effects, are good for deterring what a regime might consider awesome, particularly the regime's own extinction from foreign attack. This deterrent role is almost certainly the major reason for any interest Iranian leaders have in developing nuclear weapons. But the weapons' very awesomeness makes them too blunt an instrument for accomplishing much else. Accordingly, the record of nuclear proliferation that has already occurred around the globe does not support the notion that nuclear weapons are game-changers that facilitate regional bullying or adventurism.[9] We should have known as much from the extensive body of doctrine about nuclear weapons and escalation that was developed during the Cold War.[10] But the alarmist, conformist approach that has characterized discussion of a possible Iranian nuclear weapon has not encouraged people to crack open textbooks from the Cold War era.

Similar considerations apply to oft-repeated arguments that an Iranian nuclear weapon would somehow embolden Hamas or Lebanese Hezbollah to undertake their own forms of adventurism. Such arguments overstate the tightness of relations between Iran and these two actors. Sunni Hamas was

---

[9] Stephen M. Walt, "The mother of all worst-case assumptions about Iran," 30 November 2012, accessed at http://walt.foreignpolicy.com/?page=2, 1 January 2013; and Todd S. Sechser and Matthew Fuhrmann, "Crisis Bargaining and Nuclear Blackmail," *International Organization* 67 (Winter 2013): 173–195.

[10] A classic text is Herman Kahn, *On Escalation: Metaphors and Scenarios* (New York: Praeger, 1965). On the significance of the nuclear weapons threshold, see chapter 6.

never a client of Shia Iran, although with meager support from elsewhere, it has accepted some Iranian help. Hezbollah was very much Iran's client and is still its ally, but the power and position it has achieved in Lebanon have greatly reduced its dependence on Iran, as well as giving it important equities of its own. Whatever deterrence currently applies to Hamas and Hezbollah does not have to do with Iran's strategic situation. It instead concerns the groups' conventional confrontation with Israel and the political costs that any adventurism would have among their own constituencies and larger courts of opinion. In any event, it is not credible that Iran would assume the extremely large risks to itself of nuclear escalation on behalf of some mischief by Hamas or Hezbollah. The leaders of Hamas and Hezbollah are smart enough to realize that.

What attempts there have been to offer analysis supporting the idea of an Iranian nuclear weapon being especially dangerous show the strains of trying to make a case with a preferred conclusion. Such attempts are laden with worst-case speculation about what a nuclear-armed Iran "could" do in the region, without explaining exactly how the nuclear weapons would make a difference or how Iran could make credible a threat to escalate to nuclear war.[11] Analysis suggesting that war with Iran would be less costly and dangerous than the existence of an Iranian nuclear weapon is prone to self-contradiction, particularly by depicting an Iran that supposedly is too unpredictable to be deterred from initiating a war but that, if on the receiving end of an attack, would be a model of calmness and rationality and would be deterred from striking back.[12] Another variety of self-contradiction is to argue that an Iranian nuclear weapon might be more costly than a war because the existence of the weapon would raise fears of war (which, in turn, would adversely affect the oil market).[13]

Expressions of concern about an Iranian nuclear weapon often also posit that the introduction of this weapon would trigger a cascade of nuclear proliferation in the Middle East. As with other presumed effects of an Iranian bomb, the image of a proliferation cascade is merely held as an assumption, repeatedly referred to by politicians and others without supporting analysis. The assumption disregards how, ever since President John F. Kennedy spoke about the prospect of 15 or 20 nations having nuclear weapons by the mid-1970s, actual nuclear proliferation has lagged well behind projections

---

[11] An example is Ash Jain, *Nuclear Weapons and Iran's Global Ambitions: Troubling Scenarios* (Washington, DC: Washington Institute for Near East Policy, August 2011). For a critical commentary on this monograph, see Paul R. Pillar, "Iran's Nuclear Oats," 29 September 2011, accessed at http://nationalinterest.org/blog/paul-pillar/irans-nuclear-oats-5960, 1 January 2013.

[12] See, for example, Matthew Kroenig, "Time to Attack Iran," *Foreign Affairs* 91 (January/February 2012): 76–86.

[13] This is the main argument in the Bipartisan Policy Center report, *The Price of Inaction: Analysis of Energy and Economic Effects of a Nuclear Iran* (Washington, DC: Bipartisan Policy Center, October 2012).

about it. The assumption also does not explain why the development of nuclear weapons by Israel—which, according to Avner Cohen, the foremost historian of the Israeli program, and other researchers who have studied the subject, probably *did* have such weapons at least by the mid-1970s[14]—has not triggered a corresponding response by any of the many Middle Eastern states that have considered Israel an adversary. Most important, close examination of both the capabilities and motivations of the most-plausible Middle Eastern proliferators—particularly Egypt, Saudi Arabia, and Turkey—indicates that an Iranian bomb would be unlikely to lead any of them to cross the nuclear threshold that they so far have refrained from crossing.[15] Even if any of the states had the capability to build a nuclear weapon, negative repercussions from doing so, especially including likely damage to their relations with the United States, would be a significant disincentive.

Stepping back from the fixation on Iran's nuclear program, one has to ask—and future historians are sure to ask—how the sole superpower of the early twenty-first century could come to see this state along the Persian Gulf as posing such a supposedly immense threat. Iran, even before the damage inflicted by the most recent rounds of sanctions, has been a mid-level nation with numerous internal problems, a narrowly based economy dependent on oil exports, and almost no ability to project power at a distance. Estimates of Iranian military spending are uncertain but usually put at between one and one-and-a-half percent of U.S. defense spending, as well as being only one-fifth of military spending by the sheikhdoms on the other side of the Persian Gulf.[16]

THE ROOTS OF DEMONIZATION

The origins of the current American attitude toward Iran are thus not primarily to be found in whatever actual threat Iran poses today to U.S. interests. That raises the question of what does account for the enormous attention and alarmism centered on this subject in American political discourse today. The answer to that question begins with the historically based American way of looking at foreign adversaries. It is supplemented by the historical baggage of the past dysfunctional and strife-ridden relationship between the United States and the Islamic Republic. A further significant ingredient is the position of the government of Israel, which, because of the uncommon

---

[14] Avren Cohen, *Israel and the Bomb* (New York: Columbia University Press, 1999), 337–338; and Warner D. Farr, *The Third Temple's Holy of Holies: Israel's Nuclear Weapons* (Maxwell Air Force Base: Air War College, 1999) accessed at www.au.af.mil/au/awc/awcqate/capc-pubs/farr.htm, 4 March 2013.

[15] Steven A. Cook, "Don't Fear a Nuclear Arms Race in the Middle East," 2 April 2012, accessed at http://www.foreignpolicy.com/articles/2012/04/02/don_t_fear_a_nuclear_arms_race, 3 January 2012.

[16] Stockholm International Peace Research Institute, SIPRI Military Expenditure Database, accessed at http://milexdata.sipri.org, 2 January 2013; and Anthony H. Cordesman, "The Iran Primer: The Conventional Military," accessed at http://iranprimer.usip.org/resource/conventional-military, 2 January 2013.

role that Israel-related issues play in American politics, has done much to shape U.S. policy and discourse on Iran. All of these factors combine to maintain a political environment in which a grave Iranian threat is taken for granted and any questioning of that threat is dismissed as being outside the mainstream. This set of attitudes is further perpetuated by mutual rein-forcement with attitudes in Iran that in some respects mirror attitudes in the United States. Each side's worst presumptions about the other side en-courage words and actions that make the presumptions look true.

American Thinking about Enemies

Americans' manner of viewing foreign adversaries today is rooted in the his-tory of their country's past relations with the outside world. Their attitudes have been shaped especially by the most costly and all-consuming episodes in that history, in particular the wars—hot and cold—of the twentieth cen-tury. Not having the same experience as, say, Europeans have long had of continuous and unavoidable contact with a variety of neighbors having an assortment of conflicting and parallel interests, American attitudes are dis-proportionately molded by the great conflicts in which the United States has crossed its ocean moats to confront enemies deemed awful enough and threatening enough to warrant such expeditions. Most Americans thought of the conflicts then, and still think of them, as morally clear struggles be-tween good and bad forces, even if, as with the world wars (and worldwide communism during the Cold War), they actually were complicated multi-lateral affairs with varieties of interests within the warring coalitions. In short, Americans have a profoundly Manichean way of viewing their inter-action with the outside world and their confrontation with foreign adver-saries.

The Manichean outlook leads to demonization of the most salient of those adversaries. They are viewed not just as having interests that conflict with those of the United States, but as genuinely evil. Some of those adver-saries really have been undeniably evil, with Adolf Hitler being at or near the top of almost any such list. The lasting influence on American thinking of the experience with the Nazis stems partly from the sheer scale and dis-proportionate impact of World War II and from how the dealings with Ger-many in the 1930s were tailor-made to become the historical analogy most frequently invoked by anyone arguing that it is necessary to confront some other adversary.[17] The evil of Hitler has, in effect, been transferred by anal-ogy to various later foes of the United States.

---

[17] On the use of this and similar analogies in discourse about U.S. policy, with particular reference to the Vietnam War, see Yuen Foong Khong, *Analogies at War: Korea, Munich, Dien Bien Phu, and the Vietnam Decisions of 1965* (Princeton, NJ: Princeton University Press, 1992).

Once the United States has become locked in conflict with any adversary, especially if warfare is at least a possibility, other incentives accentuate the demonization. Gaining popular backing for an expensive war (or other expensive confrontation, such as the Cold War) is more feasible when the enemy is perceived as evil rather than being merely the other side of a conflict of interests. This aspect of gaining popular support is reinforced by the American self-image as a peace-loving people who go to war only in response to someone else's aggression. Accordingly demonization, including the Hitler analogy, played an especially important role in the selling of a war that clashed with that image: the one against Saddam Hussein's Iraq, which was an offensive war of choice and thus itself an act of aggression.[18]

Americans need a foreign villain. That has been the case since, beginning with World War II, the United States has had large and expensive overseas commitments that can be sustained only if American citizens support them and believe they understand the need for them. The need for a villain is a matter of public psychology and, because of that, also a matter of politics. As for who can play that role, Saddam Hussein is gone, and the unpleasantness of the Iraq War has provided a political incentive to erase quickly the memory of it (and along with that, some of the lessons from it). Osama bin Laden and his al Qaeda have, of course, been prominent foes over the past decade. But a terrorist group can never fill the same role as a state, and now bin Laden is gone, too. Well-suited on several counts to play the current role of villain is that other state on the Persian Gulf with oil resources and radical politics: Iran.

Current American attitudes toward Iran illustrate several consequences that commonly flow from demonization of a foreign adversary. One is a disinclination to see any reasonable basis for the adversary's actions, or at least a basis that is compatible with one's own needs or interests. Another is a tendency to underestimate how much of what the regime on the other side does may have broader support among its own population. Yet another is a tendency to see the other side's ambitions as more negative and farther-reaching than they really are. Related to this is an underestimation of the other side's willingness to compromise.

Historical Baggage
The history of Iran's relations with the United States has set the stage for the current deeply antagonistic American attitude toward it. The American view of the Islamic Republic was bound to be initially negative because of the

---

[18] Deputy Secretary of Defense Paul Wolfowitz was especially fond of applying the analogy of Hitler to Saddam Hussein. See Wolfowitz's own description of his use of the analogy, quoted in Derrick Z. Jackson, "A fatal distraction," *Boston Globe*, 26 March 2004, accessed at http://www.boston.com/news/globe/editorial_opinion/oped/articles/2004/03/26/a_fatal_distraction/, 22 January 2013.

pointedly critical view of the United States that Khomeini and his followers voiced and because they overthrew a regime that had been a significant ally of Washington. By the 1970s, the United States had come to rely on the Shah of Iran, a profuse purchaser of U.S.-made arms, as a major protector of stability and U.S. interests in the Persian Gulf. Even this aspect of the history was not enough to foreordain that the relationship would become as intensely antagonistic as it later did. During the Iranian revolution, views of it within the administration of Jimmy Carter varied, with some members of the administration disparaging the Shah as an autocrat and not mourning his departure.[19] The dominant view of the Shah's ouster, however, was as a shocking setback to U.S. interests in the region.

The experience that did more than anything to color for decades American attitudes toward the Islamic Republic of Iran was the seizing of the American embassy in Tehran in November 1979 and the holding hostage of 52 Americans for 444 days, until the day Carter left office. The hostage crisis was one of the few international events to have, largely through the medium of television, a profound and sweeping impact on the perceptions and emotions of the American public. The perpetuation of the drama for more than a year imparted a remarkable degree of public awareness and familiarity with the story, with some of the hostages and their more-outspoken family members back in the United States becoming familiar names. The popular ABC television program *Nightline* began as a nightly report on the hostage saga.

As an act of terrorism against Americans, the seizure of the embassy and its staff also identified Iran in the American consciousness as the number one terrorist state in the world. That status was further cemented over the next several years by terrorism at the hands of Lebanese Hezbollah. Americans were again victims, including in the bombing of the Marine barracks in Beirut in 1983, which was the deadliest terrorist attack against American citizens until September 11, 2001. Hostage-taking in Lebanon, with Americans among the most prominent victims, dragged on through the 1980s.

During the early years of the Islamic Republic, Iran was doing even more than this to earn a deserved reputation as the world's number one terrorist state. Operations included numerous assassinations of exiled dissidents in Europe and elsewhere, and subversive activities in the Middle East and Persian Gulf region. Iranian international terrorism later subsided as Tehran strove to improve its relations with the Europeans and came to realize that survival of the Iranian revolution did not depend on the fomenting of similar revolutions in nearby states. State-sponsored terrorism in general, however,

---

[19] Zbigniew Brzezinski, *Power and Principle: Memoirs of the National Security Adviser 1977–1981* (New York: Farrar Straus Giroux, 1983), 354–355; and Gary Sick, *All Fall Down: America's Tragic Encounter with Iran* (New York: Random House, 1985), 68–72.

also subsided during the same period,[20] and so Iran has remained in most eyes—including official ones—the leading terrorist-sponsoring state.[21] In any event, past history remains more important in shaping American attitudes about Iran than current patterns of sponsoring terrorism.

The label of arch-terrorist state is reason enough for most Americans to have a firmly embedded view of Iran as an implacable enemy. An added dimension, however, that plays directly into the preoccupation with Iran's nuclear program is the merging of terrorism, in popular fears as well as political rhetoric, with the proliferation of unconventional weapons (or weapons of mass destruction, to use the common vocabulary). Fascination with scenarios of terrorism involving such weapons has prevailed at least since the 1990s; the attack with sarin gas by the Japanese cult Aum Shinrikyo on the Tokyo subway in 1995 stimulated public interest in the subject. The George W. Bush administration's aggressive selling of the Iraq war depended on repeatedly connecting terrorism and weapons proliferation, with the President rhetorically obliterating any distinction between the two in his "axis of evil" speech.[22] The later discrediting of this sales campaign as it applied to Iraq did not seem to dispel the specter of a nuclear-armed state giving its weapons, or technology to make them, to a terrorist client. The specter gets invoked today in agitation about Iran's nuclear program.[23] It probably contributes to American public perceptions and sentiments about that program, even though there is no known instance during the entire history of the nuclear age of a nuclear-armed state—even one with terrorist clients—doing anything like that. That record is unsurprising, given the absence of any advantage in surrendering control over such weapons or materials, and the very dim prospect of the state achieving any deniability. Iran would be widely and automatically assumed to be behind any appearance of nuclear materials in the hands of a group with which it had an association, such as Hezbollah.

Alongside the history of conflict and confrontation between Washington and Tehran is a meager history of engagement. What engagement there has been has tended to discourage most Americans from more engagement. In this respect, the most significant attitude-forming event also dates from the early years of the Islamic Republic: the Iran-Contra affair of 1985–1986. A U.S. purpose of this secret initiative, which involved the sale of arms to Iran,

[20] Paul R. Pillar, *Terrorism and U.S. Foreign Policy*, 2d ed. (Washington, DC: Brookings Institution Press, 2003), chap. 6.
[21] U.S. Department of State, *Country Reports on Terrorism 2011*, 31 July 2012, chap. 3; accessed at http://www.state.gov/j/ct/rls/crt/2011/195547.htm, 5 May 2013.
[22] President George W. Bush, State of the Union Address, 29 January 2002, text accessed at http://georgewbush-whitehouse.archives.gov/news/releases/2002/01/20020129-11.html, 22 January 2013.
[23] See, for example, Elliott Abrams, "The Grounds for an Israeli Attack," *World Affairs* 175 (May/June 2012), 25–30, at 26.

was to try to secure Iranian help in the release of American hostages in Lebanon. Once revealed, the affair was quickly regarded as a scandal, not only because of the sour taste left by trading arms for hostages but also because of the illegal use of proceeds from the arms sales to fund rebels in Nicaragua, as well as efforts to cover up the entire caper. Some of those involved on the U.S. side were convicted of criminal offenses, and the affair is now seen as perhaps the blackest mark on Ronald Reagan's presidency. The episode poisoned the American political waters for anyone else thinking about initiatives to engage Iran. It also discredited the concept of "moderates" in the regime in Tehran, who were the ostensible Iranian interlocutors.

The next serious U.S. effort to reach out to Tehran, this time publicly, was by the administration of Bill Clinton in its last year in office. In a major speech in March 2000, Secretary of State Madeleine Albright expressed regret for the episodes in U.S.-Iranian history (mentioned below) that have most angered Iranians and took what the administration hoped would be the first step toward a better relationship by removing restrictions on the import of Iranian carpets, caviar, and pistachios.[24] This minor reduction in U.S. economic sanctions against Iran, however significant U.S. officials considered it to be, evidently was less conspicuous to leaders in Tehran than wording in the same speech that referred negatively to "unelected hands" as still being in control of Iranian policy. Iranian leaders took this as one more indication that Washington was less interested in dealing with the regime as it existed than in trying to replace it.[25] The initiative went nowhere, and it entered an American lore according to which the Iranians reject opportunities for a normal or cordial relationship and are the ones to be blamed for the antagonistic nature of the relationship that exists today. Clinton's administration made no further significant effort to reach out to Tehran before giving way to the neoconservative-dominated administration of George W. Bush, which had no interest in talking with the Iranian regime.

Iranian Suspicions and Grievances

The negative impact of the history of U.S.–Iranian relations on American attitudes about Iran has been amplified by the resonance it finds in some similar Iranian attitudes about the United States. The similarity starts with the psychological and political need for a foreign villain, which is at least as strong for the revolutionary regime in Tehran as it is for the United States. More specifically, this is a political need for the hard-liners who have come

---

[24] Remarks by Secretary of State Madeleine K. Albright before the American–Iranian Council, 17 March 2000, text accessed at http://www.fas.org/news/iran/2000/000317.htm, 22 January 2013.
[25] Ray Takeyh, *Hidden Iran: Paradox and Power in the Islamic Republic* (New York: Times Books, 2006), 114–115.

to dominate the regime, have drawn support from the image they have nurtured as guardians against foreign threats, and use popular perceptions of such threats as a distraction from economic and other domestic difficulties. Regardless of how open the hard-liners may be to improved foreign relations and how much they realize that the incumbent regime would benefit from improvement, in the meantime, a perception of Iran being besieged from abroad serves a domestic political purpose.

The history of U.S.–Iranian relations makes the United States the arch-enemy from the Iranian viewpoint. That viewpoint highlights different episodes in this history than the American viewpoint does. Some of the relevant history even predates the advent of the Islamic Republic. A particularly salient episode for Iranians is the coup that in 1953 overthrew the populist (and democratically elected) Prime Minister, Mohammad Mosaddegh, and was partly engineered by the United States in cooperation with Britain. Although Mosaddegh was not quite as popular as the recounting of this story sometimes makes him out to be—and although the role of Iranians was greater and the role of Britain and the United States less than in most telling of the tale—Iranians came to see the coup as an indicator of U.S. hostility toward Iran and a U.S. proclivity to trample on the rights and prerogatives of Iranians. For many Iranians, it is as much of an attitude-shaping historical landmark as the hostage crisis is for Americans.

The subsequent close U.S. relationship with Shah Mohammad Reza Pahlavi, whose power was reaffirmed with the ouster of Mosaddegh, is another part of the history that has put the United States in an unfavorable light in Iranian eyes. As the most-important foreign backer of the Shah's regime, the United States shared opprobrium generated by the regime's excesses. This is clearly the case with members of the current regime who worked to overthrow the Shah. The sentiments extend as well to many other Iranians who have unfavorable memories of repression under the Shah.

One of the most-traumatic events for a generation of Iranians is the Iran–Iraq War of 1980–1988, which began with an Iraqi invasion of Iran and in which several hundred thousand Iranians died. This, too, shaped Iranian perceptions of the United States because of a U.S. tilt in favor of Iraq, which was not undone in Iranian eyes by the later U.S. invasion of Iraq and overthrow of Saddam Hussein. U.S. support to Iraq during the war against Iran included arms, training, diplomatic support, and, during the war's final phase, the reflagging of oil tankers of Iraq's Arab allies and direct combat between U.S. and Iranian naval forces. Also during the war's closing months, a U.S. warship shot down a civilian Iranian airliner, killing all 290 persons aboard. The shooting was a mistake by a naval crew thinking it was under attack, but to this day, the Iranian government states that the downing of the airliner was intentional. Many other Iranians also probably believe it was.

Notwithstanding the historical basis for Iranians to perceive hostility from the United States and to feel hostility in return, the Iranian leadership evidently saw an opportunity for improving the relationship following the September 11 terrorist attacks, which the Iranian supreme leader, Ayatollah Ali Khameini, strongly and publicly condemned.[26] Even though Khameini also warned against launching a war in Afghanistan, once the United States did intervene in Afghanistan and oust the Taliban regime, Iranian and U.S. officials worked effectively together in midwifing a new Afghan political order under President Hamid Karzai. James Dobbins, the chief U.S. representative at the international conference in Bonn, Germany that reached agreement on creating the new Afghan government, observes that the Iranians were "particularly helpful" in that endeavor.[27] For a few weeks in late 2001 and early 2002, it looked as though Washington and Tehran were moving their relationship to a less-acrimonious path.

Then President George W. Bush declared the "axis of evil" and identified Iran as one of the points of the axis. To the Iranians, this was a shocking response to their post-September 11 cooperation. Being put in the same category as their old enemy Saddam Hussein only made the shock worse. The Iranian leadership still did not give up on the idea of an improved relationship with Washington. One indication of this was an Iranian proposal for negotiating a grand bargain of outstanding differences, with a written proposal to that effect transmitted to the U.S. government in 2003 by Switzerland, which serves as the diplomatic protecting power for the United States in Iran. Some observers have questioned the seriousness of this initiative, but the documentary evidence indicates that it was genuine.[28] The Bush administration, riding high at that moment—with Saddam Hussein having been toppled but the difficulties of the occupation of Iraq not yet having become apparent—made no reply to the overture and even reprimanded the Swiss ambassador for forwarding it. U.S.–Iranian relations were left in a bitter freeze, with no contacts at all for the next several years.

By the time Barack Obama entered the presidency, the United States and Iran were thus locked in a vicious circle of mutually reinforcing perceptions of hostility, which continues to prevail today. An action by one side

---

[26] Jim Muir, "Iran condemns attacks on US," BBC News, 17 September 2001, accessed at http://news.bbc.co.uk/2/hi/middle_east/1549573.stm, 16 January 2013.

[27] James Dobbins, "How to Talk to Iran," *The Washington Post*, 22 July 2007, accessed at http://www.washingtonpost.com/wp-dyn/content/article/2007/07/20/AR2007072002056.html, 16 January 2013.

[28] A recapitulation of this episode and links to the relevant documents are in Nicholas D. Kristof, "Iran's Proposal for a 'Grand Bargain,'" *The New York Times*, 28 April 2007, accessed at http://kristof.blogs.nytimes.com/2007/04/28/irans-proposal-for-a-grand-bargain/, 16 January 2013.

that can be interpreted as an indication of hostile intentions leads to reactions by the other side, in words or deeds, that in turn are interpreted as hostile. A perception that the other side does not want a better relationship elicits negative or suspicious reactions that the other side perceives in the same way. It is difficult, though not impossible, to get out of such a circle of mistrust and misperception. Such difficulty, far more than any conflict of national interests, inhibits improvement of the relationship today.

Influence of Israel

A major added political factor on the U.S. end of this relationship is the posture of the government of Israel. That government's insistent pushing of the theme that Iran, and specifically a nuclear-armed Iran, poses a grave threat clearly has significantly shaped the handling of the issue in American political discourse and is a leading reason the issue has the prominence that it does. The pushing does not reflect strategic analysis of the actual threat that an Iranian nuclear weapon would pose to Israel. Assessments by think tanks and scholars of the size of Israel's nuclear arsenal vary somewhat, but a typical estimate postulates a stockpile of 75–200 weapons accompanied by an assortment of modern delivery systems—a capability far superior to anything Iran could ever hope to achieve in the foreseeable future.[29] The head of the Israeli intelligence service Mossad, like many retired senior Israeli security officials who can speak on the subject even more freely, has denied the frequently heard assertion that an Iranian nuclear weapon would pose an existential threat to Israel.[30] Many ordinary Israelis understandably fear an Iranian nuclear weapon, however, based on the history of the Jewish people and vituperative anti-Israeli rhetoric from Iran, and with the fear stoked by their own government.

The government of Prime Minister Benjamin Netanyahu also has other motives for continuing its agitation on the issue. It naturally would like to maintain Israel's regional nuclear weapons monopoly. It may prefer not even to think twice the next time it uses Israel's conventional military superiority, as it has several times, in conducting operations in neighboring states or territories. The issue of Iran also serves as a distraction from the unsettled conflict between Israelis and Palestinians. The Israeli government and its supporters habitually respond to any raising of the Palestinian issue or the building of Israeli settlements in occupied territory by stating that Iran is the greatest threat to peace and stability in the region and where the

---

[29] Robert S. Norris, William M. Arkin, Hans N. Kristensen, and Joshua Handler, "Israeli Nuclear Forces, 2002," *Bulletin of the Atomic Scientists* 58 (September/October 2002): 73–75.

[30] Barak Ravid, "Mossad chief: Nuclear Iran not necessarily existential threat to Israel," *Haaretz*, 29 December 2011, accessed at http://www.haaretz.com/print-edition/news/mossad-chief-nuclear-iran-not-necessarily-existential-threat-to-israel-1.404227, 17 January 2013.

international community ought to direct its attention instead.[31] Finally, any rapprochement between Iran and the United States would threaten to weaken Israel's claim to being Washington's sole reliable partner in the Middle East.

Whatever the exact mix of motives, the Israeli agitation about Iran has a big impact on American handling of the issue because of the extraordinary role that preferences of the Israeli government play in American politics.[32] In the United States, the Iran issue has become in large part an Israel issue and a way for American politicians to demonstrate support for Israel. This dimension of the issue underlies the posture that candidate Romney took on Iran. It also has shaped the public posture on Iran of Barack Obama's administration. One of the President's strongest and most-prominent declarations that an Iranian nuclear weapon would be unacceptable was in a speech he gave during his re-election campaign to the American Israel Public Affairs Committee.[33]

The Iranian regime has no country comparable to Israel influencing its policies, but Israel itself has figured prominently in destructive Iranian rhetoric. This has especially been true of Mahmoud Ahmadinejad, Iran's President from 2005 to 2013, who found Israel-bashing to be a fruitful theme in domestic politics. Ahmadinejad's rhetoric has been taken in the United States as confirming the worst assumptions about Iranian intentions, even though the Iranian President is not the most important decision maker in the regime on foreign policy or nuclear matters. One piece of bravado seized upon more than any other was in a speech Ahmadinejad gave in 2005, in which he predicted that Israel would eventually go the way of the Shah's regime. Disputes over translation of this speech have continued ever since, but it became the basis for an oft-repeated observation that the President of Iran threatened "to wipe Israel off the map."[34] Some American politicians have gone a step further and asserted falsely that Iran has stated an intention to use a nuclear weapon to accomplish this goal—notwithstanding Iran's public posture that it does not even want a nuclear weapon.[35]

---

[31] See, for example, a speech by Netanyahu reported in "PM: Iran is greatest world danger, not settlements," *Jerusalem Post*, 8 January 2013, accessed at http://www.jpost.com/DiplomacyAndPolitics/Article.aspx?id=298796, 16 January 2013.

[32] John J. Mearsheimer and Stephen M. Walt, *The Israel Lobby and U.S. Foreign Policy* (New York: Farrar, Straus and Giroux, 2007).

[33] Remarks by the President at AIPAC Policy Conference, 4 March 2012, accessed at http://www.whitehouse.gov/the-press-office/2012/03/04/remarks-president-aipac-policy-conference-0, 17 January 2013.

[34] On the translation issue, see Uri Friedman, "Debating Every Last World of Ahmadinejad's 'Wipe Israel Off the Map'," 5 October 2011, accessed at http://www.theatlanticwire.com/global/2011/10/debating-every-last-word-ahmadinejads-wipe-israel-map/43372/, 18 January 2013.

[35] Rep. Michele Bachmann asserted this during her campaign for the Republican presidential nomination. John Bresnahan, "Bachmann: Iran would use nuke against United States, Israel," *Politico*, 18 December 2011, accessed at http://www.politico.com/blogs/politico-live/2011/12/bachmann-iran-would-use-nuke-against-united-states-107923.html, 18 January 2013.

STULTIFICATION OF POLICY

The net effect of all the influences—including history, Israel, and Iranian bombast—on American thinking about Iran is a deeply held and widely shared belief that Iran, and especially its nuclear program, poses a grave danger. In the most-recent biennial survey by the Chicago Council on Global Affairs of American attitudes on foreign policy, 67 percent of respondents said that Iran's nuclear program was a "critical threat to vital U.S. interests." This was the second-most-frequently mentioned threat, only slightly behind international terrorism.[36] Such a climate of public opinion stultifies any political action to improve relations with Iran. Political incentives push in the direction of words and policies that continue the vicious circle of hostility. Actions required to get out of that circle are politically hazardous because they are seen—and political opponents can criticize them—as being soft on Iran.

One of the specific consequences of this environment is the diffidence involved in what little diplomacy there is between Washington and Tehran, which have not had normal diplomatic relations since the hostage crisis more than three decades ago. The transition from George W. Bush to Barack Obama took the possibility of revived diplomacy out of the deep freeze, but the tentativeness each side has displayed in doing business with its bête noire is still apparent. The Obama administration made essentially a single attempt, during its first year in office, at a negotiated agreement with Iran before throwing its energy instead into gaining international support for anti-Iran sanctions. It even rejected an agreement that Brazil and Turkey extracted from Iran in 2010 that included the same Iranian concessions the United States was demanding in 2009. Diplomacy went back in the freezer, emerging only with the start of the current series of talks beginning in 2012.[37]

Another consequence is the unhelpful manner in which the sanctions have been handled, especially by the U.S. Congress. Ostensibly, the purpose of most of the sanctions is to induce Iran to make concessions regarding its nuclear program. In practice, they have instead played a different political role: as a means for American politicians to demonstrate their toughness on Iran (and their support for Israel). Repeatedly voting in favor of additional sanctions against Iran is an easy way to do this. An additional influence on American behavior regarding this subject is the hope of eventually doing away with the Iranian regime. Although regime change is not explicitly stated by most of those voting in favor of added sanctions, that hope almost

---

[36] *Foreign Policy in the New Millennium* (Chicago, IL: Chicago Council on Global Affairs, 2012), 14.
[37] The most-thorough account of the Obama administration's diplomacy on the subject is Trita Parsi, *A Single Roll of the Dice: Obama's Diplomacy with Iran* (New Haven, CT: Yale University Press, 2012).

certainly underlies much of the support for ever-increasing sanctions. Political conditions in Iran do not suggest that it is in a pre-revolutionary situation, but the upheaval in several Arab countries over the past two years has rekindled the hope.

Use of sanctions as leverage for obtaining concessions at the negotiating table requires that they be used flexibly. It is just as important for the other side to believe that relief from sanctions will result from concessions as that a lack of concessions will mean no relief. Use of sanctions as a device for political posturing or as a hoped-for way to hasten regime change, however, instead implies that the pressure from sanctions should be inflexible and unrelenting. The latter approach has prevailed. In public and congressional discussion, the sweeping and unrelenting nature of sanctions against Iran has come to be treated as an end in itself, with almost no attention to exactly how the sanctions relate to Iranian concessions beyond a simple notion that the Iranians ought to give up and cry "uncle." Meanwhile, the United States and its negotiating partners in the P5 + 1 (the permanent members of the United Nations Security Council plus Germany) have made no proposals that include any relief from sanctions other than those involving spare parts for commercial aircraft and trade in precious metals and petrochemicals.[38] The Iranians have been given no reason to believe that they would receive significant sanctions relief in return for concessions, and thus they have lacked an incentive to concede. Making promises credible is generally harder than making threats credible, and the history of mutual mistrust between the United States and Iran has made it even harder.[39] Inflexibility in the negotiating position of the P5 + 1 has made it harder still.

A similarly unhelpful pattern has characterized threats to use military force. A possible military attack on Iran was discussed originally as an alternative to a negotiated settlement as a way to prevent an Iranian nuclear weapon. The military option was discussed despite the likely counterproductive effect of stimulating an Iranian decision to build the very weapon the attack was intended to prevent. Once negotiations with Iran began but did not yield quick progress, a different purpose of a threatened military attack came to dominate discussions of the issue: the idea of such a threat as an inducement to Iran to make concessions to the P5 + 1 about its nuclear program. This idea gave greater respectability to the concept of launching an offensive war, because threatening such a war could be defended in the

---

[38] Arms Control Association, "History of Official Proposals on the Iranian Nuclear Issue," August 2012, accessed at http://www.armscontrol.org/factsheets/Iran_Nuclear_Proposals, 30 December 2012; and Arshad Mohammed, "Big powers to offer easing gold sanctions at Iran nuclear talks," Reuters, 15 February 2013, accessed at http://www.reuters.com/article/2013/02/15/us-iran-nuclear-gold-idUS-BRE91E0TP20130215, 16 February 2013.

[39] Robert Jervis, "Getting to Yes With Iran: The Challenges of Coercive Diplomacy," *Foreign Affairs* 92 (January/February 2013): 105–115, at 111.

name of aiding negotiations. The threats and saber-rattling moves to go with them have been promoted not as a seeking of war but as supposedly a necessary aid to obtaining an agreement.[40]

The threat of armed force, however, probably has impeded rather than aided the reaching of a negotiated agreement. The threats contribute to the atmosphere of hostility that for years has added to distrust and worst-case assumptions between Tehran and Washington and thereby have made rapprochement more difficult. That the reaching of an agreement would be seen as a backing down in the face of a threat of armed force adds to the political and psychological costs to Iranian leaders of making concessions. Such threats also stimulate rather than diminish Iranian interest in nuclear weapons because of their presumed value as a deterrent against major foreign attack. The more that the brandishing of the threat of military attack makes an attack seem likely, the greater will be the Iranian interest in developing nuclear weapons and the less inclined they will be to make concessions that would preclude that possibility.

The Iranians have good reason to be suspicious of ultimate U.S. and Western motivations, and threats of military force are unhelpful in that respect too. The Iranians do not have to look far to see ample evidence, including in American political rhetoric, in favor of the proposition that the primary U.S. goal regarding Iran is regime change. And they do not have to look far into the past to see a recent U.S. use of military force—participation in the intervention in Libya—that overthrew a Middle Eastern regime after it had reached an agreement with the United States to give up all its nuclear and other unconventional weapons programs. Iranian leaders would have little reason to make concessions about their own program if they believed the same thing was likely to happen to them. This is already a problem; rattling the saber only makes it worse.

Despite all these considerations, the threats continue, not only in general American discourse but in the official position of the Obama administration, which talks about all options being on the table. They continue partly because the notion of threatening an adversary into submission has a simple appeal and primitive believability. They continue also because support for military threats, like support for sanctions, serves the political function of demonstrating firmness on Iran and backing for Israel—and for some, trying to appease the Israeli government enough to dissuade it from launching its own attack.

---

[40] Among the many who make this argument are James K. Sebenius and Michael K. Singh in "Is a Nuclear Deal with Iran Possible?" *International Security* 37 (Winter 2012/13): 76–77, 89–90.

DIPLOMATIC POSSIBILITIES

The outlines of an achievable agreement between Iran and the P5 + 1 have been apparent for some time. They would include restricting Iran's enrichment of uranium to the lowest levels of enrichment, and even then in quantities corresponding to legitimate peaceful uses. Iranian production of medium-enriched (20 percent) uranium would cease, with existing stocks transferred out of the country. In return, most sanctions would be removed and Iran would be guaranteed a supply of enough 20-percent-enriched uranium to power the research reactor that uses it as fuel. Such a formula would be consistent with Iran's insistence that its nuclear program is entirely for peaceful purposes. The formula is thus attainable in a way that simply pressuring the Iranians into crying "uncle" is not.

Iran reportedly made in the summer of 2012 a proposal to the Europeans that included these basic elements.[41] The Iranian proposal as presented was unacceptable to the P5 + 1 because under it, Iran would have taken its promised steps on uranium enrichment only after the West had removed sanctions. In this respect, the Iranian proposal mirrored that of the P5 + 1, which has called on Iran to take all of its required steps before the P5 + 1 would even consider significant relief from sanctions. The resulting disagreement is common in international negotiations; each side naturally would prefer not to implement its own end of a deal until the other side makes good on its end. Also common is the resolution of such differences by negotiating a schedule of phased implementation in which each side both gives something and gets something in each phase. It is the negotiation of such an implementation sequence, as well as other details such as the exact disposition of the 20 percent-enriched uranium, that remains to be accomplished.

Political impediments to such an agreement persist on both sides but are not insurmountable. Some elements in the Iranian regime that milk foreign hostility for political benefit are unlikely to believe that an improved relationship with the United States and the West works to their advantage, but for the top leadership, this would be outweighed by being able to claim credit for the resulting advantages in economics and prestige. On the U.S. side, a likely challenge is getting congressional cooperation in lifting sanctions, some of which are designated by law as responses to human rights questions or other matters besides the nuclear issue. There also is the potential for the government of Israel, which has disdained the very idea of negotiations with Iran, to be a spoiler.

If such an accord is nevertheless achieved, it would secure for each of the parties its most important stated objectives. For the United States and its

---

[41] David E. Sanger, "Iranians Offer Plan to End Nuclear Crisis," *The New York Times*, 5 October 2012.

P5 + 1 partners, restrictions on Iran's program would preclude it from building a nuclear weapon without major difficulty and conspicuous violations of the agreement that would give ample warning well before actual construction of such a weapon. For Iran, the agreement would bestow respect and acceptance of its nuclear program and would finally gain relief from the economically debilitating sanctions.

A nuclear agreement would open the door to a better overall relationship that could bring other benefits to the United States ultimately more important than the nuclear issue itself. A reduction of tension with Tehran would permit a more relaxed and less costly U.S. military posture in the Persian Gulf, which currently is aimed overwhelmingly at Iran. There also would be a potential for positive cooperation with Iran, which, although a weakling in projecting power at a distance, has influence to be reckoned with closer to its own borders. One place with such potential is Afghanistan, where the parallel U.S. and Iranian interests that underlay the cooperation over a decade ago are still present. Another place is Iraq, where Iran is now the dominant foreign influence and where endless violence and instability serve neither U.S. nor Iranian interests.

None of this will turn Iran and the United States into close friends and allies, as they were in the time of the Shah. Differences, some of them sharp, will persist—including on matters related to Israel as long as the Palestinian issue remains unresolved. But the differences can be handled in a more normal way than in the context of the pathological non-relationship that has persisted for over three decades.

The U.S. posture toward Iran is a prominent example of how traumatic history, domestic politics, and emotions that flow from both can overpower more-sober evaluation of the U.S. interests at stake in a foreign relationship. Popular, politically charged sentiment about confronting foreign villains can have benefits; it fueled, for example, the enormous sacrifices by Americans that were necessary to win World War II. The case of Iran shows that it also can have major disadvantages.

Conceptualizing Containment:
The Iranian Threat and the Future
of Gulf Security

ZACHARY K. GOLDMAN
MIRA RAPP-HOOPER

"MAKE NO MISTAKE," DECLARED U.S. PRESIDENT Barack Obama before the 2012 session of the United Nations General Assembly, "a nuclear-armed Iran is not a challenge that can be contained."[1] In his Senate confirmation hearing, Secretary of State John Kerry echoed that sentiment: "We will do what we must do to prevent Iran from obtaining a nuclear weapon, and I repeat here today, our policy is not containment. It is prevention. . . ."[2] As part of his confirmation process as Secretary of Defense, Chuck Hagel was also asked to rule out containment as an option for dealing with a potentially nuclear-

---

[1] "President Obama's 2012 Address to UN General Assembly (Full Text)," 25 September 2013, accessed at http://articles.washingtonpost.com/2012-09-25/politics/35497281_1_libyan-people-benghazi-diplomatic-facilities, 25 February, 2013.
[2] Joe Sterling, Jessica Yellin, and Hollya Yan, "Kerry Says Iran Must Come Clean on Nuclear Program," 25 January 2013, accessed at http://edition.cnn.com/2013/01/24/politics/kerry-nomination/index.html, 24 February 2013.

ZACHARY K. GOLDMAN is a national security lawyer at the law firm WilmerHale and an adjunct professor of law at NYU School of Law. He has previously served as a policy advisor in the U.S. Department of the Treasury's Office of Terrorist Financing and Financial Crimes, and as a Special Assistant to the Chairman of the Joint Chiefs of Staff. His book *Global Intelligence Oversight* was published by Oxford University Press in 2016, and other peer-reviewed articles and opinion pieces have appeared in *Cold War History*, *The New York Times*, *The Wall Street Journal*, *Foreign Affairs*, *Lawfare*, *The Atlantic*, *The Diplomat*, *The National Interest*, and others.

MIRA RAPP-HOOPER is a Lecturer in Law and a Senior Research Scholar in Law at Yale Law School, as well as a Senior Fellow at Yale's Paul Tsai China Center. She studies and writes on US-China relations and national security issues in Asia.

capable Iran.[3] The reasons for this containment phobia are not difficult to divine: It would be politically unpalatable, both domestically and in the eyes of international partners such as Israel and Saudi Arabia, for the President or any of his closest advisers to suggest that the United States was making plans to "live with" a nuclear Iran by discussing plans to contain the Islamic Republic.

But despite their public opposition to containing Iran, as the nuclear standoff has continued, U.S. officials have hedged their bets, striving to deepen security ties with the six nations of the Gulf Cooperation Council (Bahrain, Kuwait, Oman, Qatar, Saudi Arabia, and the United Arab Emirates) in order to strengthen regional security and prepare for future contingencies. In advance of a September 2011 meeting with the leaders of the Gulf Cooperation Council (GCC), then-Secretary of Defense Leon Panetta stated that the Council was "emerging as an increasingly critical partner to advancing our common interests," and he impressed upon his counterparts the importance of a stronger Gulf security architecture.[4] At the inaugural session of the U.S.–GCC Strategic Cooperation Forum in March 2012, then-Secretary of State Hilary Clinton declared that the United States was "committed to defending the Gulf nations and we want it to be as effective as possible."[5]

Word has also been met with deed, as the United States has vastly increased arms sales to the states of the region, including F-15 and F-16 aircraft, radar and anti-missile systems, and satellite-guided bombs. Washington has also attempted to create a missile defense architecture for the region.[6] Most recently, in April 2013, the administration of Barack Obama publicized its decision to sell additional advanced fighter aircraft and sophisticated long-range missiles to the United Arab Emirates (UAE) and Saudi Arabia, as well as its provision of refueling aircraft and V-22 Ospreys to Israel.[7] Some of these sales were designed to bolster bilateral defense ties; others were aimed at coaxing the states of the region to adopt a more- integrated defense posture. Nonetheless, all had the same objective: the containment of Iran, defined as U.S. efforts to limit its regional influence. Despite

---

[3] "Remarks by the President to the UN General Assembly," 25 September 2012, accessed at http://www. whitehouse.gov/the-press-office/2012/09/25/remarks-president-un-general-assembly, 24 February 2013; "Remarks by the President at AIPAC Policy Conference," 4 March 2012, accessed at http://www.whitehouse.gov/the-press-office/2012/03/04/remarks-president-aipac-policy-conference-0, 22 February 2013; Jennifer Steinhauer, "Hagel to Meet Schumer to Discuss Policy Issues," *The New York Times*, 13 January 2013.

[4] Karen Parrish, "Clinton, Panetta to Meet with Gulf Council Ministers," *American Forces Press Services*, 22 September 2012, accessed at http://www.defense.gov/news/newsarticle.aspx?id=65431, 24 February 2013.

[5] Hillary Rodham Clinton, "Remarks Saudi Arabian Foreign Minister Saud Al-Faisal," Gulf Cooperation Council Secretariat, 31 March 2012, accessed at http://www.state.gov/secretary/rm/2012/03/187245.htm, 23 February 2013.

[6] "US Arms to Gulf Allies Hint of Strategy," 16 December 2012, accessed at http://www.washingtontimes.com/news/2012/dec/16/us-arms-to-gulf-allies-hint-of-strategy/?page=all#pagebreak, 22 February 2013.

[7] Robert Burns and Donna Cassata, "US Finalizing $10 Billion Sale of Weapons, Warplanes to Israel, Saudi Arabia and UAE," *The Associated Press*, 19 April 2013, accessed at http://www.startribune.com/nation/203776731.html?refer=y, 8 May 2013.

the rhetoric to the contrary, therefore, containment is well under way. In light of these efforts, this article outlines a number of different potential scenarios in which a regime designed to contain Iran might be useful. But as we will demonstrate, containment does not automatically mean a decision to "live with" a nuclear Iran, and may require more of U.S. partners in the Gulf than they are able to deliver.

There are two important sets of reasons that any analysis of a potential containment regime must include a discussion of the role of Gulf partners, whether or not Iran goes nuclear. First, and most directly, the Gulf states are Iran's neighbors, and along with Iraq, form the security system of which Iran is a part. The Gulf Cooperation Council was established in 1981 largely as a response to the 1979 Iranian Revolution and the outbreak of the Iran–Iraq War in 1980, and the security posture and foreign policies of the GCC states since then have been determined in part by the ebb and flow of their relationships with Iran.[8] These states have complicated, multi-faceted relationships with the Islamic Republic.[9] They will react to changes in Iran's security posture, whether it acquires the bomb or stops short of that threshold. The reactions of the Gulf states must, therefore, be accounted for in American thinking about the future security of the region. And while the United States and its partners have also begun to undertake containment efforts outside of the Arabian Peninsula, for example against Hamas and Hezbollah in the Levant, the core of Iran's military, intelligence, and sub-conventional power projection capabilities remain rooted in the Gulf. Any attempt to significantly limit Iranian influence must be directed at the region in which it maintains its most potent strengths and highly valued assets.

Second, the United States already has a large network of military bases and pre-positioned military equipment in the Gulf, as well as strong pre-existing relationships with Gulf countries, which form the core of current (and future) efforts to contain Iran. This massive extant military infrastructure provides another set of reasons that Gulf states will play an essential role in efforts to contain Iran. Indeed, the United States already makes use of critical base and port facilities for the Army, Navy, and Air Force in Bahrain, Kuwait, Oman, Qatar, and the United Arab Emirates, and has strong military and intelligence relationships with Saudi Arabia.[10] Beyond that,

---

[8] Neil Partrick, "The GCC: Gulf State Integration or Leadership Cooperation," The London School of Economics Kuwait Programme on Development, Governance, and Globalisation in the Gulf States, Research Paper No. 19, November 2011, 5.

[9] Asma Alsharif and Agnus McDowall, "Saudi Prince Turki Urges Nuclear Option After Iran," 6 December 2011, accessed at http://www.reuters.com/article/2011/12/06/nuclear-saudi-idAFL5E7N62G920111206, 21 February 2013.

[10] United States Central Command (CENTCOM), "Senate Armed Services Committee Statement of General David H. Petraeus, U.S. Army, Commander U.S. Central Command, Before the Senate Armed Services Committee on the

both Bahrain and the UAE have troops fighting with the International Security Assistance Force in Afghanistan.[11] In addition, as noted above, U.S. officials have suggested that the GCC organization itself may supply an embryonic skeleton for any future regional security structure that could be used to contain the threat posed by a potentially nuclear Iran.[12] If, therefore, the United States were to consider constructing a security architecture in the Middle East in order to contain an evolving Iranian threat, the Gulf Cooperation Council would be a logical place to start, since working through an existing multilateral organization rather than relying on new institutions could be more efficient and effective. Some policy analysts, and indeed some government officials, have already gone as far as to suggest that the GCC could serve as the NATO of the Persian Gulf,[13] making an evaluation of the viability of such a possibility important.

Despite the opposition that the American political leadership has voiced to a policy of containment, there is an active debate within the academic and policy commentary communities regarding whether the United States and its allies can contain Iran.[14] But in all of the discussion of these issues, there has been little substantive analysis of what form that containment would take and whether the construction of such a containment regime including the Gulf States is feasible. Two analysts have suggested the formation of a "regional alliance network that would marshal Arab states into a more cohesive grouping," and one has suggested formalizing the GCC as a true military alliance. Others, however, have asserted that credible new alliance commitments in the Gulf are likely to be very difficult to achieve.[15] But the

---

Afghanistan–Pakistan Strategic Review and the Posture of U.S. Central Command," 1 April 2009, accessed at http://www.centcom.mil/qatar, 23 February 2013; Ben Piven, "Map: U.S. Bases Encircle Iran," 1 May 2012, accessed at http://www.aljazeera.com/indepth/interactive/2012/04/2012417131242767298.html, 27 April 2013.

[11] "Troop Numbers and Contributions," International Security Assistance Force, accessed at http://www.isaf.nato.int/troop-numbers-and-contributions/index.php, 24 February 2013.

[12] See also: Clark Murdoch and Jessica Yeats, "Exploring the Nuclear Posture Implications of Extended Deterrence and Assurance: Workshop Proceedings and Key Takeaways," Center for Strategic and International Studies, November 2009, 57; Kenneth M. Pollack, "Security in the Persian Gulf: New Frameworks for the Twenty-First Century," *Middle East Memo*, No. 24, June 2012.

[13] Robert Haddick, "The Persian Gulf Needs its Own NATO," 18 May 2012, accessed at http://www.foreignpolicy.com/articles/2012/05/18/the_persian_gulf_needs_its_own_nato?page=full, 20 February 2013; Thom Shanker and Steven Lee Myers, " U.S. Planning Troop Buildup in Gulf After Exit From Iraq," *The New York Times*, 29 October 2011; Karen Parrish, "Clinton, Panetta to Meet With Gulf Council Ministers," *American Forces Press Service*, 22 September 2011.

[14] See, for example, James M. Lindsay and Ray Takeyh, "After Iran Gets the Bomb: Containment and its Complications," *Foreign Affairs* 89 (March/April 2010); Robert J. Reardon, *Containing Iran: Strategies for Addressing the Iranian Nuclear Challenge* (Santa Monica, CA: RAND Corp., 2012); Bill Keller, "Nuclear Mullahs," *The New York Times*, 9 September 2012; Suzanne Maloney, interview with John Donovan, "Weighing a Policy of Containment for Iran," *National Public Radio (NPR): The Talk of the Nation*, 6 March 2012, accessed at http://www.npr.org/2012/03/06/148053976/weighing-a-policy-of-containment-for-iran, 23 February 2013.

[15] James M. Lindsay and Ray Takeyh, "After Iran Gets the Bomb: Containment and its Complications," *Foreign Affairs* (March/April 2010); Kenneth M. Pollack, "Security in the Persian Gulf: New Frameworks for

fact that American political leaders have taken high-level discussions of containment off the table has had the consequence of precluding "thinking very hard about how either Iran or its neighbors would behave" if and when a more robust effort in the Gulf becomes necessary.[16]

It is clear that there is an ever-deepening American security interest in the Gulf, and ever-greater interest in whether the United States will be able to stabilize the region. This article seeks to remedy some of the gaps in strategic thinking about the future security architecture of the Gulf by considering the prospects for effective cooperation among the Gulf states to contain Iran. We examine the scenarios in which some form of containment regime against Iran might be employed. We argue that in the continued U.S. standoff with Iran, containment need not denote a "default solution" that is turned to after other attempts to prevent Iran's acquisition of a nuclear capability have failed.[17] Indeed, containment is already under way, and there are several possible futures in which containment will almost certainly be employed even if no decision to "live with" a nuclear Iran has been made.

The Iranian nuclear standoff raises the larger issue of what future Persian Gulf security may look like. One can envision numerous potential Gulf security arrangements, but for the purposes of our argument, we assume that the United States and the other countries of the Gulf region retain a strong interest in limiting Iran's influence.[18] Among these options, it is important to analyze one that relies on the existing regional security organization—the GCC. Our analysis suggests, however, that there is little hope of constructing a multilateral containment regime through existing alliance structures in the Gulf. This is because the political dynamics of the region and impediments to further American investment there will make meaningful integration of the six countries' security postures into a coherent defense structure very difficult.

The remainder of this article proceeds as follows. We begin with a brief history of the role of containment in U.S. grand strategy, and argue that containment, as currently discussed in the public debates over Iran, differs in important respects from the policy that George Kennan articulated in 1947. We contend that there are several scenarios in which U.S. policy-makers need not make a decision to "live with" a nuclear Iran, but may nonetheless want to consider a regime for containing Iran that includes the Gulf states.

---

the Twenty-First Century," *Middle East Memo*, No. 24 (June 2012): 3–7; Eric S. Edelman, Andrew F. Krepinevich, Jr., and Evan Braden Montgomery, "The Dangers of a Nuclear Iran: The Limits of Containment," *Foreign Affairs* (January/February 2011).

[16] Bill Keller, "Rethinking the Unthinkable: 'Five Myths About Nuclear Weapons,' and More," *The New York Times*, 11 January 2013.

[17] Edelman, Krepinevich, and Montgomery, "The Dangers of a Nuclear Iran."

[18] Kenneth Pollack has suggested that the Commission for Security Cooperation in Europe (CSCE) could serve as a model for a Gulf power "condominium" that includes Iran. Pollack, "Security in the Persian Gulf."

We argue that the current popular discourse, which implies a binary choice between preventing Iran from developing a nuclear weapons capability on the one hand, and "containing" a nuclear Iran on the other is, in fact, a false dichotomy.

We then demonstrate why it is unlikely that the United States will be able to establish an effective containment regime that relies upon the GCC. To do so, we analyze two historical examples of containment regimes—The North Atlantic Treaty Organization (NATO) and South East Asian Treaty Organization (SEATO)—and assess why the former thrived despite early obstacles while the latter was incontrovertibly ineffective. These two cases reveal important insights on the conditions necessary for the establishment of an effective multilateral containment regime in the Gulf. We then turn to an assessment of the Gulf itself, evaluating the prospects for enhanced co-operation among the six GCC states, and find that there are significant obstacles to further integration in the region. In particular, intra-regional rivalries and differences in how each state perceives the threat posed by Iran present serious obstacles to the creation of an integrated defense architecture for the region. This is a sharp departure from the paradigm for an effective containment regime, exemplified by NATO during the Cold War, which drew its cohesive force from the common perception of the threat posed by an external power. Whatever Iran's nuclear trajectory, if the United States intends to continue to stem its influence, containment efforts must acknowledge that there are serious limits on the prospects for intra-Gulf cooperation.

CONCEPTUALIZING CONTAINMENT, PAST AND PRESENT

Containment, as originally conceived by George Kennan, was viewed as a proactive and dynamic tool of statecraft. Kennan became convinced of the need to limit Soviet influence before the Cold War had begun in earnest, and first articulated his approach in a now-famous telegram to the State Department authored in 1946.[19] In his dispatch, Kennan described a regime that desperately needed an enemy to justify its authoritarian rule. The Soviets, he observed, were ardent nationalists and potentially subversive, but would be inclined to withdraw from attempts at power projection if they met resistance.[20] An obvious policy prescription was for the United States to devise ways to push back against the exercise of Soviet power while simultaneously providing the war-weary people of Europe with security. Kennan suggested that this strategy did not make war with the Soviets inevitable; rather, he

---

[19] Wilson D. Miscamble, *George Kennan and the Making of American Foreign Policy, 1947–1950* (Princeton, NJ: Princeton University Press, 1992), 22–25.
[20] *Ibid.*, 26.

argued that America could achieve its goals through the calibrated use of political, diplomatic, economic, and psychological tools.[21]

Kennan first used the term "containment" in 1947, and the concept became public in his famous X article that same year. Officially titled "The Sources of Soviet Conduct," Kennan argued, "the main element of any United States policy toward the Soviet Union must be that of a long- term, patient but firm and vigilant containment of Russian expansive tendencies." Containment, according to Kennan, could be thought of as the "application of counterforce at a series of constantly shifting geographical and political points."[22] This vision of containment aimed to prevent Soviet expansion by denying the Soviets influence.[23]

Several prominent scholars have argued that containment shaped U.S. grand strategy for the entire Cold War.[24] Henry Kissinger famously wrote: "George Kennan came as close to authoring the diplomatic doctrine of his era as any diplomat in our history,"[25] while Josef Joffe stated that American grand strategy during the Cold War "consisted of one word: 'containment.'"[26] This characterization, however, was almost certainly too extreme— Kennan did not author a perfect blueprint for American foreign policy that others endorsed and dutifully implemented. But he did have outsized influence during crucial years of the early Cold War, and American presidents regularly referred back to the doctrine as they formulated their own policies vis-à-vis the Soviets.

Kennan did not directly advocate for formal military alliances as vehicles for containment, but various regional security pacts formed under Presidents Harry Truman and Dwight Eisenhower were intended to ring in the Soviet threat and were inspired by Kennan's emphasis on "strongpoint defense."[27] Murmurings that the United States intends to strengthen its relationship with Gulf states evoke, and sometimes directly reference, these early Cold War alliances. Yet containment has taken on a decidedly pejorative connotation in the ongoing debate over how to handle a potentially nuclear Iran.

---

[21] George Kennan, "The Background of Current Russian Diplomatic Moves," 10 December, 1946; George Kennan, "Measures Short of War (Diplomatic)," 16 September 1946, both in Kennan Papers Box 16, as quoted in Miscamble, *Kennan*, 31.

[22] "X" [George F. Kennan], "The Sources of Soviet Conduct," *Foreign Affairs*, July 1947: 566–582.

[23] John Lewis Gaddis, *Strategies of Containment: A Critical Appraisal of American National Security Policy During the Cold War* (Oxford: Oxford University Press, 2005), 63.

[24] Miscamble, *Kennan*, 349; Gaddis, *Strategies*, 377; Stephen Walt, "The Case for Finite Containment: Analyzing U.S. Grand Strategy," *International Security*, 14 (Summer 1989): 5, 49.

[25] Henry Kissinger, *The White House Years* (Boston, MA: Little, Brown, and Co., 1979), 135.

[26] Josef Joffe, "'Bismarck' or 'Britain'? Toward an American Grand Strategy After Bipolarity," *International Security*, 19 (Spring 1995): 94.

[27] See, for example, Thomas Christensen, *Useful Adversaries: Grand Strategy, Domestic Mobilization, and the Sino-American Conflict* (Princeton, NJ: Princeton University Press, 1996), 8; Walt, "The Case for Finite Containment," 5.

In contrast to the way it was understood in the early Cold War, today's containment is articulated as an unacceptable fallback option that assumes a conscious decision by the United States to "live with" a nuclear Iran. President Barack Obama has firmly resolved to keep Iran non-nuclear. In his State of the Union Address of 24 January 2012, for example, he averred: "America is determined to prevent Iran from getting a nuclear weapon, and I will take no options off the table to achieve that goal." In March 2012, the President appeared to move one step further, declaring to the American Israel Public Affairs Committee: "Iran's leaders should understand that I do not have a policy of containment; I have a policy to prevent Iran from obtaining a nuclear weapon."[28] Two days later, Obama repeated his stance at a press conference: "My policy is not containment; my policy is to prevent them from getting a nuclear weapon—because if they get a nuclear weapon that could trigger an arms race in the region, it would undermine our non-proliferation goals, it could potentially fall into the hands of terrorists."[29] The President underscored this policy again before the United Nations General Assembly on 25 September 2012. "Make no mistake," he declared. "A nuclear-armed Iran is not a challenge that can be contained." Obama added: "The United States will do what we must to prevent Iran from obtaining a nuclear weapon." Both his first- and second-term cabinet members have also adopted this position. Congress has also pledged to prevent a nuclear weapons-capable Iran.[30]

In each of these public repudiations, containment is treated as an option that will signify that the United States has failed to prevent Iran from acquiring nuclear weapons. This new containment is, in essence, a "political dirty word."[31] It is the implicit byproduct of failed diplomacy, ineffective sanctions, and military inaction. But Kennan's containment was not a fallback or binary policy choice representing a least-worst approach to Soviet expansionism. It was, instead, a proactive tool of statecraft aimed at seizing the initiative required to push back against the Soviet threat and to achieve foreign policy goals, rather than a reluctant response to be adopted after an adversary had forced one's hand. It could also be pursued in parallel

[28] "Remarks by the President at 2012 AIPAC Policy Conference," 4 March 2012, accessed at http://www.whitehouse.gov/photos-and-video/video/2012/03/04/president-obama-2012-aipac-policy-conference#transcript, 23 February 2013.

[29] White House Press Conference, 6 March 2012, accessed at http://www.whitehouse.gov/the-press-office/2012/03/06/press-conference-president, 22 February 2013.

[30] "US Senate Reaffirms Commitment to Stopping Iran Develop Nuclear Arms," 22 September 2012, *Associated Press*, accessed at http://www.haaretz.com/news/middle-east/u-s-senate-reaffirms-commitment-to-stopping-iran-developing-nuclear-arms-1.466174, 24 February 2013.

[31] John Donvan, Host, "Talk of the Nation," *National Public Radio*, 6 March 2012. Transcript and audio accessed at http://www.npr.org/2012/03/06/148053976/weighing-a-policy-of-containment-for-iran, 1 February 2013.

with other policy options, and one important element of Kennan's containment was strengthening and supporting vulnerable allies so pressure on the Soviets would be uniformly applied. Arguments that suggest that Washington will have to choose between the two options of "pursuing a military strike to prevent Iran from going nuclear or implementing a containment strategy to live with a nuclear Iran" ignore these important nuances.[32]

Increased U.S. arms sales and closer political relations with Gulf states indicate that containment efforts, defined as actions intended to limit Iran's regional influence, are already well under way. But in the specific context of containing Iran's nuclear program, there are several possible contingencies in which the United States might wish explicitly to establish a containment regime to reassure and buttress allies in the Gulf, even if Iran does not cross the nuclear threshold. Each of these five scenarios, which we outline below, requires a realistic assessment of whether the construction of such a regime is feasible, but only one of them requires a decision by the United States to "live with" a nuclear Iran.

Colin Kahl has described two of these potential states of affairs. In early 2012, Kahl observed that the Obama administration was unlikely to choose to accept an Iranian nuclear weapons capability. But what is not often discussed is the likelihood that the most aggressive policy course to prevent the development of an Iranian nuclear weapons capacity—an American or Israeli airstrike—would also be likely to require some sort of containment regime.[33] Following an attack on Iranian nuclear weapons facilities, the U.S. would have to prepare for the possibility of a violent backlash against the Gulf states and other regional partners, which could last for months or years. There is also a good chance that the Iranians would attempt to reconstitute their program following an attack. Preventing Iran from re-establishing its nuclear program, while calming the nerves of jittery allies that would face conventional retaliation after a U.S. or Israeli strike would require an investment of major proportions in a containment regime. In these scenarios—a containment system designed to handle conventional retaliation after a strike against Iran's nuclear program, or one designed to cope with reconstitution after such an attack—the United States would need to invest in regional security architecture even after it (or Israel) undertakes military action to forestall an Iranian bomb.

But there are two additional potential scenarios that would require the establishment of a containment structure. If Iran and the P5 + 1 manage to negotiate a diplomatic settlement, it may well be one that allows Iran to keep

[32] Edelman, Krepinevich, and Montgomery, "The Dangers of a Nuclear Iran."
[33] Colin H. Kahl, "The Iran Containment Fallacy," *The Hill*, 22 February 2012, accessed at http://thehill.com/blogs/congress-blog/foreign-policy/212003-the-iran-containment-fallacy, 10 February 2013; Colin H. Kahl, "Not Time to Attack Iran: Why War Should Be the Last Resort," *Foreign Affairs* (March/April 2012).

a civilian nuclear program and some enrichment capacity, albeit with a rigorous inspection regime.[34] In this third case, it is hard to believe that Iran's neighbors would cease to fear its nuclear potential and would be eager to see Iran deterred from diverting its civilian program to nefarious military purposes. The Gulf states would probably still seek a good deal of American assurance.

Finally, a fourth scenario is possible. Even without a negotiated settlement, Iran may stop short of building the bomb, but still leave its neighbors feeling insecure. The position of the U.S. intelligence community remains that the Supreme Leader has not yet taken the decision to weaponize, and former Secretary of Defense Leon Panetta has said that analysts would observe an Iranian decision to do so.[35] Ample evidence suggests that Iran may be pursuing an incremental hedging strategy, whereby it acquires a significant nuclear capability but defers the decision to build the bomb. Iran could therefore unilaterally stop short of a nuclear weapons capability measured by a military device. If the last several years of the standoff are any indication, however, such nuclear limbo will not be comforting to Iran's neighbors, and in this scenario, some sort of containment regime would be a useful reassurance to Gulf States, and could mitigate the destabilizing effects of a breakout-capable Iran.

One can therefore imagine five possible futures in which deterring Iran and assuring regional partners would be crucial. In only one of these, a choice by the administration to live with an Iranian bomb, is containment a fallback position. In the other four, it would be an active policy that would be coupled with ongoing diplomatic efforts to influence Iran's nuclear path, continued sanctions, or even military action. Contrary to the assertions of some experts, containment is not a policy that will necessarily be reserved until Iran "has crossed the point of no return with respect to its nuclear weapons capabilities."[36] None of the four scenarios outlined above requires President Obama to go back on his red line and allow Iran to get the bomb. Efforts to deny Iran expanded regional influence are already under way, and it is difficult to imagine a scenario in which the United States *does not* continue to pursue some form of containment of the Islamic Republic.

---

[34] For a discussion of why a deal with Iran is so difficult and what a settlement might look like, see Robert Jervis, "Getting to Yes with Iran: The Challenges of Coercive Diplomacy," *Foreign Affairs* (January/ February 2013).

[35] Dan De Luce, "If Iran Builds Bomb, US Has a Year to Act: Panetta," *Agence France-Presse*, 11 September 2012, accessed at http://www.google.com/hostednews/afp/article/ALeqM5gT51_KiC2mWKHvN7oEkqJOOfyWgQ, 24 February 2013. On this point, see also Kahl, "Not Time to Attack Iran."

[36] Suzanne Maloney, Senior Fellow at the Brookings Institute's Saban Center for Middle East Policy on NPR's *Talk of the Nation* on 6 March 2012, accessed at http://www.npr.org/2012/03/06/148053976/weighing-a-policy-of-containment-for-iran, 22 February 2013.

The costs of containing Iran would, however, vary significantly among these four futures. Limiting the regional influence of an Iran that has stopped its program short of the nuclear threshold or accepted a diplomatic deal would, of course, be a less-intensive undertaking than containing and deterring military reprisals following an airstrike. When analysts suggest that the costs and benefits of military action are to be compared to those of containment, however, they ignore the fact that containment in some form will almost certainly appear on the ledger whatever policy option is chosen.

Whether the United States chooses air strikes, opts for continued diplomacy and sanctions, or brokers a deal with Iran, we must seriously evaluate whether and how containment might work in the Gulf. What would be required for a containment regime in the region to function as "strongpoint defense" against an emerging adversary? Can the existing regional security organization, the GCC, serve as a viable structure? Two historical examples of multilateral containment efforts—NATO's success and SEATO's failure—give us a baseline for analyzing this crucial question.

NATO: ENTANGLEMENT BY INVITATION

The NATO alliance serves as the paradigm of successful containment, and the reasons for its endurance highlight some necessary conditions for a multilateral effort aimed at Iran. The U.S. decision to join NATO represented a sharp break with its foreign policy past; from 1800 to 1949, the country had purposely avoided standing peacetime alignments with European powers.[37] Until the North Atlantic Treaty, the country had more or less heeded George Washington's warnings against "entangling alliances," and respected the hemispheric divide enshrined in the Monroe Doctrine.[38] U.S. senators of an isolationist bent vigorously opposed the NATO treaty, but it mustered sufficient support because its architects believed that the country would not actively be involved in European affairs forever.

America chose to bind itself to NATO to counter the Soviet threat and to recreate a balance of power in Europe.[39] The Americans spent NATO's early years navigating these twin commitments, and in the process, increased their financial and military investments in the alliance, as well as their willingness to become enmeshed in internal European affairs. At the time of the alliance's founding, the United States believed that the paramount danger in Europe was not a Soviet invasion but a European loss of heart and political

---

[37] Lawrence S. Kaplan, *NATO and the United States: The Enduring Alliance* (New York: Twayne, 1994), 8.
[38] Ibid.
[39] Timothy P. Ireland, *Creating the Entangling Alliance: The Origins of the North Atlantic Treaty Organization* (Westport, CT: Greenwood, 1981), 4–5.

will necessary to rebuild in the postwar years.[40] The initial American commitment to NATO came in the form of a political security guarantee that relied on the threat of nuclear retaliation for the defense of Europe.[41] The Atlantic Alliance only became an integrated military organization as the Americans responded to external pressures. In particular, three external events—the Soviet development of a nuclear weapon, the North Korean invasion of the South, and, to a lesser extent, the Berlin Blockade—all challenged the notion that the Americans would be able to provide for NATO's security from afar.

The first Soviet nuclear test in September 1949 came as a shock, shattering the American nuclear monopoly, and suggesting that the United States could no longer depend solely on homeland-based bombers to keep the Soviets out of Europe.[42] An American-based deterrent was seen as less reliable and reassuring if deterrence was mutual and the Soviets could return an American nuclear blow. Just nine months later, the North Koreans launched an attack on the South, with Joseph Stalin's advance approval, and Truman officials believed that unanswered communist aggression would invite it elsewhere. They also considered the striking parallel between Korea and Germany, two tenuously divided countries.[43] NATO allies could not help but fear a similar attack on Germany, and China's entry into the Korean War in September appeared to be evidence of a monolithic communist military threat. The Berlin Blockade also laid bare the weakness of the U.S. military position in Europe. With only two-and-one-third divisions on the ground in 1948, the Americans could not attempt to break the blockade with an armed convoy without taking the decision to mobilize.[44] By the spring of 1950, the United States and its European allies all realized that a security guarantee supported by a far-off nuclear deterrent was insufficient.

Soon after the first Russian nuclear test, the United States began to consider a major increase in ground forces.[45] NATO's first strategic concept was approved in December 1949, setting guidelines for how each member would contribute to the broader military mission. The alliance's integrated force structure was devised in 1950.[46] Early in the Korean War, the United States tripled its defense budget, with only a fraction of the increase going to the war itself. Most of the increase was to provide for an active, forward military

[40] Robert Jervis, *The Meaning of the Nuclear Revolution* (Ithaca, NY: Cornell University Press, 1989), 206–212.

[41] Robert E. Osgood, *NATO: The Entangling Alliance* (Chicago, IL: University of Chicago Press, 1975), 32.

[42] Osgood, *The Entangling Alliance*, 52.

[43] Marc Trachtenberg, *A Constructed Peace: The Making of the European Settlement, 1945–1963* (Princeton, NJ: Princeton University Press, 1999), 100.

[44] Osgood, *The Entangling Alliance*, 29.

[45] Ibid., 61.

[46] Kaplan, *NATO and the United States*, 43.

defense of Western Europe. American divisions were permanently stationed on European soil beginning in 1951, with an American general commanding NATO troops as the Supreme Allied Commander (SACEUR).[47] In the words of historian Marc Trachtenberg, this was the only strategy "that could hold the western alliance together over the long run."[48] The United States therefore chose military entanglement lest its security guarantee to Europe seem empty at a perilous time.

The forward defense strategy, however, required not only a robust troop presence, but also the tackling of some thorny intra-alliance issues. The strategy hinged upon the defense of Germany, which required energetic German cooperation. But if Germany was to be defended by the alliance, it was only natural that it should contribute to the effort.[49] The new integrated command structure made it clear that Germany would have to become more of an alliance member, as opposed to an occupied country. Western Europe could not be defended without German troops.[50] But both the French and the Soviets were deeply concerned about German rearmament. To assuage these fears, the Americans bound themselves to the NATO military structure, so that German participation would only occur under American supervision. The United States made its forward troop commitment and acceptance of the SACEUR position contingent upon allied acceptance of German rearmament, and West Germany was eventually admitted to NATO in 1954.[51]

The external threats of the 1949–1950 period made it clear that the defense of Europe would have to be a forward and active one. Concerns about Germany meant that American leadership (and by extension, entanglement) was the only way to accomplish this while holding the alliance together. The American commitment to NATO began as an arms-length guarantee, but the alliance survived its early years because the United States became deeply involved in European affairs, vastly increasing its material commitment. Hastings Lionel Ismay's oft-quoted statement that the alliance's goal was "to keep the Russians out, the Americans in, and the Germans down," could not have been accomplished any other way.[52]

SEATO: GUARANTEED IN NAME ONLY

The failure of the Southeast Asian Treaty Organization in some ways foreshadowed the potential difficulties involved in trying to encourage security cooperation among the Gulf states, and was a marked contrast to NATO's

---

[47] Ibid., 45.
[48] Trachtenberg, *Constructed Peace*, 100.
[49] Ibid., 101–103.
[50] Trachtenberg, *Constructed Peace*, 107.
[51] Ibid., 108.
[52] Ismay, as quoted in David Reynolds, *The Origins of the Cold War in Europe: International Perspectives* (New Haven, CT: Yale University, 1994), 13.

success. The Manila Treaty established SEATO in 1954, following the conclusion of several other security guarantees, including U.S. pacts with Japan and South Korea, and the trilateral Australia/New Zealand/United States (ANZUS) agreement. The Eisenhower administration had wholeheartedly embraced "nuclear umbrella" alliances as a tool for managing communist threats. SEATO originated at the Geneva conference of April–July 1954, and its birth was hurried along by the French collapse at Dien Bien Phu.

In light of NATO's early successes, American officials believed that a regional containment organization could be helpful in combating the threat of communist subversion and potential Chinese aggression in Southeast Asia. From its first days, however, it was clear that this would not be a new NATO. The member states of SEATO had a variety of reasons for joining the alliance, and their incongruent motivations were only exacerbated by the fact that the military means at SEATO's disposal were ill suited to the end of preventing communist subversion in the region. These factors meant that SEATO lacked the resources and the collective will necessary to evolve into a coherent or capable organization.

The founding Manila Treaty members included the United States, Britain, France, Australia, New Zealand, Thailand, the Philippines, and Pakistan. All shared an interest in the stability of the region and believed that an American military presence could help to bring this about, but their common vision ended there. The Americans supported SEATO for its deterrent value against communist foes, and hoped that it would facilitate swift military entry into Indochina and elsewhere if it became necessary.[53] The British were interested in a less-militaristic and more-flexible pact and preferred to focus on police and intelligence operations that might be useful against subversion. They were interested in clinging to their remaining colonial holdings in the region.[54] The French also desired to protect their interests in Indochina, and hoped that SEATO would translate into an American commitment to defend the region without requiring much real U.S. presence.[55]

Beyond the pact's great power sponsors, Australia and New Zealand were interested in gaining the support of the United States, Britain, and France. Thailand felt threatened by the Viet Minh and Pathet Lao presence in Laos, and wanted great-power aid. The Philippines hoped for a more solid security guarantee from the Americans but had no immediate interests in Vietnam, Laos, or Cambodia. Pakistan sought military assistance, and

---

[53] Leszek Buszynski, *SEATO: The Failure of an Alliance Strategy* (Singapore: Singapore University Press, 1983), 15.
[54] Buszynski, *SEATO*, 22–26.
[55] Ibid., 26–28.

hoped that SEATO would have some marginal impact on its conflict with India over Kashmir, despite the fact that the treaty did not apply there.[56]

The member states' divergent goals were evident in their early commitments to SEATO. At the Manila Conference in September 1954, the Americans announced that they wanted the pact to apply only to cases of "communist aggression." The other members refused to amend the treaty in this direction, because each had hoped, in its own way, to secure broader American involvement in the region. So Secretary of State John Foster Dulles attached a note to the treaty explaining that the Americans would interpret their commitments as being specific to communist foes.[57] In another harbinger of the trouble that was to come, SEATO members also disagreed on the nature of the military capacity that the organization should have. Many of the smaller powers had hoped for a NATO-like integrated command structure with SEATO-dedicated troops. The Americans, however, refused to participate in deep military cooperation, citing a need to maintain "mobile striking power."[58] A standing SEATO organization was nonetheless created, but it had no meaningful kinetic power at its disposal. Where communist threats were concerned, the organization could identify them and propose joint action, but counter-subversive operations were the responsibility of member governments.[59]

SEATO's structural shortcomings were first laid bare in the Laotian crisis of 1960–1961. Despite the fact that Thailand felt deeply threatened by incursions into Laos, the Manila Pact members could not decide whether this was grounds for intervention and ruled that the situation was "too complex" to activate the alliance.[60] Later, the Manila Pact served as part of the initial justification for American intervention in Vietnam, although the British and French did not support it and reduced their roles in the organization. By the time the Vietnam War was over, it was abundantly clear that SEATO did not serve a purpose. The alliance had been unable to act coherently in Laos, and was unwilling to do so in Vietnam. The diverging priorities of the member states and the fact that SEATO had few means to further its supposed mission meant that this containment effort against communist subversion was hamstrung before it began. NATO's ability to overcome early obstacles and SEATO's paralysis and demise impart some useful lessons for the possibility of a multilateral containment regime in the Gulf. As the NATO case instructs, a successful containment effort requires not only great

---

[56] Ibid., 33, 42; Henry W. Brands, Jr., "From ANZUS to SEATO: United States Strategic Policy Toward Australia and New Zealand, 1952–1954," *The International History Review* 9 (May 1987): 250–270, at 268.

[57] Brands, "ANZUS to SEATO," 269.

[58] American Foreign Policy, 1950–1955 (Washington, DC: Department of State, 1957), I, 917.

[59] Buszynski, *SEATO*, 55.

[60] Ibid., 76.

material resources from its sponsors, but a willingness to navigate and engage the internal politics of the region. It also requires a flexibility of commitment and a capacity to increase vastly one's alliance obligations if internal and external threats so require. SEATO, on the other hand, demonstrates starkly that a constellation of states with nominally compatible goals is insufficient for containment success. Members must specify and agree on how their containment strategy will achieve their political ends, and those who are providing the resources must be committed in more than name alone. Without this cohesion, alliance members cannot advance, and might even undercut, their objectives.

Containment regimes aim first and foremost to limit an adversary's influence and deter aggression. Sending strong deterrent signals means that partners must work assiduously to communicate their commitments to adversaries. An important part of this is a shared understanding of external threats among security partners. A deterrent threat is supported by the capability and intent to follow it through. America's commitment to NATO began with intent, but commensurate capability followed quickly and in spades. American commitments to SEATO lacked in both categories (and France and Britain did little to make up for that fact).

If the United States were to spearhead a containment effort with the states of the GCC, there would be at least two requirements for success. First, the membership would need to evince a coherence and level of commitment that is robust enough to send clear signals. They would need to share an understanding of the Iranian threat, and demonstrate the ability to coordinate effectively to meet it. Second, the United States would have to be prepared to devote significant political and military resources to providing for an integrated Gulf defense effort, and to successfully navigating intra-Gulf politics. We now turn to the question of whether such an effort may be possible among the Gulf states, and between them and the United States.

CONCEPTUALIZING CONTAINMENT: THE GULF STATES AND IRAN
The Origins of the Obstacles
The Gulf Cooperation Council was established in 1981 to provide a platform for the leadership of the six member countries to cooperate on issues of mutual interest.[61] The organization formed as a response to the Iranian Revolution and the outbreak of the Iran–Iraq war. But despite the establishment of a Peninsula Shield Force in the 1980s to provide the group with a limited military capability, the GCC has never developed into a formal mutual defense alliance.

---

[61] Partrick, Gulf State Integration, 2.

This section evaluates the prospects for enhanced security cooperation among the six member states of the Council in order to contain Iran. As the cases of NATO and SEATO suggest, the prospects for an effective containment regime in the Gulf will depend on whether the states in the region can achieve sufficient unity of purpose and integration on security issues to deter Iran. It will also depend on whether the United States can devote the necessary political and military resources to the GCC to help it become an effective organization.

Since the United Kingdom withdrew from the region in 1971 and the Gulf became an independent security system, however, there have been persistent challenges to integration on defense issues, driven largely by two phenomena. First, contests for power and influence among the Arab Gulf states have stood in the way of the development of the degree of trust and coherence necessary to build a truly effective containment regime. This dynamic manifests itself in a number of ways, but was perhaps illustrated most clearly when the sheikhdoms of the lower Gulf—what is today Bahrain, Qatar, and the United Arab Emirates—achieved independence from the United Kingdom and such internal rivalries frustrated an early attempt at unity.

Second, the states in the region "view threats primarily through the lens of regime security" rather than more conventional balance-of-power considerations.[62] Indeed, even the "external" threat posed by Iran is in important senses internal—many Gulf states see Iran primarily as a political challenge to their domestic authority because of the Islamic Republic's perceived ability to undermine the authority of the (Sunni) ruling families.[63] Because each state perceives the danger posed by Iran differently, however, they are not all willing to take the same combination of measures against it that would be required to create a robust, unified containment architecture. This poses a stark contrast to NATO, where member states agreed on relatively specific goals with respect to an external threat that was similar in kind for the member states.[64]

We begin this section by examining an early attempt at regional unity among the nine sheikhdoms that became Bahrain, Qatar, and the UAE. This abortive effort took place between 1968, when the United Kingdom announced its intention to withdraw from the region, and 1971, when the British actually withdrew, and illustrates some of the enduring features of regional security relationships. The attempt to establish the Federation of the

---

[62] F. Gregory Gause III, *The International Relations of the Persian Gulf* (New York, NY: Cambridge University Press, 2010), 1.

[63] See, for example, Abdul-Reda Assiri, *Kuwait's Foreign Policy: City-State in World Politics* (Boulder, CO: Westview Press, 1990), 89.

[64] See, for example, F. Gregory Gause, III, "Threats and Threat Perception in the Persian Gulf Region," *Middle East Policy*, XIV (Summer 2007): 120.

Arab Amirates (FAA) in 1971 was perhaps the most important effort to pool sovereignty among the sheikhdoms in order to achieve security objectives in the modern history of the region.[65] Analyzing the reasons for its failure, in turn, discloses persistent features of the Gulf's security dynamics that remain to this day, and which have frustrated more modern attempts to integrate control over security-related issues.

After analyzing the failed attempt to create the FAA in 1971, we then examine two more recent attempts at integration to achieve security objectives in the Gulf and find that they failed for reasons similar to those that doomed the FAA. We then turn to an examination of the prospects for U.S. cooperation with and commitment to a more-robust constellation among the GCC states. We argue that intra-Gulf rivalries and differing perceptions of the (largely internal) threat posed by Iran, as well as fiscal and political barriers to a deeper U.S. commitment, place significant limits on the prospects for a robust, multilateral effort to contain Iran.

Achieving Independence: A Stillborn Attempt at Unity

Between 1820 and 1916, the United Kingdom established treaty relationships with the sheikhdoms of the lower Gulf to ensure regional stability and protect commerce with India.[66] But in the post-World War II era, the demands on the United Kingdom had changed, and by 1961, amidst a growing tide of Arab nationalist sentiment, Kuwait achieved independence.[67] By the late 1960s, under pressure from serious economic and political constraints at home,[68] the United Kingdom announced its intention to withdraw its forces from the Far East and all of the states of the Persian Gulf before the end of 1971.[69]

Despite the British withdrawal, however, the region remained strategically important to the United Kingdom and to the United States, and so both sought ways to secure their interests in the face of a new post-imperial security landscape. At the time of the British withdrawal, the United States defined its specific interests in the region as the free flow of oil (the Gulf provided 85 percent of the oil used by U.S. forces in Southeast Asia), the continued use of communications and intelligence facilities in Iran, and the perpetuation of landing rights in Saudi Arabia.[70]

---

[65] See, Partrick, Gulf State Integration, 3.

[66] W. Taylor Fain, *American Ascendance and British Retreat in the Persian Gulf Region* (New York: Palgrave MacMillan, 2008), 14–15.

[67] Fain, *American Ascendance*, 19.

[68] Sohei Sato, "Britain's Decision to Withdraw from the Persian Gulf, 1964–1968: A Pattern and a Puzzle," *Journal of Imperial and Commonwealth History* 37 (March 2009): 99, 112.

[69] Jacob Abadi, *Britain's Withdrawal from the Middle East, 1947–1971: The Economic and Strategic Imperatives* (Princeton, NJ: The Kingston Press, 1982), 212–214.

[70] Paper prepared by the National Security Council staff: Persian Gulf, 4 June 1970, U.S. Department of State, *Foreign Relations of the United States* (FRUS) 1969–1976, Vol. XXIV, 257.

The United States saw instability among the Gulf states as the primary threat to those interests, as it could be exploited by Arab radicals or by the Soviet Union.[71] Such chaos, the United States and Britain feared, would arise from the vacuum left after the British withdrawal, when political subversion would make the states of the region vulnerable;[72] a threat that the United States regarded as more plausible than external aggression.[73] At the same time, officials like National Security Adviser Henry Kissinger were acutely aware of the limited direct influence of the United States in the region, and of the fact that the United States, bogged down in Vietnam, was unable at that time to physically replace the British as the regional security guarantor.[74]

Because of their limited ability to directly protect their interests after the British withdrawal, the United Kingdom, supported by the United States, endorsed the creation of a single political entity, the FAA, in order to stabilize the nine sheikhdoms of the lower Gulf that were to achieve independence (Abu Dhabi, Ajman, Bahrain, Dubai, Fujairah, Qatar, Ras al-Khaimah, Sharjah, and Umm al-Quwain). The FAA was a part of Britain and America's attempt to forestall the activation of longstanding latent disputes that they feared would surface after the British withdrawal, including border rows between Iran and Iraq, Iran and Bahrain, Iraq and Kuwait, and Saudi Arabia and Abu Dhabi.[75]

In this potentially volatile context, U.S. officials believed that a federation among the nine emirates of the lower Gulf "represent[ed] the best hope for stability among the Arab Shaykhdoms."[76] After substantial effort, however, the attempt to establish the FAA out of the nine emirates failed, and in 1971, Bahrain and Qatar achieved independence, while the remaining seven emirates eventually joined together as the UAE.[77] Examining the reasons for this failed attempt at integration sheds light on persistent features of the security system of the Gulf, with important implications for the future ability of the Gulf states to achieve the degree of integration needed for an effective regime to contain Iran today.

---

[71] Paper prepared by the National Security Council staff: Persian Gulf, 256.

[72] Memorandum from the President's Assistant for National Security Affairs (Kissinger) to President Nixon, 22 October 1970, *FRUS* 1969–1976, Vol. XXIV, 280; telegram from the embassy in Iran to the Department of State, 4 February 1970, *FRUS* 1969–1976, Vol. XXIV, 246.

[73] Memorandum of Conversation, 13 January 1971, *FRUS* 1969–1976, Vol. XXIV, 289.

[74] Memorandum from the President's Assistant for National Security Affairs (Kissinger) to President Nixon, 22 October 1970, *FRUS* 1969–1976, Vol. XXIV, 280.

[75] Charles Kupchan, *The Persian Gulf and the West: The Dilemmas of Security* (Boston, MA: Allen & Unwin, 1987), 34; Richard Young, "Equitable Solutions for Offshore Boundaries: The 1968 Saudi Arabia–Iran Agreement," *The American Journal of International Law* 64 (January 1970): 152–157.

[76] Memorandum from Peter Rodman of the National Security Council Staff to the President's Assistant for National Security Affairs (Kissinger), 31 December 1969, *FRUS* 1969–1976, Vol. XXIV, 245.

[77] Rosemary Said Zahlan, *The Origins of the United Arab Emirates: A Political and Social History of the Trucial States* (New York: St. Martin's Press, 1978), 195.

First, contests for leadership and power among the states of the region, driven in large part by differences in development and oil wealth, were an important factor dooming integration efforts in the period leading up to independence. Indeed, a U.S. National Intelligence Estimate published a few months before Bahrain, Qatar, and the UAE became independent noted that despite the best efforts of the United Kingdom, "[t]here is little prospect that British-sponsored efforts to organize a federation of these tiny sheikhdoms will come to fruition."[78] This failure was due predominantly to the "mind-boggling jealousies and tribal prerogatives that affect regional cooperation among the Gulf states."[79] General disputes among the proposed members of the FAA manifested themselves as disagreements about which powers should be delegated to the proposed federation, and where the capital of the FAA should lie.[80] Bahrain was also unable to arrive at a satisfactory power-sharing arrangement with the less-developed emirates in the proposed Federation.[81]

Such contests for power and influence do not mean, however, that the Gulf states were unable to act in concert when it suited their interests to do so. Indeed, in February 1971, while negotiations about the FAA were ongoing, Saudi Arabia, Qatar, and Abu Dhabi worked with Iraq, Iran, and Kuwait to re-negotiate the terms of their agreements with international oil companies.[82]

The sheikhdoms of the region, however, had differing perceptions of the threat posed by Iran to the security of the ruling regimes. These distinct views on Iran dictated different approaches by each state to the Islamic Republic and stood in the way of deeper integration among the Gulf states, both at independence and today. Around the time of independence, as today, some of the sheikhdoms of the lower Gulf considered Iran to be their chief rival. Shortly after the United Kingdom announced its intentions to leave the region in 1968, for example, Iran re-asserted its perennial claims to sovereignty over Bahrain, which it has intermittently declared since the late eighteenth century.[83] Ultimately Iran's claims were resolved by a 1970 UN-sponsored "survey," which determined that the population of the island preferred inde-

---

[78] National Intelligence Estimate, 1 April 1971, *FRUS* 1969–1976, Vol. XXIV, 306.

[79] Memorandum from Harold Saunders and Rosemary Neaher of the National Security Council staff to the President's Assistant for National Security Affairs (Kissinger), 19 May 1971, *FRUS* 1969–1976, Vol. XXIV, 314.

[80] Memorandum from Harold Saunders and Rosemary Neaher of the National Security Council staff, 313.

[81] Memorandum of Conversation, 13 January 1971, *FRUS* 1969–1976, Vol. XXIV, 294; Zahlan, *The Origins of the United Arab Emirates*, 195.

[82] Intelligence Memorandum prepared in the Central Intelligence Agency, March 1971, *FRUS* 1969–1976, Vol. XXIV, 298.

[83] Rosemary Said Zahlan, *The Making of the Modern Gulf States: Kuwait, Bahrain, Qatar, and the United Arab Emirates* (London: Ithaca Press, 1998), 61–62.

pendence to Iranian control, but difficulties in Iran's relationship with the island persist to this day. Tensions also flared between Iran and the UAE when the former seized three islands in a dispute that remains unresolved.

Some of the lower Gulf sheikhdoms, in contrast, considered Iran to be an ally with whom their interests converged in the period surrounding their independence. In 1973, for example, the Shah of Iran sent troops to Oman to assist the Sultan in putting down a leftist rebellion,[84] and in doing so, helped cement the position of the Omani ruler. Oman today continues to enjoy cordial relations with the Islamic Republic, and in 2011, mediated the release of two American hikers taken captive in Iran. Tense relations between the states of the GCC and other regional actors are not limited to Iran. Each, for example, has a differing perception of the threat posed by Iraq, with Saudi Arabia, and others, failing to open Embassies in Baghdad because of mistrust of the government of Nouri al-Maliki.[85] Kuwait, by contrast, has a functional embassy there.

These sorts of differences constitute an important obstacle to closer regional integration because they condition each state's threat perceptions, and thus the degree to which they will be willing to cede or pool sovereignty in order to protect themselves. It also determines, in large part, the degree to which various GCC states will commit themselves to a containment structure designed to deter Iran. As demonstrated by the history of NATO and SEATO, a shared understanding and approach to an outside threat is important for the formation of an effective, well-integrated containment regime.

Persistent Challenges to Integration

Far from being mere historical artifacts, the tendencies identified above—contests for regional power and influence and differing threat perceptions, particularly with respect to Iran—continue to pose obstacles to closer security integration in the region. Indeed, two specific initiatives launched in recent years to more closely integrate the states of the GCC have failed for reasons similar to those that prevented the countries of the region from achieving unity in the years immediately after independence.

The first initiative was aimed at creating an integrated missile defense radar system to provide early warning and to deter against an Iranian missile attack.[86] The United States has sold billions of dollars of missiles and related radar equipment to GCC countries on a bilateral basis in recent years, but it has struggled to achieve a truly integrated, region-wide missile defense capability. Indeed, as General James Mattis, then-Commander of

---

[84] Fred Halliday, *Arabia Without Sultans* (London: Saqi Books, 2002), 352–353.
[85] Jack Healy, "Saudis Pick First Envoy to Baghdad in 20 Years," *The New York Times*, 21 February 2012.
[86] Patrick M. Cronin, "Can U.S. help Gulf shield itself against Iran?" *CNN*, 14 August 2012, accessed at http://edition.cnn.com/2012/08/14/opinion/cronin-missile-shield/, 22 February 2013.

U.S. Central Command noted, effective air and missile defense requires comprehensive collaborative planning and direction between the United States and regional partners; effective and interoperable command, control, and communications capabilities; planned integrated air and missile defense responses to enemy action; and common rules of engagement and missile defense firing doctrine.[87] In short, it requires a truly integrated defense architecture among the states of the GCC.

But while closer integration has long been a goal, these efforts have not been successful. This is due in large part to the fact that political challenges stemming from historic rivalries have inhibited the kind of close cooperation among GCC states that would be necessary for such a missile defense system to function effectively.[88] Specifically, disagreements about the conditions for sharing data among the elements of the system located in different countries and the location of a command center have prevented the creation of a missile defense system as well-designed and closely integrated as analogous systems in Europe.[89] Indeed, the states of the region have failed to agree on the location of a missile defense command center, largely because of the presumptive control over the system that such a command center would provide. Such disputes also doomed the GCC's efforts to create a common currency; the location of a regional central bank similarly became a bone of contention, shelving any possibility of an agreement.[90]

The second initiative consists of a December 2011 proposal by Saudi King Abdullah to more closely unify the states of the GCC into a "single entity."[91] The primary motivation for the proposal was the uprisings of the Arab Spring in general, and in particular, the revolt in Bahrain, in which a Shiite majority and other liberal protesters challenged the rule of the Sunni al-Khalifa family. But despite the fact that the fear of contagion from the Arab Spring posed a direct threat to the domestic stability of all of the ruling families of the region, that fear was insufficient to draw the six states of the

---

[87] General James Mattis, Remarks before International Symposium on Air Defense in Saudi Arabia, *Press Release, United States Central Command*, 17 April 2011, accessed at http://www.centcom.mil/press-releases/u-s-central-command-commander-addresses-international-symposium-on-air-defense-in-saudi-arabia, 22 February 2013.

[88] Thom Shanker, "U.S. and Gulf Allies Pursue a Missile Shield Against Iranian Attack," *The New York Times*, 8 August 2012.

[89] Andrew Quinn, "U.S., Gulf Countries Seek to Advance Missile Defense Plan," 28 September 2012, accessed at http://www.reuters.com/article/2012/09/28/us-un-assembly-gulf-usa-idUSBRE88R1GW20120928, 23 February 2013.

[90] Mahmoud Habboush, "Analysis: Gulf States Struggle to Agree on Missile Shield," 30 April 2012, accessed at http://www.reuters.com/article/2012/04/30/us-gulf-missile-defence-idUSBRE83T0QB20120430, 20 February 2013.

[91] Angus McDowall and Asma Alsharif, "Gulf Arabs Back Unity After Hinting at Iran Threat," *Reuters*, 20 December 2011, accessed at http://www.reuters.com/article/2011/12/20/us-saudi-gulf-idUSTRE7BJ1MF 20111220, 21 February 2013.

region more closely together; a year and a half after King Abdullah's proposal, it appears to have encountered serious obstacles.[92] This is largely due to fear on the part of states like the UAE and Qatar that any such union would inevitably be dominated by Saudi Arabia—precisely the kind of intra-regional rivalries for leadership that prevented the unity of the lower Gulf states upon independence. The forces that prevented Gulf unity in 1971 appear to be alive and well today.

Prospects for Patronage: The United States and the GCC

Beyond the internal obstacles to greater integration among the Gulf states, there are also significant obstacles to the United States serving as the guarantor for any enhanced regional security structure in the Gulf akin to the role it played in NATO. In the past, such investments have required significant military footprints, including forward troop deployments, a robust schedule of joint training and exercises, some degree of inter-operable equipment, and even integrated war planning. More importantly, any such defense pact would require a web of established relationships between military and civilian bureaucracies, and indeed the creation of shared institutions devoted to military planning, political coordination, and intelligence sharing, and the development of joint military doctrine for use in case of hostilities.

While this exists today to some degree, there are at least two broad sets of reasons why the United States is unlikely to invest in the creation of even more-robust independent institutional structures in the Gulf in the years to come. The first, and most important, has to do with continued budgetary pressure, including on military spending, in the United States. In an environment of fiscal austerity, and with the United States coming out of more than a decade of combat in the Middle East and South Asia, there will probably be little appetite for a major investment in the creation of a comprehensive new defense architecture in the region. And while the United States is perfectly willing to sell tens of billions of dollars worth of advanced military equipment, investing in the creation of collaborative institutions and doctrines is another matter entirely. Indeed, even a proposed sale of $60 billion worth of arms to Saudi Arabia in 2010 prompted 198 Members of Congress to write to the Secretaries of State and Defense to question the rationale for the sale.[93] If that was the reaction when the

---

[92] Andrew Hammond, "Analysis: Saudi Gulf Union Plan Stumbles As Wary Leaders Seek Detail," *Reuters*, 17 May 2012, accessed at http://www.reuters.com/article/2012/05/17/us-gulf-union-idUSBRE84G0WN20120517, 24 February 2013.

[93] Josh Rogin, "Congressional Letter Questioning Saudi Arms Sales Gets 198 Signatures," *Foreign Policy*, 12 November 2010, accessed at http://thecable.foreignpolicy.com/posts/2010/11/12/congressional_letter_questioning_saudi_arms_sales_gets_198_signatures, 24 February 2013.

United States proposed to sell billions of dollars worth of arms to its allies, it can be expected that a long-term commitment to investing in new or enhanced institutions needed for a robust security architecture would probably provoke fatal opposition. Fiscal constraints have already placed important limitations on U.S. forward deployment to the Gulf.[94] Moreover, the Obama administration's strategy of "pivoting" toward East Asia does not augur well for a more robust Gulf commitment.

A second obstacle to greater American involvement lies in the political difficulties for the states in the region that would be caused by a deeper and more-overt U.S. military presence in the region. The presence of American troops in Saudi Arabia after the 1991 Persian Gulf War became a rallying cry for al Qaeda,[95] and in 2003, after more than a decade with a significant military presence in the Kingdom, the United States withdrew the vast majority of its forces from Saudi soil.[96] While the United States retains extensive bases throughout the Gulf, in many cases, it keeps a low public profile to avoid provoking domestic opposition to its presence. In this context, it would probably prove difficult for the United States to expand its presence sufficiently to create a robust defense architecture.

Taken together, the current fiscal climate and general wariness toward the U.S. military presence in the region suggest that a more-resource-intensive commitment to an integrated defense architecture in the Gulf, whether through the existing structure of the GCC or through some other means, is unlikely to be forthcoming. The persistent obstacles to integration among the Gulf states themselves and the impediments to greater U.S. involvement there suggest that encouraging defense integration among Gulf Arab states to contain Iran, as some analysts have suggested, is unlikely to be a viable path forward.

CONCLUSIONS: TOWARD A "STRONGPOINT DEFENSE"

As we have demonstrated, there are four plausible scenarios in which a robust containment regime may be necessary even if the United States does not decide to "live with" a nuclear Iran. In each of these, strengthening and reassuring jittery regional partners would be a top priority if the United States hopes to ensure a modicum of stability in the Gulf. But as the history of NATO and SEATO demonstrates, multilateral containment regimes are not reserve options, selected after all other choices have been exhausted. Rather, they are

---

[94] Eyder Peralta, "Citing Uncertainty, Pentagon Will Not Deploy Aircraft Carrier to Persian Gulf," 6 February 2013, accessed at http://www.npr.org/blogs/thetwo-way/2013/02/06/171300433/citing-uncertainty-pentagon-will-not-deploy-aircraft-carrier-to-persian-gulf, 24 February 2013.

[95] Thomas Hegghammer, *Jihad in Saudi Arabia: Violence and Pan-Islamism since 1979* (New York, NY: Cambridge University Press, 2010), 113.

[96] Eric Schmitt, "U.S. to Withdraw All Combat Forces from Saudi Arabia," *The New York Times*, 29 April 2003.

laboriously constructed political entities that also often entail the creation of integrated institutions and strategic doctrines. They require unity of purpose and a degree of integration among the member states of the containment regime, and also the close support of an outside power like the United States.

As we have shown, however, the states that comprise the GCC have faced significant obstacles to the kind of integration that would be necessary for a robust multilateral alliance. The United States is also highly unlikely to be able to devote the resources or political capital needed to help shape the states of the region into a unified defense structure. This does not, however, suggest that there is no hope for the United States to limit Iran's influence through the support of allies and regional security—it simply suggests that this goal should not be pursued collectively or formally.

Because the states of the GCC vary in their perceptions of the Iranian threat, as well as in their ability to work with one another, the United States should instead expect to shoulder the primary burden of containing Iran, working with the states of the region whenever and in whichever ways possible. Like Otto von Bismarck's alliance strategy in the late nineteenth century, or the U.S. approach in northeast Asia, a "hub-and-spokes" configuration of defense ties would allow the United States to provide the region with the political and military assistance it needs to contain Iran, without requiring that it engage deeply with intra-Gulf politics. Unlike the German Chancellor's or the mid-century American alliance strategies, however, this engagement strategy does not require a series of formal military alliances.

The failure of SEATO is a poignant reminder of how an alliance strategy may founder if the states in a threatened region do not share the same defense priorities and goals as their superpower patron. The varied nature of the relations between the United States and some GCC states, and the gulf states' uneven perception of the Iranian threat, suggest that security paradigms are not close enough to sustain a formal, specific guarantee over the long term. Flexible, informal relations are preferable. Indeed, when the NATO alliance was proposed in 1948, Kennan himself was skeptical of its permanence and its inherently militarized approach. Containment, in his eyes, relied on political, psychological, and economic tools as much as on kinetic ones, and required a dynamism that could be undermined by a complex, rigid, standing defense organization.[97]

While the region may never come together into a single integrated containment structure, the United States can still leverage the comparative advantage possessed by each state in the region to create a security system in which the whole is greater than the sum of the parts. The United States will ultimately have to undertake the primary role of operationalizing much of

---

[97] See Miscamble, *Kennan*, 129; 133–134; 139–140.

the containment systems on its own, working individually with its GCC partners as appropriate. But each state will contribute what it is capable of adding to the U.S.-led regime without the United States having to invest in the institutions required by new collective security regimes for the Gulf. Some, like the UAE, may provide bases for the United States to forward-deploy advanced fighter jets;[98] others, like Saudi Arabia, may continue cooperation in intelligence and counterterrorism,[99] contending against Iran's asymmetric avenues of influence. In all cases, the United States should assist each state in building the capabilities that both it and the region need to diffuse Iran's influence, without indulging in the desire to invest in additional institutions.

There are signs that the United States has embarked upon a path of pursuing stronger, informal bilateral ties with the Gulf states, selling billions of dollars of offensive and defensive weaponry to the states of the Gulf in the last several years. It should continue this course, conscious that efforts to integrate these weapons sales into a more-robust and coherent regional security architecture are unlikely to prevail. A more-difficult challenge may arise, however, if the long-simmering standoff over Iran's nuclear program boils over and a strike occurs, or Iran appears to move toward an actual weapons capability. As with the first Soviet nuclear test in 1949, the Korean invasion in 1950, or the French defeat at Dien Bien Phu in 1954, a full-blown crisis in the Gulf may superficially appear to be a catalyst for enhanced regional cohesion and U.S. commitment. For an integrated containment structure to prevail, however, it is not allies' short-term incentives in a crisis that matter, but rather long-term security priorities that must cohere.

If, indeed, Iran is a threat that can be contained, "strongpoint defense" in the Gulf will look nothing like NATO or SEATO. It must depart from the security paradigms of the past, accepting, rather than obscuring the profound obstacles to Gulf security integration that have defined the region since its independence, and maintaining the flexibility to respond to whatever regional conflicts arise. The answers to the Gulf's containment conundrum will not simply materialize when the current crisis peaks. As Kennan might advise, U.S. policymakers must seize the initiative and plan for a modern, dynamic, security system in the Gulf that acknowledges twenty-first century resource constraints and political realities. Regional stability, whether in the aftermath of an airstrike or in the wake of a settlement, demands it.*

* The authors would like to thank Robert Jervis, Edward Fishman, and the anonymous reviewer for helpful comments.

---

[98] Anshel Pfeffer, "U.S. Upgrades Strike Capabilities Against Iran, Stations 'Stealth' Fighters in Gulf," *Haaretz*, 27 January 2013, accessed at http://www.haaretz.com/misc/iphone-blog-article/u-s-upgrades-strike-capabilities-against-iran-stations-stealth-fighters-in-gulf.premium-1.496668, 21 February 2013.

[99] Greg Miller and Karen De Young, "Brennan Nomination Exposes Criticism on Targeted Killings and Secret Saudi Base," *The Washington Post*, 5 February 2013.